The Commercial Society

STUDIES IN ETHICS AND ECONOMICS

Series Editor
Samuel Gregg, Acton Institute

Economics as a discipline cannot be detached from a historical background that was, it is increasingly recognized, religious in nature. Adam Ferguson and Adam Smith drew on the work of sixteenth- and seventeenth-century Spanish theologians, who strove to understand the process of exchange and trade in order to better address the moral dilemmas they saw arising from the spread of commerce in the New World. After a long period in which economics became detached from theology and ethics, many economists and theologians now see the benefit of studying economic realities in their full cultural, often religious, context. This new series, Studies in Ethics and Economics, provides an international forum for exploring the difficult theological and economic questions that arise in the pursuit of this objective.

Titles in the Series

Intelligence as a Principle of Public Economy / Del pensiero come principio d'economia publica, by Carlo Cattaneo

And Why Not?: The Human Person at the Heart of Business, by François Michelin

Faith and Liberty: The Economic Thought of the Late Scholastics, by Alejandro A. Chafuen

The Boundaries of Technique: Ordering Positive and Normative Concerns in Economic Research, by Andrew Yuengert

Within the Market Strife: American Economic Thought from Rerum Novarum *to* Vatican II, by Kevin E. Schmiesing

Natural Law: The Foundation of an Orderly Economic System, by Alberto M. Piedra

The Church and the Market: A Catholic Defense of the Free Economy, by Thomas E. Woods Jr.

The Constitution under Social Justice, by Antonio Rosmini, translated by Alberto Mingardi

The Commercial Society: Foundations and Challenges in a Global Age, by Samuel Gregg

The Commercial Society

Foundations and Challenges in a Global Age

Samuel Gregg

LEXINGTON BOOKS

A division of
ROWMAN & LITTLEFIELD PUBLISHERS, INC.
Lanham • Boulder • New York • Toronto • Plymouth, UK

LEXINGTON BOOKS

A division of Rowman & Littlefield Publishers, Inc.
A wholly owned subsidiary of The Rowman & Littlefield Publishing Group, Inc.
4501 Forbes Boulevard, Suite 200
Lanham, MD 20706

Estover Road
Plymouth PL6 7PY
United Kingdom

British Library Cataloguing in Publication Information Available

Library of Congress Cataloging-in-Publication Data

Gregg, Samuel, 1969-
  The commercial society : foundations and challenges in a global age / Samuel Gregg.
    p. cm. — (Studies in ethics and economics)
  Includes bibliographical references and index.
  ISBN-13: 978-0-7391-1993-8 (cloth : alk. paper)
  ISBN-10: 0-7391-1993-1 (cloth : alk. paper)
  ISBN-13: 978-0-7391-1994-5 (pbk. : alk. paper)
  ISBN-10: 0-7391-1994-X (pbk. : alk. paper)
  1. Free enterprise—History. 2. Democracy—Economic aspects. 3. Economic history.
  I. Title.
  HB95.G74 2007
  330.1—dc22   2006030116

Printed in the United States of America

♾™ The paper used in this publication meets the minimum requirements of American
National Standard for Information Sciences—Permanence of Paper for Printed Library
Materials, ANSI/NISO Z39.48–1992.

A.M.D.G.

CONTENTS

ACKNOWLEDGMENTS

The promise and challenges of commercially orientated societies have long fascinated me. The debate about whether commercial society contributes to or diminishes civilizational development is a discussion that has been occurring for centuries and shows no immediate sign of resolution. Readers of this book will soon comprehend that the author—though conscious of the flaws that mark anything shaped or built by man—regards commercial society as a phenomenon that has made a generally positive contribution to the human project and hence worthy of reflection and deeper understanding.

Completion of this book represents the fruition of much thought on this subject over a period of several years. In undertaking this journey, I have benefited from the insights and observations of many great minds, both alive and deceased. Though much of the preparation and writing of this text occurred in the United States, sections of it were composed while lecturing and speaking in Europe, Latin America, and Australia. One could not help but be provoked, stimulated, and challenged by the various manifestations of market-orientated orders in these settings. Fortunately there were many fine minds to help me think through these phenomena and to place them into a coherent theoretical context. Particular contributions, both witting and unwitting, that merit special attention include Stephen Bainbridge, Philip Booth, Mariya Chernyavskaya, Alejandro Chafuen, Ricardo Crespo, Jude Chua Soo Meng, Ramón Díaz, Ian Harper, Pierre Garello, Brian Griffiths, Ralph Harris, Carlos Hoevel, Harold James, Oskari Juurikkala, Robert G. Kennedy, Leonard Liggio, Heinrich Liechtenstein, Mart Laar, Greg Lindsay, Kris Alan Mauren, Daniel Mahoney, C. J. McCloskey, Jennifer Roback Morse, Jean-Yves Naudet, Michael Novak, Ramón Parellada, Anthony Percy, Alberto Piedra, Andrea Schneider, Robert Sirico, the late Rafael Termes, Manfred Spieker, Christian Watrin, Gabriel Zanotti, and Christof Zellenberg.

Though this book is directed to those with interests in political thought, law, economics, and philosophy. It is, I hope, written in a manner designed to be accessible to undergraduate and graduate students working in these disciplines. Though the text does not purport to be an exhaustive treatment of its subject matter, I am optimistic that it may encourage some students to immerse themselves further in the rich history of ideas and events associated with the rise of commercial society. In this small way, I hope to return some of the debt I owe to students who, over the years, have asked me questions about this book's subject matter and many related issues.

Above all, I thank my wife Ingrid Gregg for her support and gentle urging to look more carefully at the thought of those who first engaged in profound philosophical reflection upon modern commercial society, especially those associated with the still-underestimated Scottish Enlightenment. My debt to her is inestimable. A more intangible contribution to this text was made by our daughter Madeleine.

The universal movement prevailing in the United States, the frequent reversals of fortune, and the unexpected shifts in public and private wealth all unite to keep the mind in a sort of feverish agitation which wonderfully disposes it toward every type of exertion and keeps it, so to say, above the common level of humanity.

—Alexis de Tocqueville

Commerce tends to wear off those prejudices which maintain distinction and animosity between nations. It softens and polishes the manners of men. It unites them, by one of the strongest of ties, the desire of supplying their mutual wants. It disposes them to peace, by establishing in every state an order of citizens bound by their interest to be guardians of public tranquility. As soon as the commercial spirit gains ... an ascendant in any society, we discover a new genius in its policy, its alliances, its wars, and its negotiations.

—William Robertson

PREFACE

The American lives in a land of wonders; everything around him is in constant movement, and every movement seems an advance. Consequently, in his mind the idea of newness is closely linked with that of improvement. Nowhere does he see any limit placed by nature to human endeavor; in his eyes something which does not exist is just something that has not been tried yet.

—Alexis de Tocqueville

When one of France's greatest political thinkers, Count Alexis de Tocqueville, arrived in the United States of America on May 11, 1831, he quickly realized that he was not simply encountering another nation. Within days of stepping ashore in New York Harbor, Tocqueville understood that he had stumbled across something quite foreign to his experience, both as an aristocrat and a Frenchman. He had for the first time entered a commercial republic.

It was not as if commerce did not exist in his native country. Though Tocqueville's France had been slower to embrace many of the economic changes that had commenced in Britain in the early eighteenth century, it did possess a commercial middle class as attached to private property and as hostile to excessive taxation as any nineteenth-century American businessman.

The difference between France and America, Tocqueville realized, was that a type of enterprising spirit permeated American society, embracing both the most humble and the grandest in the land. In one of the especially perceptive parts of his biography of Tocqueville, André Jardin brings to life just how different the United States visited by Tocqueville and his friend Gustave de Beaumont was from Continental Europe. Jardin points out, for example, that the salons of Restoration France were dominated by men holding public office as well as gentlemen of leisure devoted to disinterested scholarship. Hence, "[O]ne of the first surprises for Tocqueville and Beaumont in New York was that at gatherings during the evening one would rub shoulders with men who had spent the day in an office or a bank—lawyers, businessmen, bankers. The pleasures of society came at the end of a day in which they had waged a fierce battle for profit."[1]

As Tocqueville and Beaumont traveled throughout the still young America, neither could help comparing the habits, culture, and institutions of the United States with the daily practices, customs, and organizational patterns of their native France. It is only in this light that the full import of Tocqueville's *Democracy in America* becomes apparent. American manners, for example, immediately revealed to Tocqueville a society in which classes were much less distinct than in Europe. The negative result was that, unlike France, America lacked a sophisticated elite with a refined education. Nevertheless Tocqueville also perceived that even the most ordinary sales clerk did not have what he called the "bad form" of the French working classes. The Americans, in Tocqueville's eyes, were essentially a commercial people. On May 15, 1831, Tocqueville scribbled in his diary under the title "First Impressions" that "the entire society seems to have melted into a middle class."[2]

Another feature of America that struck Tocqueville was the relatively small presence of government and the corresponding vitality of what might be broadly called civil society. It was not that civil servants in the United States were less well thought of than any other group. They were simply considered people like any other. By contrast government officials were the objects of a particular respect, even awe, in France. Tocqueville also quickly discerned that American political life was not dominated by a hectic and corrosive struggle for power between very distinct political parties. Tocqueville came from a country where legitimists, republicans, Bonapartists and Orléanists had been engaged in precisely this form of conflict for decades.

Tocqueville indicated to his readers that they needed to understand that American commercial society reflected some fundamental cultural transitions from the world of Old Europe. Patriotism, he noted, permeated American society, but it was not overly associated with an instinctive love for the land of one's ancestors. The character of American patriotism had been shaped by the same moral sensibility that helped to give commerce such a salient place in American society. This attitude was one of rational self-interest properly understood, a mindset which somehow allowed each individual to identify his rational self-interest with the interest of all Americans. A rational regard for self was thus linked to feelings of pride in the moral, economic, and legal institutions that allowed as many Americans as possible to pursue their freely chosen goals, primarily through commercial activity. Tocqueville recognized that such sentiments were quite different from the attachment to the state that had marked the citizenry of the ancient world, or even the citizenry envisaged by the likes of Voltaire, Jean-Jacques Rousseau, and eventually Maximilian Robespierre.

It was, then, a civilization dominated and shaped by commercial activity that captured Tocqueville's imagination during his brief time in America. His encounters with less-commercial and non-commercial cultures in North America during this same period only sharpened the contrast. Tocqueville likened the inhabitants of the French-populated settlements of Québec to a lost fragment of *ancien régime* France and underscored the unwillingness of most of the French inhabitants to stray too far from the banks of the St. Lawrence River. The various Native Americans encountered by Tocqueville ranged from those who he described as "brutalized by our wines and liquors" in whom there was "no trace of any of those lofty virtues born of the spirit of freedom,"[3] to hunter-nomads who, while ferocious in battle, possessed the qualities of gravity, endurance, and a sense of honor that Tocqueville considered characteristic of a warrior nobility.

Tocqueville's sensitivity to the distinctly commercial character of the society that he surveyed in the United States did not blind him to the young Republic's difficulties. Not least among these problems was the existence of slavery in the southern states. A passionate abolitionist, Tocqueville was especially sensitive to this issue. Slavery in America, he believed, encouraged the persistence of a type of economy in the South that was rapidly becoming archaic. He also held that slavery shaped for the worst the cultural habits not only of slaves but also their masters. Ultimately, the United States was to be torn asunder by the question.

Tocqueville himself was rather guarded about the likely future of America's commercial republic. He was not as fond of making predictions as many think. Yet while he did not regard commercial civilization as an unmixed blessing, Tocqueville did believe that America's particular blend of moral-cultural habits and legal and economic institutions had the potential to allow the vast majority of its citizens a relatively stable and prosperous future in which the endeavors and disruptions created by people's use of their liberty were stabilized by a context of social order.

Though it discusses the foundations of commercial society and the challenges it faces across the globe, this book is no more a text about economics than was Adam Smith's *The Wealth of Nations*. Smith well understood that commercial society is about much more than economics. Nor does this book present a great deal that will be new to those who have studied commercial society in any systematic way. As the economist Joseph Schumpeter was fond of stating, Smith's *Wealth of Nations* "does not contain a single analytic idea, principle, or method that was entirely new in 1776."[4] The *Wealth of Nations* true significance lies in the synthesis it represents and its expression of particular ideas at a critical point of history. Though this book does not claim to replicate Smith's particular achievement, it does seek to be expository, attempting to outline the foundations of contemporary commercial society in relatively simple sketches. This book is, however, also critical insofar as it seeks to specify perennial threats to commercial society, and concludes by asking whether it is possible to build commercial societies in particular cultural settings as opposed to waiting for them to evolve under their own volition.

While this book is not directed at any one group, it is written in the hope that it will be of assistance to two particular audiences. The first is those nations struggling to break the cycle of poverty. Though endowed with many natural resources, much of the developing world continues to live in conditions that most in the developed world would find unbearable. For developing nations, the moral-cultural, economic, and legal foundations of commercial society, rather than direct aid, represent their best chance of overcoming the economic poverty that contributes to death rates that ought to be relegated to the pages of history. Some of these countries, especially in Africa, have barely begun this long journey. Others, such as some Latin American countries, are further along the path, but prey to doubts about their direction and tempted by the siren calls of those who would pursue populist paths.

The second audience is those nations who, after decades of unprecedented economic growth, now find themselves mired in economic stagnancy. One cannot help but think of the many countries of the European Union, especially some of the original signatories to the Treaty of Rome, where high levels of unemployment have become the norm, where even relatively modest attempts at reform encounter fierce resistance, and where increased activity from the state in the economy is routinely advocated across the political spectrum as the solution to economic malaise and decline. Such reactions should not surprise us. In a global age of commerce, Mauricio Rojas sagely reminds us:

> Old structures, patterns of life and positions of power are threatened. The breathtaking pace of development is exerting an enormous pressure on individuals and enterprises to transform the way they work. The pressure on regions and nations is greater still. And it is at this level where opposition to change is usually greatest, precisely because the transformations of earlier eras have brought powerful institutions, vested interests and ingrained attitudes which now stand in the way of the renewal necessary for continuing success. What were once strengths have become weaknesses. The nations that used to lead the way in development now risk languishing in backwaters.[5]

This is not to suggest that the pace of change engendered by commercial society is a new phenomenon. Those eighteenth-century scholars such as Adam Smith, Guy de Montesquieu, William Robertson, and Adam Ferguson, who first realized that commercial society represented an alteration of the social order that dwarfed previous transformations, were keenly aware of the scale of the effects and responded to them in different ways. The difference between now and then lies in the truly global proportions being assumed by commercial society's foundations and the corresponding rise in the significance of the perennial challenges that appear to have always limited and sometimes threatened the growth of commercial society.

Hence while this book seeks to define and explain the moral-cultural, economic, and legal foundations of commercial order, it also examines the contemporary challenges faced by these societies. The stakes today are considerably higher from the time of the eighteenth century, when commercial society was very much an "Anglo-Saxon" phenomenon. With commercial order now taking on global dimensions, both misunderstanding of commercial society's foundations as well as failure to recognize and comprehend the challenges it confronts may well weaken the ability of such societies to resist the subtle self-enslavement that Tocqueville described as soft-despotism. Of course, neither oppression nor tyranny is unfamiliar to human beings. They have been the norm for much of human history. The true terror of soft-despotism is that those who endure it have ceased to recognize their enslavement.

Notes

1. André Jardin, *Tocqueville: A Biography*, trans. Lydia Davis with Robert Hemenway (Baltimore and London: Johns Hopkins University Press, 1998), 109.

2. George Wilson Pierson, *Tocqueville in America* (Baltimore and London: Johns Hopkins University Press, 1999), 69–70.

3. *Voyage en Amérique*, in Alexis de Tocqueville, *Oeuvres Complètes*, ed. J. P. Mayer (Paris: Gallimard, 1951–), V, 1, 223.

4. Joseph Schumpeter, *History of Economic Analysis*, ed. E. B. Schumpeter (London: Allen & Unwin, 1954), 184–85.

5. Mauricio Rojas, *The Rise and Fall of the Swedish Model* (London: Social Market Foundation, 1998), x–xi.

1

Toward Commercial Order

The bourgeoisie has played a most revolutionary role in history. The bourgeoisie has been the first to show what man's activity can bring about. It has accomplished wonders far surpassing Egyptian pyramids, Roman aqueducts, and Gothic cathedrals: it has conducted expeditions that put in the shade all former migrations of nations and crusades.... The bourgeoisie has given a cosmopolitan character to production and consumption in every country. The bourgeoisie, by the rapid improvement of all instruments of production, by the immensely facilitated means of communication, draws all nations, even the most barbarian, into civilization.

—Karl Marx

Though often regarded as one of the more prominent critics of the society that began to emerge in the wake of the Industrial Revolution, Karl Marx was under no illusions concerning the revolutionary transformation associated with commercial society. What Marx portrayed as the new capitalist order was, to his mind, infinitely preferable to the feudal-mercantile society that preceded the growing dominance of a commercially orientated middle class. He also believed that the advent of this new society would help to create the proletariat who would, Marx maintained, replace the bourgeoisie as the engine of historical transformation. The advent of commercial society thus brought humanity closer to what

Marx envisaged would be the end of history: a communist world in which it would be possible for all people who survived the inevitable rigors of the transformation "to do one thing today and another tomorrow; to hunt in the morning, fish in the afternoon, breed cattle in the evening and criticize after dinner, just as I please."[1]

In his writings, Marx offered many reasons to explain these social transformations, but central to his argument was his attention to changes in man's relationship to the means of production. While feudalism was held in place, Marx claimed, by a particular vision of the world much shaped by Christianity, his primary explanation for the organization of feudal society concerned people's relationship to the means of production in a predominately agricultural economy. Those who owned large amounts of productive land or enjoyed special privileges over the land were therefore in a superior position to those who merely worked the land or whose ownership was contingent upon performance of specific duties such as paying feudal dues. Hence, Marx held, as the dominant means of production shifted away from land and agricultural methods toward industry and commerce, there was an inevitable power-shift away from the land-owning nobility and toward the emerging commercial classes.

The attraction of Marx's theory is its apparent concurrence with shifts in the dominant modes of economic production that have occurred over time. The difficulty is that this is too simple an explanation. It fails to account not only for observable facts in the history of economic life, but also changes in the way that people have thought about the production and consumption of materials. This includes practical insights such as Adam Smith's attention to the manner in which the specialization of labor facilitated greater efficiency in the production of goods, alongside a web of supporting ideas about the nature of human beings, the demands and consequences of human liberty, and the character and purposes of different institutions that have evolved over time. Commercial society is far too complex a phenomenon to be rooted solely in economic theory.

The very expression "free exchange," for instance, necessarily implies that a commercial society depends upon more than just the exchange of goods and services. It demands a *free* as opposed to a *coerced* exchange. The word *free* indicates in turn that the economic processes that characterize commercial society presuppose a certain understanding of human beings that differs from the view of man promoted by, for instance, Marxist and other deterministic visions of human life.

Commercial society thus embraces dimensions and suppositions that go beyond the economistic visions of Marx and his disciples. It follows that if commercial society is to endure, then a wider and deeper understanding of these presuppositions—its foundations—is necessary. Not only does the diffusion of such knowledge help to refute false ideas about commercial society; it may also assist commercial societies to cope with some of the real challenges they face across the globe. By challenges, we do not primarily have in mind the threats posed from outside commercially orientated societies such as Islamic terrorism. While these are important, our attention is directed primarily to those challenges that continually emerge *within* these societies.

There were few more robust defenders of commercial societies than the twentieth-century Swiss-German economist Wilhelm Röpke. Yet for all his critiques of communist, socialist, and corporatist alternatives, Röpke shared Alexis de Tocqueville's concern that the same pressures and developments that facilitated commercial society also led to the emergence of phenomena—such as a fixation with equality—that could prove antithetical to the long-term preservation of commercial society. Though their lives were separated by many decades, both Röpke and Tocqueville asked themselves how commercial societies could avoid such problems without undermining the very foundations that had done so much to promote human liberty and reduce material poverty.

It is with these concerns in mind that this book is written. Part One outlines and analyzes commercial society's moral, economic, and legal foundations and underlines the connections between them. By "foundations," we mean certain habits, procedures, and institutions, the absence of which raises questions about the ability of commercial society to emerge and sustain itself. This is not to intimate that these foundations, ranging from moral qualities such as trust or legal structures such as rule of law, are somehow unique to commercial society. Clearly they are not. Yet without these particular features, the long-term preservation of commercial society becomes more tenuous. In Part Two, we examine what might be called the perennial core challenges that emerge within modern commercial societies. Prominent among these are the expansionary tendencies of the political sphere, the demands of various equalizing tendencies, as well as particular developments associated with the advent and spread of democracy.

Before examining the foundations of commercial society and the challenges they confront, we need to define what is meant by "commercial society." There is a tendency to associate commercial society with economics and even more specifically free-market economics. Though commercial society is correctly associated with what might be called capitalist modes of economic production, excessive focus on this dimension of commercial order is likely to result in insufficient attention to the critical role played by certain ideas in the rise of commercial order—ideas that have acquired institutional form over many centuries.

One of the first twentieth-century thinkers to speculate upon such matters was another Swiss-German intellectual, Max Weber. Attention to his analysis of the rise of capitalism is important, for though there are significant flaws in his theory, his arguments allow us to begin identifying some of the ideas driving commercial society's emergence and expansion across the globe. Weber was one of the first commentators who established—contra Marx—that capitalism's development could be explained in more profound terms than simply alterations in the means of production. According to Weber, changes in the way that people thought about themselves and their world were central to facilitating significant transformations that in turn undermined the feudal-mercantilist social order.

A Capitalist Ethic?

Though Weber wrote many texts, he is perhaps most well known for associating the rise of commercial order with changes generated by the religious schism that split Western Christianity in the first half of the sixteenth century.[2] Weber's *Die protestantische Ethik und der Geist des Kapitalismus* (1905) was his first published work following a well-documented period of mental instability that began with Weber's initial nervous collapse in 1898 and continued with time spent in and out of mental institutions until 1903. The book itself was based upon lectures given by Weber during a visit to the United States in 1904. Significantly, Weber never expanded his ideas on this subject beyond this work.[3]

Weber took the view that capitalism involved more than just the production and exchange of goods within a particular institutional setting. Commercial orders, he believed, were firmly rooted in a particular state of mind. They were driven by rationality and the subordination of emotion, custom, tradition, folklore, and myth to the workings of instrumental reason.[4] Rationality, Weber believed, was crucial for the development of the disciplined investment patterns and division of labor that, he posited, began to surface across Western Europe during the sixteenth century.

Weber declared that this linkage of rationality with economic practices occurred primarily in Europe's predominately Protestant areas, especially those with significant numbers of ascetically-inclined Protestants in their midst. He particularly had in mind countries such as England and the Netherlands which, Weber held, were among the first to develop powerful commercial orientations. By inculcating a belief among its adherents that they needed to avoid superficial pursuits and totally commit themselves to whatever calling to which God had summoned them, ascetic Protestantism, Weber theorized, played a major role in endowing Western Europe with a form of economic life largely unknown in the non-European world.

In theological terms, Weber asserted that some forms of Protestantism, especially Puritan versions of Calvinism and its central doctrine of predestination, fostered the type of discipline required by commercial economies. Ascetic Calvinists and Puritans, in Weber's opinion, were convinced that it was not possible to do good works to attain heaven in the next world. One was either among the elect or one was not. One indication of election, according to Weber's interpretation of John Calvin, was wealth. The accumulation of wealth thus encouraged people to see themselves as destined to be saved. This in turn fostered a spirit among people that directed them toward the rational accumulation of wealth.

The objections to Weber's analysis can be categorized as theoretical and empirical. In the case of the former, his suggestion concerning Protestantism's facilitation of the emergence of the rational mindset seems to imply that a concern for reason and, more specifically, instrumental reason, was largely absent from pre-Reformation Europe. One need only consult the works of Thomas

Aquinas to discover that this is not true. It also ignores the writings of Renaissance figures such as Nicolai Machiavelli, many of whom discoursed long and eloquently in a Catholic world about forms of reasoning that closely resembled what Weber meant by rationality.

There are also questions about the adequacy of Weber's portrait of sixteenth-century Protestantism. His association of the apparent laicizing of the idea of calling with Protestantism does not survive peripheral study of pre-Reformation Christian theological reflection about the concept of vocation. The writings of Aquinas, for example, indicate that he believed that the very nature of human society meant that different men were destined to fulfill different tasks. Even in the post-Reformation period, Catholic religious orders such as the Jesuits went to significant lengths to stress the need for men to regard their diverse occupations as a calling from God.[5] Nor is it clear that Calvin associated the idea of the elect and good works with material success in this world. A survey of Calvin's *Institutes* indicates that he did not regard works as having much to do with the growth of wealth or financial profit. "Works," Calvin taught, essentially concerns those spiritual acts that require obedience to God's Law. A similar picture emerges from study of the Westminster Confession, the profession of faith that has dominated much Puritan, Calvinist, and Presbyterian theology since the sixteenth century, and upon which Weber relied heavily in building his theory. The Westminster Confession makes a clear distinction between each person's heavenly and earthly callings. An individual's earthly vocation was not regarded as a positive contribution to man's salvation—a position that contradicts Weber's analysis. The Confession also stresses that believers must ensure that their earthly tasks do not distract them from pursuing their heavenly destiny. Christians are in fact called upon to choose "that employment or calling in which you may be most serviceable to God. Choose not that in which you may be most honorable in the world; but that which you may do most good and best escape sinning."[6]

The empirical evidence against Weber's thesis is also compelling. In the 1920s and 1930s, the Italian political thinker Amintore Fanfani (no friend of commercial society) pointed out that capitalism had begun to emerge at least a century before Luther and Calvin.[7] Fanfani especially had in mind what he described as the "commercial spirit" that characterized Northern Italy's city-states, not to mention the Venetian republic that dominated the Mediterranean's merchant and trading life for several hundred years. Areas of Europe such as the Low Countries and England had begun to embark upon commercial paths years before Luther nailed his Ninety-Five Theses to a church door in Wittenberg. Double-entry bookkeeping was born in Italy long before 1519 and was quickly taken up by other merchants throughout Western Europe.[8]

To establish these points is not to assert that modern commercial societies owe more to a Jewish, Catholic, or secular ethic than to a Protestant ethic. It is simply to state that Weber's particular conclusions are very questionable. For all the problems with Weber's thesis, he was surely right to identify the emergence of new ways of thinking as crucial to the character of what he called capitalism.

His failure lay in his inattentiveness to the manner in which crucial concept and patterns of thought that lie at the heart of commercial society first appeared in a somewhat systematic form during the Middle Ages, especially through the particular attention accorded during this period to the importance and implications of human liberty, private property, free exchange, the rule of law, and civility.

Pre-Modern Traditions of Commerce

The Europe predating the great sixteenth-century religious schism is often regarded as dominated by an essentially communal mindset. Cary Nederman has indicated that while Medieval Latin Christendom could not be described as collectivist, the phrase "communitarian" best summarizes the nature of the prevailing social, economic, and political order.[9] The Western European feudal system was based upon a web of mutual obligations that different social groups such as the nobility and the peasantry were held to owe each other. While various forms of commerce existed in this period, all these activities and institutions were meshed in what the political theorist Antony Black calls the widespread diffusion, even dominance, of corporatist values within rural areas, villages and towns.[10]

By *corporatist*, Black does not mean "corporate" in the sense of the modern business corporation. Rather he has in mind the prevalence of particular ideas about the social order that flowed in part from Christianity's emphasis upon brotherly love, as well as ideals concerning the nature of friendship and mutual assistance promoted in the works of classical Roman thinkers. According to Black, it was the medieval guilds found in every village and town throughout Europe that gave particular form to such notions and spread them throughout society along with a range of institutional structures and expectations. Terms associated with the life of guilds such as *fraternitas, confraternitas*, and *bruderschaft* evoked notions of brotherhood, while phrases such as *communion* and *consortium* spoke of comradeship and fellowship.[11] They also indicated a range of concrete obligations that guild members owed each other. In practical terms, membership of a guild not only endowed people with a certain social status. In many instances it determined who could and could not engage in certain occupations or produce certain goods and services, and thereby effectively constituted what would be regarded today as "closed shops." Significantly, membership of many guilds was regarded as eternal rather than a matter of voluntary contract and explicitly linked to a certain understanding of justice. Black describes this as

> the duty to produce work of a certain standard and the right to secure employment. The chief means to do this was the restriction on craft entry. Rules stipulating maximum hours and so on comprised a large part of guild regulations … The main purpose of the corporate legal rights claimed by guilds was to ensure a secure livelihood. In this way their sense of justice led to a belief in approximate equality of output and of the returns due to all craft members; their main

opponent here was the merchant-capitalist … who, by employing more men and working them harder, undercut their price and ruined their livelihood.[12]

Though ideas and culture associated with guilds were widespread in the medieval world, this state of affairs did not go unchallenged. The canonist and Cardinal-Bishop of Ostia and Velletri, Henry of Segusio (better known as Hostiensis, d.1261) stated that the legal rights of guilds needed to be understood "without prejudice to their lord if they have one." Neither guilds nor their corporate claims, according to Hostiensis, were above the law of the realm or the city. There is also evidence to suggest that the rulers of cities would often limit guild regulations and even occasionally dissolve guilds in order to protect the interests of consumers. Though they generally acknowledged that guilds could create their own rules and regulations, medieval legal thinkers stressed that any guild regulations were subordinate to the demands of natural justice. Some scholastic theologians such as Bartolus of Sassoferrato (1313–1357) even argued that guilds were not permitted to make "a law by which another is prejudiced, as for instance if they make a law that only certain persons and no others can exercise that craft."[13] Nor is it insignificant that while scholastic thinkers generally attached great importance to the ideas of friendship and mutual aid, they did not view guilds as morally significant communities in the way that the family and the state were considered natural communities.

The dominance of corporatist-communalist theories and practices was also challenged in the same historical period by the emergence of concepts that were to help define commercial order. Black holds that this "complex of ideas" was present in Europe at least as early as the thirteenth century. He summarizes them as:

> first, personal security in the sense of freedom from the arbitrary passions of others. And freedom from domination in general. This involves freedom (or security) of the person from violence, and of private property from arbitrary seizure. But these … can only be maintained if legal process is credible and successfully enforced as an alternative to physical violence, in settlement of disagreements, and in redressing wrongs committed by violence. This leads to the notion of legal rights (whether or not so called), both in the sense of the right to sue in court on equal terms with everyone else—legal equality—and in the sense of claims, for example, to property, recognized and upheld by the law.[14]

This attention to *liberty* appears to have flowed primarily from Christianity's distinctive stress upon freedom. Aquinas emphasized, for instance, that, unlike animals, people could only acquire what they needed through using their "reason and hands" freely and creatively.[15] At an even deeper level, the Christian accent upon man being freed from the burden of sin, not to mention its insistence upon the reality of free will and therefore of free choice, underlined the idea that human beings were, by God's grace, free. Saint Paul spoke of everyone being called "to liberty" through Christ. While there was—and is—a way of discussing this in

Christian theology that focused upon man's interior liberation from sin, the conviction that all people were called to freedom had profound political, social, and economic implications. Slavery, for instance, began to acquire negative moral connotations that it did not have in a pre-Christian world. Though Christianity affirmed that social groups, law, and the secular authorities had legitimate roles to play in shaping the social order, it avowed that there were limits to what these bodies and even the Church could do when it came to influencing people's exercise of their freedom. In the words of the medieval theologian John of Salisbury, though virtue and ultimately communion with God was the proper and natural end of man, people could not achieve this "without liberty, and the loss of liberty shows that perfect virtue is lacking."[16]

Having emphasized that human freedom implied limits to the power of secular and religious authorities, it is hardly surprising that one of the great institutional expressions of these limits and a prerequisite for a commercial society—*private property*—also received much attention in the Middle Ages. Following Aristotle, Aquinas outlined three reasons why appropriation of property to particular owners is morally licit and even necessary. First, people tend to take better care of what is theirs than of what is common to everyone, since individuals tend to shirk a responsibility which is nobody's in particular. Second, if everyone were responsible for everything, the result would be confusion. Third, dividing up things generally produces a more peaceful state of affairs, whilst sharing common things often results in tension. Individual ownership, then—understood as the power to manage and dispose of things—is justified.[17]

This explanation is attentive to what Christianity stresses as the effects of sin upon human beings. Aquinas' argument assumes that it is generally unreasonable to expect fallen human beings to own things in common for long periods of time. Sin, Aquinas implies, limits man's capacity to be other-regarding in an altruistic sense. Aquinas appears conscious of the fact that each individual's *self-interest* and its workings cannot be ignored in any reflection upon the social order.

In other writings, Aquinas stressed that the fact that property is generally owned *privately* creates limits to what the state can tell people to do with their goods and lives. He wrote, for instance, that the power of households to manage their own economic affairs—a power that depends on the assurance associated with property ownership—is the foundation of their ability to tell the state's rulers that their powers are limited. It is not surprising therefore that Aquinas' statements about unjust law in his *Summa Theologiae* seem at least partly directed against the tendency of rulers to impose unfair taxation burdens.[18] One of Aquinas' likely disciples, John of Paris, went so far as to assert that, with respect to the goods of laymen, no member of the clergy enjoyed any lordship or even stewardship.[19] Such goods, in his view, did not come by gift or grant to a community but rather were acquired by individual laymen "through their own skill, labor and diligence."[20] Here we should note that medieval legal thought was primarily shaped by reflection upon the second tablet of the Decalogue: the so-called negative commandments. Thus the importance attached to property that emerges in the medieval period was shaped in part by excavation of the meaning of the Decalogue's prohibitions against stealing and killing innocent life.

Another implication of medieval attention to the importance of private property was that it suggested that, subject to the demands of law and natural justice, people could *freely exchange* what they privately owned. Certain rights concerning the free trade of privately-owned goods thus began to receive formal legal recognition in twelfth and thirteenth-century civil law. By the thirteenth century, the willingness and legal authority to buy and sell different forms of property had become so widespread in England and facilitated such low-transaction costs in the exchange of goods as well as relatively easy capital-formation that the historian Alan MacFarlane has described this society as "an open, mobile, market-orientated nation."[21] This was especially true of towns, where those who became residents were generally able to enter into business partnerships, contracts, and exchanges without requiring the local lord's agreement.

With the moral validity of freely buying and selling goods becoming a given fact of economic life in towns and cities, it was inevitable that the concept of *contract* became widespread in these societies. The idea of contract was already well-established in Roman law and was implicit in the nature of many feudal obligations. With the spread of private ownership and free exchange in medieval Europe, it became more widely understood that fulfillment of promises, as well as legal provision to enforce unreasonable failures to perform promises, was a prerequisite for ensuring that services and goods would be delivered in return for payment. This led many medieval lawyers to spend considerable energy ensuring that people distinguished the obligations incurred by contract from those that proceeded from membership of, for example, a guild. Thus figures such as Hostiensis emphasized that the purpose of contracted business partnerships and associations was "more favorable profit and richer gain"[22] rather than expressions of brotherly solidarity commonly presented as being the purpose of guilds.

Last, we should recall that the idea of *civility*, much popularized during the Scottish Enlightenment, was also associated in the minds of some medievals with the growth of trade and commerce. Another of Aquinas' likely disciples, Ptolemy of Lucca, stated that business affairs in cities needed to be conducted with politeness, gentility, and "a certain civility."[23] By this was meant that people in urban commercial settings needed and therefore tended to treat each other as formal equals (regardless of social or economic status) under the law and with a certain degree of kindness and gentleness, even if their primary contact was through business transactions.

Many of these ideas concerning liberty, exchange, property, contract, and civility were presented by Renaissance Christian humanists as increasingly characteristic of the cities of their time. It was common for Renaissance writers to portray self-made and entrepreneurial individuals who pursued personal gain in a way consistent with Christian morality and the law as among the city's greatest treasures.[24] As one commentator states, this was directly contrary to the usual guild objective of limiting output to a level that all could achieve.[25] Other Renaissance scholars such as Leonardo Bruni of Arezzo (1369–1444) penned essays linking the persistence of commercial liberty with rule of law and civility. "The magistrates," Bruni wrote, "are set up for the sake of justice ... lest the power of any person should surpass that of the laws in the city."[26] He described the people of Florence as a commercial people who were "industrious, liberal ... affable, and above all urbane."[27] Mario Salamanio (1450–1532) even advised the readers of his *De Principatu* that just as contractual arrangements were the basis for business partnerships, so too were contracts also "the means by which the state is arranged and preserved."[28] He thus employed a legal concept increasingly used to facilitate ease and predictability in commercial life to define the character of the state and implicitly the limits of its powers. For just as a business partnership could be voided by violation of the contract, so presumably could the authority of the ruler. A contemporary of Salamanio, the Italian humanist Brandolinus (1440–1497), emphasized that the prevalence of liberty and rule of law in many Italian city-states were central to the emergence of a spirit of free enterprise and the encouragement of commerce and trade across Europe:

> Our citizens enter into commerce and partnerships freely with all nations, open up the whole world for their own gain, and come to the aid of all men with their industry [*industria*] and skills [*artibus*]; and all nations from everywhere flow together into our cities as into markets common to all peoples [*communia gentium emporia*].[29]

On the Brink of a New World

Though the emerging world of Christian humanism was shattered by the religious wars that shook Western Europe, the ideas and institutions associated with commercial order were not. While mercantilism became the dominant mode of economic life as absolutist governments began to establish a grip over much of Protestant and Catholic Europe, it is also true that previously unimaginable commercial possibilities emerged. Adam Smith once described the discovery of the Americas and of a passage to the East Indies via the Cape of Good Hope as two of the most important events recorded in human history. In terms of their significance for the expansion of commerce throughout the world, Smith did not exaggerate. The gradual conquest and settlement of the New World by Spanish adventurers, not to mention the Dutch and Portuguese expansion into Africa and Southeast Asia, transformed Western Europe's economic life, especially in the Netherlands, Italy and the Iberian peninsula. International trade expanded at an unprecedented rate. As Spanish colonies were established in the Americas, they became the source of a growing demand for basic and luxury products made in Castile and Aragon.[30]

One consequence of these developments was the rise and expansion of the commercial classes. Cities like Seville—the destination of the treasure fleets from America—grew in size as they attracted merchants and traders from the rest of Europe. Skills such as valuing and accounting became highly valued. The center for merchant activity in Europe began to shift toward Spanish merchant families, many of which were of foreign origin, having first established themselves in North Italy and the Low Countries before gravitating toward Spanish markets. The effects of Spain's growing commercialization throughout the sixteenth century were not limited to the social and political realm. For this was a society in which most people, peasant or aristocrat, believed that their free choices could mean the difference between their salvation and damnation. Though a moderate profit on sales was viewed as acceptable, the increase in the volume of credit transactions in the Spanish economy only reminded people of the traditional prohibition of usury. Many merchants and traders, being desirous of salvation, turned to their confessors for guidance.

Confronted with this and other moral questions in their consciences and the confessional, many priests turned to those charged with the responsibility of providing guidance on such subjects: that is, theologians and canon lawyers. The response of many theologians was to reflect upon the wisdom of medieval scholars and thinkers of antiquity and apply their insights to the new situation enveloping Spanish, and more broadly, Western European life. The application of medieval scholastic and Aristotelian thought to the commercial upheavals of the time resulted in the publication of an unprecedented number of lengthy treatises on the moral dimension of economic life. Some of the most detailed descriptions of sixteenth century commercial life are contained in these writings. The Austrian economist and philosopher Friedrich von Hayek did not exaggerate when he indicated that the tradition of liberty under law—so strong in continental Europe during the Middle Ages—was kept alive

> by the Schoolmen after it had received its first great systematization, on foundations deriving from Aristotle, at the hands of Thomas Aquinas; by the end of the sixteenth century it had been developed by some of the Spanish Jesuit philosophers into a system of essentially liberal policy, especially in the economic field, where they anticipated much that was revived only by the Scottish philosophers of the eighteenth century."[31]

Written by late-Scholastic scholars such as Francis de Vitoria, Domingo de Soto, and Tomas de Mercado, these works sought to determine which of the new commercial practices conformed to the demands of morality, and distinguish them from those that did not. In his discussion of money-changing, for example, Tomas de Mercado informs his reader that he wants to help confessors "who, abstracted as they are from the world, cannot understand the ways of these entangled dealings."[32] The inquiries of the late-Scholastics consequently embraced activities and practices as varied as taxation, coinage, foreign exchange, credit, prices, and interest. They also analyzed the workings of the banking business of their time, and showed how the fluctuations in foreign exchange were related to changes in the purchasing power of different currencies. One unforeseen result of these reflections, according to some historians, was the theoretical conceptualization of important aspects of commercial life. These include the subjective theory of value, the identification of all the determining factors of price, a simple version of the quantity theory of money, as well as new insights into how coinage debasement facilitated inflation.[33]

Though many late-Scholastics generally regarded commercial activity as morally indifferent,[34] some ascribed positive moral characteristics to trade and commerce. The economic historian Henry Robertson records that the Jesuits Francisco Suarez and Luis de Molina were unashamed promoters of the social benefits of enterprise, financial speculation and the expansion of trade.[35] Another late-Scholastic, Domingo de Soto, even portrayed commercial activity as evidence of civilizational development:

> Mankind progresses from imperfection to perfection. For this reason, in the beginning barter was sufficient as man was rude and ignorant and had few necessities. But afterward, with the development of a more educated, civilized and distinguished life, the need to create new forms of trade arose. Among them the most respectable is commerce, despite the fact that human avarice can pervert anything.[36]

In other late-Scholastic texts, one finds awareness that there was something new and energetic about this expansion of commerce. Bartolomé de Albornóz described commercial activity as "the nerve of human life that sustains the universe. By means of buying and selling the world is united, joining distant lands and nations, people of different language, laws and ways of life. If it were not for these contracts, some would lack the goods that others have in abundance and they would not be able to share the goods that they have in excess with those countries where they are scarce."[37] Likewise in Mercado's manual, we encounter a sense of wonder concerning the commercial life of Seville, where a "banker traffics with a whole world and embraces more than the Atlantic, though sometimes he loses his grip and it all comes tumbling down."[38]

Unfortunately this period of financial and intellectual prosperity did not persist in Spain. Heavy taxation necessitated by Spain's almost continuous involvement in war throughout the second half of the sixteenth century, the population decline throughout the Iberian Peninsula, unfavorable trade balances, and the European-wide rise in prices contributed to a slow deterioration in the economic situation. In other parts of Europe, however, other important intellectual developments were occurring that would further stimulate the emergence of commercial society. This is especially true of the seventeenth-century English philosopher John Locke. Articulating many of the ideas outlined above, Locke integrated them with the concept that a person's work could be viewed as something that could be bought and sold; he even went so far as to describe a person's labor as their property.[39] This made it possible to speak of a labor market in which people could freely sell their labor or purchase the labor of others in the form of wages.

An important effect of these ideas was their provision of a stronger moral and legal basis for labor to escape the confines and regulations of the guilds and other labor-restricting organizations, thus facilitating a free market in labor and a high degree of occupational mobility.[40] This becomes clearer when we consider that once a society begins to define work obligations less in terms of hereditary duties and more in terms of freely agreed contractual arrangements, it changes at a fundamental level. The pace at which this took effect varied from country to country. In England, the effects were speedier because its legal system had already begun moving in this direction. In his *Puritanism and Revolution* (1962), Christopher Hill illustrates that England's seventeenth-century Chief Justice Sir Edward Coke (1552–1634) regarded guilds as nothing more than institutions of monopoly. Coke consequently worked to undermine their restrictive labor practices by arguing that they were contrary to the freedom enjoyed by all the Crown's subjects. This theme, according to Hill, became a standard argument of the Parliamentary party in its struggle against royal absolutism, partly because of the Crown's attempts to impose royal monopolies as an alternative to parliament as a revenue source.[41]

Another idea much associated with Locke that proved vital for commercial society was that of *tolerance*. While Locke had much to say on subjects such as private property, his most significant contribution to commercial society may have been his anonymously published *Letter Concerning Toleration* (1689). Like others of his time, Locke evoked the death and destruction that had flowed from the intolerance showed by Protestants and Catholics alike during Western Europe's religious wars. For Locke, one way of resolving this issue was through what he called "toleration." This embraced many facets, but at the heart of Locke's argument was the notion that the state should refrain from interfering in the religious beliefs of its subjects, save when these religious beliefs lead to behaviors or attitudes that run counter to the security of the state and the legitimate demands of public order.[42]

On one level, Locke's understanding of toleration could be viewed as a logical extension of the civility that medieval and renaissance writers associated with commercial activity. Being polite to others with whom one disagrees about, for instance, religious and political questions is surely implicit to the idea of civility. In practical commercial terms, the gradual acceptance of tolerance allowed people to travel for trading purposes without fearing that those with whom they exchanged goods and services would denounce them to the public authorities for the particulars of their faith or politics. The Britain of Locke's time was, of course, a far from religiously tolerant country. Nonetheless, the demands of commerce appear to have contributed over time to the spread of a de facto toleration of religious differences throughout England. Voltaire commented upon this when visiting London in the middle of the eighteenth century. Though he stressed the established Church of England's political dominance and its intolerance of other faiths, Voltaire remarked in his *Philosophical Letters* upon the tolerance encouraged by commerce:

> Go into the Exchange in London, that place more venerable than many a court, and you will see representatives of all the nations assembled there for the profit of mankind. There the Jew, the Mahometan, and the Christian deal with one another as if they were of the same religion, and reserve the name of infidel for those who go bankrupt.[43]

The soothing effects of this activity upon other social interactions did not go unnoticed by Voltaire. As he put it: "On leaving these peaceable and free assemblies, some go to the synagogue, others in search of a drink." Generally, Voltaire concluded, "all are satisfied."[44]

A Modern Commercial Tradition

Though other correspondence and acts by Voltaire indicate that his own commercial ventures did not diminish his own prejudices against various categories of people, including Jews,[45] his observations of the London Stock Exchange reflected heightened awareness of how commercial activity changed the character of social relationships in other arenas. Still, neither Voltaire nor the medieval, Renaissance and post-Reformation thinkers posited that a new society was coming into being. In some instances, their thoughts about commerce led them to reason that private property and the necessity of certain economic certitudes such as a stable value of money necessarily implied new limits to state power. What we do not find in their works is a realization that a fundamental shift toward a new social order was underway.

Yet by the middle of the eighteenth century, we see distinct signs that consciousness of such a sea change was becoming apparent. Reflecting on this period, the French political philosopher Pierre Manent writes:

> During the eighteenth century, in England, Scotland, and France, perceptive observers felt able to describe the workings of a new social bond, which went by the generic name of commerce, not rarely qualified as *doux commerce*. Commerce then is not just a human activity among a number of human activities; it connotes a new regime of human action itself, and its development aids the axis of human progress. The radical newness of commerce in this comprehensive meaning consisted in this, that people were now linked to one another without commanding each other, and without necessarily sharing a common way of life.[46]

In his *Spirit of the Laws* (1748), the French philosopher Guy de Montesquieu drew a picture of a world unfolding between two poles. One pole was the ancient world, in which republican virtue predominated; the other was England, a society in which commerce and liberty held sway. "The political men of Greece," Montesquieu wrote, "who lived under popular government recognized no other force to sustain it than virtue. Those of today speak to us only of manufacturing, commerce, finance, wealth, and even luxury."[47] In the end, it was a group of thinkers on the outskirts of Western Europe who were to "discover" that a new society was emerging and to analyze its nature and consequences. Like Montesquieu, Adam Smith and others associated with the eighteenth-century Scottish Enlightenment sensed that momentous changes were underway as the basic engine of commercial society—"the desire to better one's condition"— began to take on an unprecedented momentum. In studying these changes the Scots certainly drew upon the intellectual resources of the past, but sharpened points of reflection into the discussion.[48]

Members of the Scottish school ranging from William Robertson to Adam Ferguson followed the then-common European tradition of integrating and presenting different fields of study as a cohesive whole rather than promoting a rigid segmentation of areas of knowledge. This may have heightened their sensitivity to the societal-wide implications of economic changes. This is almost certainly true of Henry Home, a philosopher and historian better known to history as the Scottish jurist Lord Kames. Like others before him, Kames underlined the significance of property for social and legal order. Societies and laws came into existence, he emphasized, in part because all people who owned things wanted some guarantees of its protection. "It is ... a principle of the law of nature," Kames added, "and essential to the well-being of society that men be secured in their possessions."[49] This in turn led to people devising rules that not only enforced the protections implicit to property, but also educated people in property's importance for social order and each person's security. These laws became especially important, according to Kames, when social development reached a particular point—that being what Kames called commercial society.

Kames regarded commercial society as one that represented a progression upon the agricultural stage which had in turn evolved from pastoral-nomadic communities that had developed out of hunting-fishing societies. The more complex social and economic arrangements of agricultural society, Kames held, had required laws to achieve what the customs of nomadic societies could not. There were, for example, relationships such as those between landowners and those who rented the land which generated a range of new freely undertaken obligations between people, the violation of which undermined social order. Elaborating upon this thesis, Kames proposed that as the locus of economic activities began to shift away from villages and fields toward towns and cities, further changes in law were necessitated. For once the buying, selling, and exchange of goods reached the level of sophistication characteristic of commerce, Kames believed new societies would start to surface which allowed ever-increasing numbers to enjoy greater ease and material prosperity. Under such influences, he proposed, how could the entire pattern of life *not* change in some fundamental ways?

The social developments generated by commercial society, especially in terms of the prospect of greater wealth it held out for increasingly larger numbers of people, went beyond the economic. The Scottish philosopher David Hume, for one, was fascinated by the manner in which commerce

> rouses men from their indolence; and presenting the gayer and more opulent part of the nation with objects of luxury, which they never have dreamed of, raises in them a desire of a more splendid way of life than what their ancestors enjoyed.... Imitation soon diffuses all these arts; while domestic manufactures emulate the foreign in their improvements.... Their own steel and iron become the equal to the gold and rubies of the *INDIES*.[50]

In his *History of the Reign of Emperor Charles V* (1769), Hume's contemporary, William Robertson, described how commerce's spread throughout Western Europe was reconfiguring the cultural tone of large communities. "In proportion as commerce made its way into the different countries of Europe," he wrote, "they successfully ... adopted those manners, which occupy and distinguish polished nations." Civility, in short, was both necessary for commercial society as well as a by-product. It embraced a range of characteristics such as self-restraint, politeness, self-confidence, and charity. Robertson also stressed that civility helped to diminish some of commercial society's sharper edges. He was not afraid to acknowledge that an element of self-interest was involved insofar as such behavior made life more pleasant for everyone and facilitated a greater ease and predictability in commercial transactions.

With commerce creating such incentives for change, Kames and other Scots realized that it could not help but break down those features of feudal, agricultural, and medieval society that created barriers to sustained wealth-creation for the majority of the population. This was especially true of the guilds. These attracted particular ire from many Scottish writers. Not only, Smith contended, did guilds restrict people's ability to use their talents and abilities in the market place but, also paradoxically enough, they failed to produce skilled workers.[51] Decades earlier Montesquieu had assailed the influence of the guilds, insisting that "Laws which oblige every one to continue in his profession, and to devolve it upon his children, neither are nor can be of use in any but despotic kingdoms."[52]

Throughout eighteenth-century England and Scotland, the ability of guilds to control a range of industries was undermined in an unprecedented manner. All across Great Britain, the Smith scholar Jerry Muller remarks, "The 'freedom' of the guilds—the exclusive legal right to practice a trade or craft within an incorporated town—were being challenged, ignored, or regarded as unenforceable."[53] Watching and encouraging such developments, Adam Smith highlighted the manner in which commercial society broke the power of guilds across Europe to inflate wages, prices, and profits artificially. The demise of guilds in commercial society, Smith stressed, weakened their ability to protect whole categories of people from the most important form of economic discipline: their customers.[54]

The disintegration of guild-like, mercantile economic arrangements did not mean that the commercial society portrayed by the Scots lacked an organizing principle. Though medieval and Renaissance thinkers devoted considerable attention to the effects of the pursuit of self-interest, it was the Scots who explored the workings of rational self-interest in the greatest detail. Interestingly, their interpretation of self-interest was not monolithic. It assumed a variety of manifestations. One was the notion, promoted by the philosopher Francis Hutcheson, that the pursuit of virtue was itself in man's self-interest. Who, after all, would want to be hedonistic or corrupt? Virtue itself was the essence of happiness. This, in Hutcheson's view, meant that each person's use of his freedom would be guided, if sufficiently cultivated, by an innate moral sense. Another understanding of self-interest may be found in Smith's attention to the self-regarding element present in all human beings, though he was careful to underline each person's ability to balance this by placing himself in the position of an external assessor of his own behavior. Then there is David Hume's idea of self-interest as being essentially concerned with self-gratification, unmoderated by right reason, as Hutcheson understood it, or even what Smith would call a type of "fellow feeling" he believed was in every person.

Though the differences between these three conceptions of self-interest were considerable, their authors shared the belief that everyone's pursuit of self-interest was paradoxically enough in the best interests of all and central to the growth of commercial society. Echoing Bernard Mandeville, Smith famously wrote, "It is not from the benevolence of the butcher, the brewer, or the baker, that we expect our dinner, but from regard to their own interest."[55] And while Smith affirmed Mandeville's view that the pursuit of self-interest facilitated greater independence of action as people pursued their interests in increasingly creative ways, he parted with Mandeville's radical individualism by noting that it also meant that people were increasingly interdependent upon each other. In Smith's vision of commercial society, no man could be an island—the liberty to pursue one's self-interest created reciprocity as people engaged in mutually beneficial exchange.

This is not to say that the Scottish school was oblivious to potential problems facing this new commercial order. Adam Smith is often praised for identifying the increasing specialization of labor as crucial for commercial society's economic dynamism, even though his teacher, Frances Hutcheson, had already made this point in his *System of Moral Philosophy* (1755). Less well-known is Smith's concern that this specialization had the potential to narrow human horizons. In one of his lectures written several years before the appearance of *Wealth of Nations*, Smith taught that "Another bad effect of commerce is that it sinks the courage of mankind, and tends to extinguish martial spirit. In all commercial societies the division of labor is infinite, and everyone's thoughts are employed about one particular thing … The minds of men are contracted, and rendered incapable of elevation, and heroic spirit is utterly extinguished."[56]

This criticism of commercial society was mild compared to that contained in Adam Ferguson's *Essay on the History of Civil Society* (1767). Like his fellow Scots, Ferguson traced the history of civilizational development in terms of an ascent from a barbarous state toward the commercial way of life. In the latter, the sources of wealth are increased at an unprecedented speed, technology improves, and the division of labor is used by merchants and entrepreneurs to reduce their costs and increase their profits. Simultaneously, the prevalence of rule of law replaces conflict with order and thus allows a greater sphere of individual liberty. In this "age of separations," Ferguson wrote, there is an "air of superior ingenuity"[57] compared to previous ages.

Unfortunately, the same society becomes, according to Ferguson, a victim of its own success. While civility reigns in commercial society, both polished manners and the prevalence of order are gradually undermined by the very engines of commercial prosperity. There is, he deduced, a tendency for people in commercial society to become disinterested in public life. This in turn degenerates into a sphere in which people pursue extremely narrow sectional interests. The division of labor that fosters commercial society, Ferguson believed, breaks down non-commercial bonds of association as people become fixated on a single-minded pursuit of wealth. Beneath a façade of politeness and good manners, people begin to behave in a largely mercenary fashion, while others become what Ferguson described as "servile" and "effeminate."[58] In his own time, Ferguson believed, "the individual considers his community only insofar as it can be rendered subservient to his personal advancement and profit."

The long-term problem, Ferguson alleged, is that commercial society's apparent sapping of people's public spiritedness and its excessive constriction of their horizons opens the way to tyranny. The non-commercial associations that limit state power begin to disappear and people start to look to the state to reforge public bonds and protect them against the uncertainties of commercial life. While the state might be able to preserve rule of law and protect property, Ferguson recognized that those who exercised the state's authority were not immune from the temptations and potentially corrupting effects of political power. Nor did their government service, Ferguson held, preserve them from the general contraction of vision that occurred in commercial society. "The boasted refinements, then, of the polished age," Ferguson concluded, "are not divested of danger. They open a door, perhaps, to disaster, as wide and accessible as any they have shut."[59]

Not all of Ferguson's fellow Scots agreed with his dark predictions. Though not denying a possible diminishing of imagination, Smith held that commercial society was morally and materially superior to its primitive and agricultural predecessors. He and other Scots affirmed, for example, that the expansion of trade and the increase and spread of wealth provided increasing numbers of people with more resources and time to deepen their knowledge of the finer things of life and the study of more abstract subjects. In the Glasgow in which Adam Smith spent much of his life, service industries dealing in luxury goods became more prevalent, as did the availability of architecture and the arts. The jurist John Erskine underlined the manner in which commercial society discouraged law-lessness. With more and more people acquiring substantial property and business interests, they had a greater interest in the prevalence of rule of law. Then there was the way in which commerce changed the manner in which people thought about each other. In a point reminiscent of Voltaire, Scottish thinkers stressed that, while the significance of a person's social status, religion, or nationality could never be obliterated, commerce encouraged more people to see others in a new light—as consumers, producers, owners, customers, and clients—and pay less attention to their religious and political differences. Commercial society thus encouraged people to see themselves as individuals who cooperate with each other voluntarily rather than as members of groups who adhere to caste or tribal patterns of social interaction. Smith also had much faith in the power of educa-tion to ensure that people did not lose sight of the importance of non-commercial activities and interests such as the philosophy that Smith pursued with perhaps greater passion than his study of economics.

A Universal Society?

The commercial society depicted by the eighteenth-century Scots was not one that they regarded as being limited to Great Britain or even Western Europe. Though not blind to cultural differences, the Scots genuinely viewed commercial society as universal in meaning and potential application. This appears to have been a correct assumption. Versions of what figures such as Smith, Robertson, and Hume would recognize as commercial society soon spread beyond the British Isles. Throughout the late eighteenth and nineteenth centuries, regulations, monopolies, guilds, and corporate structures across much of the world were diminished and replaced by basic foundations of commercial society such as freedom of contract, private property, economic liberty, and free trade.[60] Today commercial society crisscrosses the planet as these foundations have spread and become integrated across national and regional boundaries. Many of the features of political, legal, and economic life which are often corralled under the term "globalization" are effectively universalizations of the foundations of commer-cial society.

These developments raise the question of whether commercial society is the eventual and inevitable direction in which all nations and cultures are headed. This theory constituted part of the thesis famously put by Francis Fukuyama in *The End of History and the Last Man* (1992). For Fukuyama, what he called "the worldwide liberal revolution" that preceded and continued after Communism's collapse in the former Soviet Union and Eastern Bloc constituted "further evidence that there is a fundamental process at work that dictates a common evolutionary pattern for all human societies."[61] A rather different interpretation is offered by the economist Paul Henderson. Though Henderson does not dispute that Fukuyama's contention might possibly be true for democratic forms of government, he expresses uncertainty whether the same can be said for what he calls "economic liberalism." There has, Henderson points out, "been no consistent trend to economic liberalism"[62] over the past 250 years. While there was, he states, progress from the late eighteenth century onward, this pattern began to change in the late nineteenth century. Reversals to the spread of commercial society include, according to Henderson, the introduction of tariffs at the level of international trade, increasing government involvement in income redistribution, the establishment of state social welfare systems, government provision of the bulk of education and health services, and closer state regulation of labor markets. While the last quarter of the twentieth century represented a partial shift in some countries toward freer economic arrangements in the wake of Communism's collapse, the decline of economic nationalism, and the contracting of the boundaries of state ownership or enterprises, Henderson reminds us that public spending levels have barely altered (if anything, they have risen), labor markets in most countries (especially in Europe) remain highly regulated, and services ranging from health care to education continue to be dominated by state monopolies. He also comments that in some parts of the world, particularly Western Europe, there remains great resistance to the cultural, political, legal and economic changes associated with commercial society—what is popularly referred to as "Anglo-Saxon capitalism" throughout continental Europe. Even in many countries that underwent significant economic liberalization in the 1980s and 1990s (including the United States, Great Britain, Australia, and New Zealand) and reaped considerable economic growth as a consequence, high levels of animosity against many aspects of commercial society persist.

Some reasons for this acrimony are easy to identify. While commercial societies generate more wealth and raise everyone's standard of living, they neither resolve nor necessarily reduce economic inequality. Commercial society even assumes a certain degree of economic inequity which translates into inequities in other areas. This remains a major source of complaint for many on the political right and political left. Also controversial is the notion of self-interest, which is commonly equated with selfishness. Nor should it be forgotten that the rise of commercial society has not diminished the persistence of corporate guild-like attitudes and values within many cultures. According to Black, these have often manifested themselves in the growth of trade unions and the integration of workers' representatives into the governing bodies of businesses of a certain size (what is called *Mitbestimmung* in Germany). Then there are the various modern theories of corporatism that first acquired expression in the schools of solidarist thought which flourished in Wilhelmine Germany and the Austro-Hungarian Empire. Promoted by figures such as Chancellor Engelbert Dollfus in pre-World

War II Austria as well as through industrial policies advocated (if somewhat loosely implemented) by regimes of a fascist nature or with fascist leanings such as Nazi Germany, Mussolini's Italy, and Franco's Spain, corporatist thinking has also exerted significant influence throughout much of Latin America. Socialism, many believe, is dead. Its ghost, however, lives on in the guise of corporatist and neo-corporatist thought and structures, all of which drain commercial society of its energy, genius, and cultural esprit.

Yet despite the ongoing challenges to commercial society, clear explanation and analysis of the moral-cultural, legal, and economic foundations of commercial society remain relatively rare. While it is not difficult to find strictly economic defenses of free markets, the economic liberalization associated with the revival and revitalization of commercial society in the last quarter of the twentieth century surely requires an accompanying explanation of social order. As Paul Kelly has noted, economic liberalization moves capital quickly from one location to the next, breaks social ties, and uproots long-established communities and work habits. These, he hints, are just some of the reasons why the ongoing progress of economic liberalization tends to facilitate increasing resistence to such change. Arguments promoting the merits of economic efficiency are not enough, it seems, to persuade significant numbers of people of commercial society's merits.[63] A fresh presentation of the foundations of commercial society does, however, have the potential to establish a theory of social order that grounds and explains the ideas and policies associated with the spread of economic liberalization while similtaneously revealing the civilizing potential of commercial order.

Notes

1. Karl Marx and Friedrich Engels, *Works*, vol. 3 (London: Penguin, 1971), 33.

2. Weber acknowledged that others such as the English economist William Petty, had attempted to associate the rise of capitalism in the West with its specific religious trajectory. Weber's contribution was to fill out this position by associating it with particular forms of Christianity that began to emerge in the sixteenth century.

3. This section draws on Samuel Gregg, "La fin d'un mythe: Max Weber, le capitalisme et l'ordre médiéval," *Journal des Economistes et des Etudes Humaines*, 13, no. 2/3, 2003: 185–96.

4. See Max Weber, *The Protestant Ethic and the Spirit of Capitalism* (London: Allen & Unwin, 1930), chap. 1.

5. See J. W. O'Malley, *The First Jesuits* (Harvard: Harvard University Press, 1995).

6. See D. Kelly, *The Westminster Confession of Faith: An Authentic Modern Version* (New York: Summertown Texts, 1992).

7. See A. Fanfani, *Catholicism, Protestantism, and Capitalism* (Notre Dame, Ind.: University of Notre Dame Press, 1984). On this general topic, see Rodney Stark, *The Victory of Reason: How Christianity Led to Freedom, Capitalism, and Western Success* (New York: Random House, 2006).

8. Peter Ackroyd's biography of Sir Thomas More provides modern readers with a profound sense of the vibrant life of commerce, banking and trade that permeated much of Catholic England before Henry VIII embarked on his quest to obtain a divorce and Puritanism first began to emerge anywhere in the British Isles. See Peter Ackroyd, *The Life of Thomas More* (London: Vintage, 1999). Supporting empirical evidence that further disproves Weber's thesis may be found in the work of the economic historian, Jacques Delacroix. He methodically outlines a range of facts that simply cannot be accounted for by Weber's theory. He notes, for example, that "Amsterdam's wealth was centered on Catholic families; the economically advanced German Rhineland is more Catholic than Protestant; all-Catholic Belgium was the second country to industrialize, ahead of a good half-dozen Protestant entities." J. Delacroix, "Religion and Economic Action: The Protestant Ethic, the Rise of Capitalism, and the Abuses of Scholarship," *Journal for the Scientific Study of Religion* 34 (1995): 126–27.

9. See C. Nederman, "Freedom, Community and Function: Communitarian Lessons of Medieval Political Theory," *American Political Science Review* 86 (1992): 977–86.

10. See Antony Black, *Guild and State: European Political Thought from the Twelfth Century to the Present* (London: Transaction Publishers, 2003), xvii.

11. The following three paragraphs draw upon ibid., 13–19.

12. Ibid., 16.

13. Bartolus of Sassoferrato, *Commentaries on the Digest* (Turin: 1577), 47.22.4. Lord Robbins, it seems, was not quite correct when he wrote, "Only in the middle of the eighteenth century did men begin to conceive of a world in which privilege to restrict should itself be restricted and in which the disposition of resources should obey, not the demands of producers for monopoly, but the demands of consumers for wealth." Lionel Robbins, *Economic Planning and International Order* (London: Macmillan, 1937), 233.

14. Black, *Guild and State*, 32. See also C. W. Bynum, "Did the twelfth century discover the individual?" *Journal of Ecclesiastical History* 31 (1980): 1–17.

15. Thomas Aquinas, *Summa Theologiae*, ed. T. Gilby (London: Blackfriars, 1963), I-II, q.95, a.1. Hereafter *ST*.

16. John of Salisbury, *Policraticus*, vol. 2, ed. C. Webb (Oxford: Typographeo Clarendoniano, 1909), 217.

17. See *ST*, II-II, q.66, a.2. Aquinas states that the *use* of things is a different matter. In regard to use, one is not justified in holding things as exclusively one's own (*ut proprias*) but should rather hold them as common, in the sense that one must be ready to share them with others in need. For Aquinas, private property is the normative way of realizing this principle of common use, but it is not absolute.

18. See *ST*, I-II, q.96, a.4.

19. See John of Paris, *On Royal and Papal Power*, trans. J. A. Watt (Toronto, Ont.: Pontifical Institute of Mediaeval Studies, 1971), chap. 7.

20. Ibid., 103.

21. See A. McFarlane, *The Origins of English Individualism: The Family, Property and Social Transition* (Oxford: Oxford University Press, 1978), 163. See also John F. McGovern, "The Rise of New Economic Attitudes—Economic Humanism, Economic Nationalism—During the Later Middle Ages and the Renaissance, A.D. 1200–1500," *Traditio* 26 (1970): 217–54.

22. Hostiensis, *De Syndicis*, in *Summa Aurea Super Titulis Decretalium* (Venice, 1570), fol. 104r.

23. Ptolemy of Lucca in *De Regimine Principum*, bks. II–IV, in Thomas Aquinas, *Opuscula Omnia Necnon Opera Minora*, vol. 1, *Opuscula Philosophica*, ed. J. Perrier (Paris: Cerf, 1949), bk. II, chap. 8. *De Regimine Principum* is a continuation of an earlier unfinished work (probably by Aquinas) to which Ptolemy began adding approximately halfway through Book Two. Books Three and Four are entirely by Ptolemy.

24. See Quentin Skinner, *The Foundations of Modern Political Thought*, vol. 1 (Cambridge: CUP, 1978), 74.

25. See Black, *Guild and State*, 15.

26. Leonardo Bruni, *Laudatio Florentinae Urbis* [*Eulogy to the City of Florence*], ed. H. Baron, *From Petrarch to Leonardo Bruni* (Chicago: University of Chicago Press, 1968), 259. See also G. Holmes, "The emergence of an urban ideology at Florence, c. 1250–1450," *Transactions of the Royal Historical Society*, 5, no. 23 (1970): 111–134; and G. de Lagrade, "Individualisme et corporatisme au moyen âge," *Université de Louvain, receuil de travaux d'historie et de philology*, 3, no. 18 (1943): 57–134.

27. Bruni, *Laudatio*, 263.

28. Mario Salamonio, *De Principatu*, ed. M d'Addio, *Pubblicazioni dell'istituto de diritto pubblico dell'Universita di Roma*, vol. 4 (Milan: Giuffrè, 1955), 28.

29. Aurelius Brandolinus, *De Comparatione Reipublicae et Regni ad Laurentium Medicem Libri Tres*, in *Irodalomtörteneti Enlekek*, vol. 2, *Plaszorszagi XV Szazadbeli Iroknak*, ed. A. Jenö (Budapest, 1890), 123–24.

30. See *Economic Thought in Spain: Selected Essays of Marjorie Grice-Hutchinson*, ed. Laurence S. Moss and Christopher Ryan, trans. Christopher K. Ryan and Marjorie Grice-Hutchinson (Aldershot: E. Elgar, 1993).

31. F. A. Hayek, "Liberalism," in *New Studies in Philosophy, Politics, Economics and the History of Ideas* (Chicago: University of Chicago Press, 1978), 123.

32. Tomas de Mercado, *Summa de tratos y contractos*, ed. R. Sierra Bravo (Madrid: IEP, 1975), 313.

33. This summary is drawn from Murray Rothbard's summary of the late-Scholastics in *Economic Thought Before Adam Smith*, vol. 1, *An Austrian Perspective on the History of Economic Thought* (Aldershot: Edward Elgar, 1995), 97–136.

34. See Alejandro Chafuen, *Faith and Liberty: The Economic Thought of the Late Scholastics* (Lanham, Mich.: Lexington Books, 2003).

35. See Henry Robertson, *Aspects of the Rise of Economic Individualism: A Criticism of Max Weber and His School* (Clifton: A. M. Kelly, 1973).

36. D. de Soto, *De Iustitia de Iure* (Madrid: IEP, 1968), VI, q.II, a.2.

37. Bartolomé de Albornóz, *Arte de los Contratos* (Valencia: 1573), VII, 29.

38. Mercado, *Summa*, 10.

39. See John Locke, *Two Treatises of Government*, ed. P. Laslett (Cambridge: CUP, 1967), 305–7.

40. See Black, *Guild and State*, 155.

41. See C. Hill, *Puritanism and Revolution: Studies in Interpretation of the English Revolution of the 17th Century* (London: Mercury Books, 1962), 28.

42. Toleration need not mean that the law must commit itself to agnosticism or skepticism about moral good or evil of different choices and actions. Locke did not, for instance, suggest that stealing should be tolerated. To steal, in Locke's view, was to violate that natural law accessible to people of all faiths and none. Toleration was thus neither an absolute nor an end in itself. Locke himself did not extend toleration to atheists,

anyone whose religious faith involved allegiance to a foreign power, and those whose religious faith did not allow them to extend to others the toleration they claim for themselves. Atheists, Locke argued, could not be tolerated because he believed that it was impossible for atheists to have any moral principles and thus they could not be trusted to adhere to promises and oaths. Though he mentioned Muslims as examples of the other two cases, he probably had in mind Roman Catholics.

43. Voltaire, "On the Presbyterians," *Philosophical Letters*, trans. Ernest Dilworth (New York: Macmillan Publishing Company, 1961), letter six.

44. Ibid.

45. See the discussion of Voltaire's financial dealings in the context of his difficult relationship with King Frederick the Great of Prussia in Robert Asprey, *Frederick the Great: The Magnificent Enigma* (New York: Ticknor & Fields, 1988).

46. Pierre Manent, *Modern Liberty and its Discontents*, ed. and trans. Daniel J. Mahoney and Paul Seaton (Lanham, Md.: Rowman & Littlefield, 1998), 222.

47. Guy de Montesquieu, *The Spirit of Laws*, ed. David Wallace Carrithers (Berkeley: University of California Press, 1977), bk. 3, chap. 3.

48. This is not to underestimate the differences between different contributors to Scottish Enlightenment thinking about commerce. The implicit atheism and philosophical skepticism of a David Hume contrasts sharply with the Christian belief and acceptance of natural law by a William Robertson or a Francis Hutcheson.

49. Lord Kames, *Sketches of the History of Man*, vol. 2, 3d ed. (Dublin: 1779), 85.

50. David Hume, "Of Commerce," in *Selected Essays*, ed. Stephen Copley and Andrew Edgar (New York: Oxford University Press, 1993), 196.

51. See Adam Smith, *Glasgow Edition of Works and Correspondence of Adam Smith*, vol. 2, *An Inquiry into the Nature and Causes of the Wealth of Nations*, ed. R. H. Campbell and A. S. Skinner, rev. ed., (Oxford: Oxford University Press, 1979), I.x.c.13–14.

52. Montesquieu, *Spirit*, bk. 20, chap. 22.

53. Jerry Z. Muller, *Adam Smith in His Times and Ours: Designing the Decent Society* (Princeton: Princeton University Press, 1993), 31.

54. See Smith, *Wealth of Nations*, I.x.c.17.

55. Ibid., I.ii.2.

56. Cited in Arthur Herman, *How the Scots Invented the Modern World* (New York: Crown Publishers, 2001), 186.

57. Adam Ferguson, *An Essay on the History of Civil Society*, 6th ed., (London: 1763), 183–84.

58. Ibid., 220.

59. Adam Ferguson, *An Essay on the History of Civil Society* (Edinburgh: Edinburgh University Press, 1978), 65.

60. See Rojas, *Rise and Fall of the Swedish Model*, 19.

61. Francis Fukuyama, *The End of History and the Last Man* (New York: Avon Books, 1993), 48.

62. David Henderson, *The Changing Fortunes of Economic Liberalism: Yesterday, Today and Tomorrow* (London: Institute for Economic Affairs, 1998), 11.

63. See Paul Kelly, *The End of Certainty: Power, Politics & Business in Australia* (Sydney: Allen & Unwin, 1994), 418–20.

Part 1

FOUNDATIONS

2

Neither Angel nor Beast

At what ethical level, in general, must we situate the economic life of a society that puts its trust in the market economy?

It is rather like the ethical level of average man, of whom Pascal says: "L'homme n'est ni ange ni bête, et le malheur veut que qui veut faire ange fait la bête" To put it briefly, we move on an intermediate plane. It is not the summit of heroes and saints, of simon-pure altruism, selfless dedication, and contemplative calm, but neither is it the lowlands of open or concealed struggle in which force and cunning determine the victor and the vanquished.

—Wilhelm Röpke

Perhaps one of the greatest outcomes of commercial society is the manner in which it provides greater wealth to increasing numbers of people and progressively diminishes poverty at an unprecedented rate.[1] It is not a coincidence that Adam Smith's *Wealth of Nations* begins by highlighting the state of those nations that have not yet embraced commercial order. They are, he writes, "so miserably poor, that, from mere want, they are frequently reduced, or, at least, think themselves reduced, to the necessity sometimes of directly destroying, and sometimes of abandoning their infants, their old people, and those afflicted with lingering diseases, to perish with hunger, or to be devoured by wild beasts."[2]

Commercial society's impact upon poverty is, however, not simply a result of the unintended consequences of market exchange. It owes much to commercial society's particular moral foundations. By *moral foundations*, we mean particular values and habits of action indispensable for the workings of commercial society. This is an area of much controversy, not least because as Michael Novak remarks in his *Spirit of Democratic Capitalism* (1982), many contemporary reflections about commercial life are still "disproportionately colored by the values of the ancient, aristocratic order."[3] This does not necessarily mean that values viewed by many as characteristic of pre–1789 Europe such as honor ought to be dispensed with. Rather Novak avows that much modern reflection upon what principles ought to shape the moral culture of civilized society tended to be barely tolerant if not dismissive of the values that Novak associates with commercial order.

This may owe something to the tendency to reduce the worth of commercial society to its economic efficiency and wealth-creating ability. Neither economic efficiency nor wealth creation are unimportant in themselves; but the moral foundations of commercial society are more complex and numerous.[4] Man does not live by utility alone. What follows is an attempt to describe commercial society's basic moral foundations. Taken together, these habits and values do not suffice for a society that wishes to merit the title humane or civilized. Nor are they exclusive to commercial society. Trust and peace, for instance, can exist in a range of social orders. The values identified below should therefore be understood as distinctly pronounced in commercial society, while their absence compromises a society's capacity to be recognized as commercial in character and reality.

Self-Interest, Rightly Understood

Any system of social and economic life that aspires to be truly humane needs to reflect the nature of human beings. Communism imploded, at least in part, because it denied certain truths about humans, most notably the fact that we possess the unique ability to make free choices. By attempting to replace market mechanisms of supply and demand with a top-down command approach, both socialist and communist economic theory ascribed abilities to humans that are possessed by no individual or group. One was the assumption that any one of us can look ahead and foresee all the possible needs of an entire society at any one point of time in the near or distant future. No matter how sophisticated the available methods of economic modeling, such foresight is beyond any human intelligence. There are good reasons why economic forecasting is often described as more of an art than a science.

Another failure of real socialism to comprehend human nature was its inability to appreciate the observable fact that at most times, the vast majority of people prefer to place the ownership of things in private hands. This is not to claim that people are never willing to ascribe ownership of certain things to wider associations of people (such as businesses with multiple shareholders) or even the state. In some situations, such as wartime, people are willing to accept certain restrictions on their ownership. Nonetheless, private ownership remains the preferred norm in virtually all societies. With its in-principle opposition to private ownership, communism was unable to account for this reality.

Why then do people tend to favor private over communal ownership? One reason is that they are aware, as Aristotle and Aquinas witnessed long ago, that when things are owned in common, the responsibility and accountability for their use disappears, precisely because few are willing to assume responsibility for things that they do not own. Our everyday experience reminds us of the tragedy of the commons. The early advocates of socialism were well aware of these objections. Their response was to hold that all that was needed was a change of mind and heart on the part of people as well as profound structural change: a change that would not only produce a new system of ownership, but also a "new man"—the socialist man much trumpeted by the former Soviet Union.

Commercial society rejects this vision of man as well as the means proposed for realizing such an economic order. For the understanding of humans that pervades commercial society is one of *realism*. It does not assume that human beings can always be other-regarding when it comes to acts of economic exchange. Many of commercial society's legal and economic structures are thus predicated on a decidedly non-altruistic understanding of humans and their world. Contracts exist, in part, because there will always be some people who will unreasonably decide not to fulfill their promises. Likewise, the network of free exchange assumes that people normally engage in exchanges in order to meet their own needs rather than from a specific concern for the well-being of those with whom they are exchanging goods and services. The type of exchange characteristic of commercial society thus differs from the system of mutual obligation from that which existed in some medieval societies whereby peasants, for instance, were required to pay money to the nobility in return for the protection accorded by the nobility against brigands and foreign invaders. Commercial society requires *free* exchanges into which people enter in pursuit of their *own* interests.

Commercial society does not therefore attempt to eliminate human fallibility. Instead it holds that there is nothing unnatural about self-interest. To speak about self-interest, as Manent notes, is to "designate a powerful and universal resort of human action."[5] It is not an abstract principle without grounding in reality. Those who followed commercial society's early development noted its ability to align human weakness and self-regard with a society's overall progress toward a more prosperous state of well-being. Adam Smith's reference to the "invisible hand" perplexes some, but is simply a metaphor for the idea that through allowing people to pursue their self-interest, unintended but beneficial social consequences for others will follow. As individuals pursue profit, they unintentionally add to the sum total of the wealth in society, unintentionally

allow people from different nations to come to know each other, unintentionally
promote civility and peace, unintentionally allow others to benefit from more
and better jobs, and unintentionally contribute to technological development.[6]
None of this means that commercial society does not afford opportunities for
people to act altruistically. Rather, it is precisely because increasingly large numbers of people in commercial society are able to accumulate sums of capital that
exceed their immediate needs and acquired responsibilities, they begin to develop
opportunities to be generous to others.

Despite this, the pursuit of self-interest by individuals and groups alike
remains perhaps the most controversial moral-cultural feature of commercial
societies. As suggested in Chapter 1, there was considerable disagreement among
Scottish Enlightenment thinkers about the meaning of self-interest. When twentieth-century economic historians such as R. H. Tawney portrayed the age of
commerce as the age of acquisitiveness, they associated the pursuit of self-
interest with the indulgence of greed, the effective endorsement of depravity, and
a type of ruthlessness when it comes to achieving the ends chosen by individuals.
Such observations rarely account for the fact that the "self" is capable of being
other-regarding and even critical of his own behavior. Nor do they acknowledge
that every self is enveloped in a web of relationships, ranging from the contractual to the familial and communal, all of which moderate and check our acquisi-
tive instincts. It is also worth considering that hedonism, decadence, and greed
are hardly unique to commercial societies. They are present at all times and
places where human beings exist. As noted by Max Weber:

> The impulse to acquisition, the pursuit of gain, of money, of the greatest possi-
> ble amount of money, has in itself nothing to do with capitalism. This pursuit
> exists and has existed among waiters, physicians, prostitutes, dishonest offi-
> cials, soldiers, brigands, crusaders, gamblers, and beggars—among all sorts and
> conditions of men, in all times and in every land on earth where the objective
> possibility of it has existed or exists. This naive conception of capitalism ought
> to be given up once and for all in the nursery school of cultural history.
> Unbridled avarice is not in the least the equivalent of capitalism, still less of its
> "spirit." Capitalism may actually amount to the restraint, or at least the rational
> tempering, of this irrational impulse.[7]

Properly understood, self-interest has little in common with such features. It is
even possible to speak of a reasonable self-love. When Aristotle, Aquinas, and
other thinkers of the classical moral tradition underlined the imperative of people
pursuing virtue, they did so because they regarded this as a natural result of people engaging in a reasonable form of self-regard. This is, for Aquinas, a reasonable love of self.[8]

Tocqueville's observations of the American commercial society of the 1830s
echo similar themes. In *Democracy in America*, Tocqueville presented his readers with the paradox that self-interest properly understood was the primary means

by which Americans combated radical individualism. He recorded that the tendency in pre-commercial societies was for the very rich and powerful to despise self-interest.[9] In the new post-aristocratic world of America, Tocqueville was adamant that all people, rich and poor, believed that "by serving his fellows man serves himself and that doing good is to his private advantage."[10] Hence, far from objecting to people pursuing their own interests, the Americans "do all they can to prove that it is in each man's interest to be good."[11] The efficacy of self-interest properly understood, according to Tocqueville, is that it is "within the scope of everyone's understanding," not least because "it is wonderfully agreeable to human weaknesses."[12] Self-interest properly understood, Tocqueville stresses, also sets people against what might be their narrowly selfish concerns. "Every American," Tocqueville insisted, "has the sense to sacrifice some of his private interests to save the rest."[13] Though self-interest rightly understood does not immediately produce virtue, it does exert a "discipline" that "shapes a lot of orderly, temperate, moderate, careful, and self-controlled citizens."[14] While its prevalence may lead to less moral heroism in a society, Tocqueville asserted that self-interest properly understood would make "gross depravity" less common. It was, in Tocqueville's view, a moral outlook peculiarly suited to "men of our time" and their "strongest remaining guarantee against themselves."[15]

More contemporary figures such as the economist Kenneth Arrow have indicated that no one's choices and preferences need be determined by an emaciated concept of self-interest.[16] There are many good reasons, he demonstrates, why people may prefer a marginal rather than a large immediate increase in their own material well-being. The self-interest of a rational businessman indicates that, rather than immediately acquiring vast wealth by cheating his shareholders before fleeing to a safe haven, he should ensure that his firm meets its fiduciary responsibilities to its shareholders if he is serious about growing the company, becoming wealthier in legal ways, and leading a peaceful existence rather than that of a fugitive. Likewise, rational self-interest suggests that we should abide by all legitimate law, even if we disagree with the content and aims of a particular law, for no reasonable person would want to encourage contempt for legitimate law. Considered in these terms, we see the wisdom of Tocqueville's remark that while self-interest properly understood may not be a "sublime doctrine,"[17] its workings in commercial society can have more than material benefits.[18]

In practical terms, there are a number of ways in which the pursuit of rational self-interest is stimulated by commercial society. First, commercial society contains fewer of those social conventions and organizational structures that inhibit both aristocrat and peasant from pursuing their rational self-interest. Second, commercial orders provide wider scope than other societies for people to make choices about what—in light of their particular skills, education, and circumstances—is truly in their economic self-interest to pursue. Third, the competition associated with commercial society encourages people to think ahead as they pursue their self-interest and consider the financial and extra-financial costs and benefits of different choices over the short and long term. Last, people's self-interest in the success of their commercial enterprises pushes them toward common sense rather than wild speculation, prudent risk-taking rather than foolishness, and self-reliance rather than excessive dependency.

The Liberty of Commerce

The pursuit of self-interest rightly understood is preconditioned upon our ability to discern what that self-interest in particular circumstances might be and then to act freely in order to bring about the realization of that chosen end. Liberty is thus essential for commercial society in the same way that the negation of freedom is fundamental to the workings of a socialist or communist economic system.

In notes written during his travels in England and Ireland, Tocqueville underscored this ultimate dependence of commercial society upon liberty. "Considering the world's history," he wrote, "I can find some free peoples who have been neither manufacturers nor traders. But I can find no example of a manufacturing and, above all, a trading people who have not been free ... there must be a hidden relationship between those two words: *liberty* and *trade*."[19] Interestingly, Tocqueville added that he disagreed with Montesquieu's contention that it was commercial society that leads to the expansion of human freedom. "People say," Tocqueville jotted down, "that the spirit of trade naturally gives people the spirit of liberty. Montesquieu asserts that somewhere." While conceding that Montesquieu was partly right, Tocqueville held that "it is above all the spirit and habits of liberty which inspire the spirit and habits of trade."[20]

The essence of Tocqueville's argument is that particular moral qualities essential for freedom are also conducive to commercial success. "To be free," he claims, "one must have the capacity to plan and persevere in a difficult undertaking, and be accustomed to act on one's own; to live in freedom one must grow used to a life full of agitation, change and danger; to keep alert the whole time with a restless eye on everything around: that is the price of freedom. All those qualities are equally needed for success in commerce."[21] Tocqueville goes on to describe how the spirit of commerce flows from those who rely upon themselves, who are inspired by a sense that they can do anything and who look restlessly at the present and imagine how it can be transformed. Hence, Tocqueville writes, "I am in no hurry to inquire whether nature has scooped out ports for him, and given him coal and iron. The reason for his commercial prosperity is not there at all: it is in himself."[22]

While commerce may contribute to the spread of freedom, there is no possibility of widespread commerce without liberty. This becomes more evident when we consider the ways in which commerce relies upon people exercising a variety of liberties. If, for instance, there is not a considerable degree of freedom concerning what people can buy and sell, then trade and free exchange are impossible for both potential consumers and vendors. Likewise, unless people are free to associate with whom they choose, there is no possibility of commercial legal mediums such as contracts. The freedom to decide to discontinue one form of commercial association and to opt for another is essential for the type of competitive behavior that underlies a free market. Competition also relies upon the liberty of people to offer a similar good or product at the same or less expensive price as other individuals and organizations. So too does the system of free movement of prices that enables consumers to judge for themselves the relative availability and competitiveness of goods and services and which permits producers to set their own prices. The very essence of economic entrepreneurship is a high degree of freedom of private initiative. Indeed, if people are to take advantage of new opportunities, their ability to realize their objectives may depend upon their freedom to move from their current place or even country of residence.

While these liberties are often taken for granted in much of the modern world, this was not always the case. Many of these freedoms, such as the relatively free movement of prices, existed in many pre-commercial societies. Nonetheless, most such liberties were strictly limited in their application or largely denied to entire categories of people. In pre-revolutionary Europe, most social groups were severely limited in their ability to exercise some of the freedoms listed above. Not only were those who subsisted in the status of serfdom only allowed to engage in the most basic forms of commerce, but it was common for the nobility in countries such as France, Prussia and Russia to be prohibited from engaging in bourgeois-like activities—the expectation being that they would engage in some form of service to the state, either in the military or civil service, or live the life of a semi-feudal landowner. Prior to 1789, an aristocrat in France could even temporarily lose his noble status if he engaged in commercial activity in order to restore his family's wealth.[23] Likewise the ability of serfs, peasants, and aristocrats to travel was often limited by law throughout much of pre-revolutionary Europe. Observing Czarist Russia, Montesquieu commented:

> As all the subjects of the empire are slaves, they can neither go abroad themselves nor send away their effects without permission ... Commerce itself is inconsistent with the Russian laws. The people are composed only of slaves employed in agriculture, and of slaves called ecclesiastics or gentlemen, who are the lords of those slaves; there is then nobody left for the third estate which ought to be composed of mechanics and merchants.[24]

This is not to imply that the liberties underpinning commercial society somehow involve people being free "from" law. It is simply to note that commercial society is impossible without people being able to exercise a particular range of liberties. It follows that a state that seeks to place unreasonable limits upon these freedoms, either through excessive coercion or failure to uphold key institutions such as rule of law, is likely to inhibit the growth of commercial society.

The Creative Imperative

A key freedom associated with the emergence of commercial society and the undermining of legal and social obstacles to such a society is that of entrepreneurship. Private initiative rarely occurs unless considerable incentives exist to encourage people to exercise it. At the same time private initiative is closely associated with another habit of action essential for commercial society—creativity. Marx was aware of this connection:

> The bourgeoisie cannot exist without constantly revolutionizing the instruments of production, that is to say productive conditions, and thus all social conditions. Preservation intact of the old mode of production, by contrast, was the first precondition for all earlier industrial classes. The ongoing revolution in production, the uninterrupted shaking of all social conditions, the perpetual uncertainty and motion characterize the epoch of the bourgeoisie in contrast to all others.[25]

Man, it seems, is designed in such a way that his very capacity for survival depends upon his unique ability to create new objects as well as to discover how to create and use things already in existence in faster, more efficient, and cost-effective ways, which can be further transformed through the further application of man's creative insight. The created world, it seems, is full of potentialities to be actualized by human reason and insight. Thus, while the natural world can produce much food of its own accord, there is tremendous scope for humans to accelerate the growth, augment the amount, and transform the character of man's material sustenance. The sources of wealth and economic growth in commercial society depend far less upon the possession of natural resources and much more upon human insight and creativity.

Creativity is not a morally neutral activity. We can certainly question the worth and prudence of creating any number of substances, objects and organizations. The fact that man has used his mind to discover new, more effective means of destroying his fellow human beings does not acquire moral redemption by virtue of the creative insights that allowed such things to be produced. The moral worth of creativity is rather demonstrated by reflection upon its opposite—passiveness and excessive dependency.[26] It concerns the attitude of being unwilling to look beyond one's present circumstances or even consider whether change might be necessary. In some cases, passivity can reflect an instinctive opposition to change for sake of resistance to change or an excessive and unthinking dependence upon the past. The resilience of commercial society does, as we will see, require a high degree of trust in, and even dependence upon, long-established institutions and conventions with which we tamper at our peril. But quietism results in the slow suffocation of the human ability to foresee new possibilities, including those of a commercial character.

Creativity of thought, action, and association literally transforms humanity's outlook from one of a static or cyclical view of history and life to a vision of the world as open to transformation and uplifting through human endeavor. It permits people to break out of set and sometimes stagnant patterns of life. Creativity allows people to imagine a future different from the present in which they exist—a future in which their well-being and that of their children in terms of tangibles such as material wealth and education have all multiplied. This creativity is not limited to one choice or one action on the part of one individual. It invariably involves building upon the creative choices and insights of people living now and those long dead. This collaborative creativity can occur informally or in a more structured environment such as a business. Many such organizations even possess entire departments devoted exclusively to creative purposes. The creativity that flourishes in commercial society is thus rarely that of an isolated individual. It is invariably social in character.

Practical Wisdom

Human insight and creativity spring from the human mind and are thus inseparable from human intelligence. They nonetheless require the disciplined ordering of practical intelligence that allows creative insights to become real. Innovation in itself is not enough for commercial society. For a service or good to become real, we need people who possess the habits of long-term strategic thinking, organizational ability, and the capacity to think about *how* to realize a new product, efficiency, or industry. Centuries ago the medieval theologian Bernardino of Sienna wryly observed, "Very few are capable of doing this."[27]

Reason and rationality have many facets, ranging from the capacity to think abstractly (such as in the realm of physics) to people's ability to know the nature of good and evil. Another manifestation of reason is the ability to understand which form of reason is appropriate for resolving the problem at hand and which is not. Instrumental or scientific reason is not, for example, capable of resolving moral dilemmas. Nor is moral wisdom capable of discerning the nature of the laws of gravity.

Practical wisdom is an especially important moral habit for commercial society. Success in commerce requires a high degree of common sense, thrift and self-reliance; the capacity to make sound business judgments; a strong sense of prudence; an attention to efficiency; a determination to overcome obstacles; the capacity to assimilate knowledge of prices, qualities and costs quickly; attentiveness to detail; and the ability to assess risks and estimate profit opportunities. A particularly important element of practical wisdom is the use and organization of time. The expression "time is money" reflects the awareness that we need to organize ourselves and others in ways that allow many moments of our lives to be directed toward transforming the future in effective and efficient ways. Early voyagers to the United States noticed the extent to which the young American republic embodied this practical wisdom. Everyone, Tocqueville wrote, was calculating, weighing, and computing.

They like order, without which affairs do not prosper, and they set an especial
value on regularity of mores which are the foundation of a sound business; they
prefer the good sense which creates fortunes to the genius which often dissi-
pates them; their minds, accustomed to definite calculations, are frightened by
general ideas; and they hold practice in greater honor than theory.[28]

One reason for this state of affairs, according to Tocqueville, was the tendency
of people in commercial America to distinguish between three types of science.
"The first," he wrote, "comprises the most theoretical principles and the most
abstract conceptions whose application is either unknown or very remote. The
second comprises general truths which, though still based in theory, lead directly
and immediately to practical application. Methods of application and means of
execution make up the third."[29] In Tocqueville's view, the practical instincts of
Americans led them to place a high value on the second and third of these sciences. "But," he added, "hardly anyone in the United States devotes himself to
the essentially theoretical and abstract side of human knowledge."[30] For people
of a commercial frame of mind, Tocqueville writes, "every way of getting new
wealth more quickly, every machine which lessens work, every means of diminishing the costs of production, every invention which makes pleasures easier or
greater, seems the most magnificent accomplishment of the human mind."[31]

Practical wisdom, then, is wary not only of wild speculation but also of tendencies to utopianism. Nor is it the stuff of mundane activity. Among the
Americans who obeyed its maxims, Tocqueville thought they "put something
heroic into their way of trading,"[32] especially in the way that Americans were
willing to engage in significant privations in order to match or outbid their competitors. Tocqueville drew a parallel here between the bravery of Americans
engaged in business and the courage displayed by the French in time of war.[33]

Trust

While a society may embody great resources of creativity and practical wisdom,
commercial development is equally dependent upon a more commonplace moral
quality. For all its reputation for rugged individualism, commercial society is
very reliant upon the element of trust. In commercial terms, trust refers to an
aspect of a *relationship* between two or more parties in which a given situation is
mutually understood and commitments are made toward different actions
designed to produce one or more desired outcomes. The trust required in commercial society extends to faith in people as well as a confidence that certain
rules will always, save in exceptional circumstances, be followed and that certain
institutions such as courts will follow consistent patterns of behavior.

In pre-commercial societies, trust was not unknown. Nevertheless, it tended
to remain relatively weak outside families and to be grounded in expectations
attached to different social roles. In feudal society, there was a strong sense that

clergy, nobles and commoners would fulfill various responsibilities ascribed to them by customary and feudal law. While this qualified as a form of trust, it was more limited in scope and application than the type of trust essential for commercial society. Loyalty and trust in pre-commercial situations might well be expanded to a broad concept of family of the type that existed in the Scottish Highland clans or even some of the banking houses of Renaissance Italy. Outside these confines, deep suspicion of the stranger is often the rule.

The emergence of commercial society requires an extremely widespread diffusion of the willingness to trust others, even total strangers, and to make and keep promises. The legal philosopher Roscoe Pound did not exaggerate when he wrote, "Wealth, in a commercial age, is made up largely of promises."[34] The economist Wolfgang Kasper neatly summarizes the place of trust in commercial society:

> Whenever individuals interact with others they have to trust that their counter-parts will behave in predictable ways, fulfilling the promises they made. This fact is so fundamental that we frequently lose sight of it. When you hand a sum to a bank teller to pay an account, you trust that the teller will not steal the money and the bank will remit the funds to their intended destination. When you sign an employment contract, you trust that many matters which are not spelt out in the contract will be handled reasonably and without your boss exerting undue arbitrary power. When you order a book from an overseas supplier over the Internet and give your credit card number to pay for it, you rely on a large number of people, whom you have never met and will never meet. When foreign exchange dealers conclude telephone contracts worth billions of dollars every day, they often deal with complete strangers in other countries whom they must trust.[35]

Adam Smith traces this fostering of trust to the workings of rational self-interest: "Whenever dealings are frequent, a man does not expect to gain so much by any one contract as by probity and punctuality in the whole, and a prudent dealer, who is sensible of his real interest, would rather choose to lose what he has a right to than give any ground for suspicion ..."[36] The growth and spread of banking practices exemplify the importance of trust for everyday commercial life.[37] Depositing one's surplus capital in a bank instead of storing it in one's house demands an act of trust on the part of depositors in that bank. The same depositors have to be willing to trust bankers who want to make loans and sometimes grant unsecured credits to people that the original depositors will never know. The same trust permits banks to assume the roles of remitting money and supplying paper circulation within a country. While this may reflect a widespread realization that an efficient way of circulating money in a society is to allow banks to issue bank notes that complement (and perhaps even eventually supersede) metal currencies, it also requires people to trust banks to do so in a responsible manner.

Modern commercial banking is based on a peculiar and unprecedented trust that exists on a massive scale between thousands of people, depositors and debtors who usually do not know each other. To this extent, bankers are mediators of trust. As institutions, banks are founded on a series of promises to pay certain amounts of money that exist between the bank, its depositors, its debtors, and other clients. While the bank prospers on the basis of its ability to make a profit on the spread between lending and borrowing rates that have been contracted between the various parties, such prosperity would be impossible without trust.

Some societies are quicker to develop this factor of trust than others. This in turn has economic consequences for a community's ability to build the surplus capital that any commercial society needs for expansion and growth. In nineteenth-century Britain, for instance, there were many banks and many depositors. By contrast, checkbooks in France were rare, as was the practice of keeping running accounts at banks. While savings for major investments were often lodged at banks, most individuals and families in France made separate arrangements for the storage of their money. Thus Walter Bagehot was moved to remark in 1872:

> If a "branch," such as the National Provincial Bank in an English country town, were opened in a corresponding French one, it would not pay its expenses. You could not get any sufficient number of Frenchmen to agree to put their money there.... Deposit banking is a very difficult thing to begin, because people do not like to let their money out of their sight, and especially do not like to let it out of sight without security—still more, cannot all at once agree on a single person to whom they are content to trust it unseen and unsecured.[38]

Trust is equally essential to a medium as characteristic of commercial society as the forming and fulfillment of contracts. While legal guarantees secure some protection against unreasonable failure to fulfill the contract, the contract itself is unlikely to come about unless there is a minimum of trust. When people make a contract, they are engaging in a commercial convention and a recognized legal practice. Such an activity presupposes a basic exercise in promise-making in which we make a reasoned choice to commit ourselves to perform certain actions while relying on others to bind themselves to doing particular things. Contracts are in fact null and void without such prior commitments. They therefore enlist our willingness to trust others and to merit their trust.[39] If commercial society required all agreements to receive formal contractual endorsement, its ability to prosper would be limited. By necessity, trust in commercial society extends beyond what is formally endorsed by commercial law. Most economic exchanges do in fact involve making promises which carry only minimal and sometimes no legal weight. Most things are bought and sold in commercial society without extensive checks that the goods and services being exchanged are in fact what the buyers and sellers hold them to be. There is a prevailing expectation that, in most situations and most of the time, people will do what they said they would do and there will generally be little need to have recourse to legal remedies.

But perhaps the importance of trust in commercial society is best understood by considering how people in commercial orders deal—both legally and informally—with those who demonstrate through words or deeds that they are in fact untrustworthy. Investors, entrepreneurs, and everyday consumers who break promises made during various transactions (and thus violate the trust of others) are often severely restricted by law from being allowed to engage in a wide range of activities. Others who incur even the suspicion of being guilty of fraud or breaking the rules that govern commercial life are often isolated and shunned (often even in the absence of formal legal sanctions) by others precisely because they have broken the bonds of trust. It is little wonder that many commercial enterprises will go to significant lengths to ensure that a buyer who finds himself burdened with a faulty product or service is more than adequately compensated for the business's failure to provide what it promised. The reason is simple: the desire to protect the company's reputation for being worthy of trust, both with the aggrieved consumer and anyone to whom the consumer might mention his disappointment.

Civility and Restraint

The giving and receiving of trust assumes a certain willingness to treat others in particular ways until they prove that they are unworthy of such trust. It thus involves behaving toward others in a certain manner—not necessarily in the way that people interact with close friends but certainly in a manner best described as *civil*. Scottish Enlightenment thinkers viewed this as especially characteristic of commercial order, often associating it with the habit of politeness. They saw commercial society as bound together not only by market relations underpinned by rational self-interest, but also a culture of civility, gentleness, and mutual respect that paid no heed to a person's background or status in society. The historian of ideas J. G. A. Pocock employs the phrase "commercial humanism"[40] to describe this aspect of the Scots' understanding of commercial society.

While figures such as Adam Smith and William Robertson drew upon the Aristotelian and Christian attention to the importance of a virtuous citizenry in describing the content of commercial society, they emphasized that the type of virtues developed often depended upon the culture in which people lived. "In general," Smith wrote, "the style of manners which takes place in any nation, may commonly be said to be that which is most suitable to its situation."[41] Hence while their conception of civility did embrace the habit of being polite to each other while engaging in competition in the market place, it also encompassed a range of characteristics and habits that soften and facilitate the business of commerce.

In the pre-commercial world, the type of behavior commonly regarded as civil was normally linked with lifestyles often associated with the nobility. Reflecting upon this, Tocqueville ventured that, "Among an aristocratic people each caste has its own opinions, feelings, rights, mores, and whole separate existence. Hence its members are not at all like members of all the other castes. They have not at all the same way of thinking or feeling, and they hardly manage to think of themselves as forming part of the same humanity."[42] This did not mean that the different groups, Tocqueville hastened to add, did not provide each other with mutual support or were invariably rude to each other. A certain degree of brutishness, however, was often assumed to be an aspect of the life of those who were not aristocrats.

In commercial society, civility is no longer associated with an inherited social caste. The civilizing project effectively moves away from a small group and embraces increasing numbers of people as levels of wealth rise across society. In commercial society, many people have for the first time the possibility of having sufficient means to be generous, to learn to defer immediate gratification, to follow lives marked by graciousness, and to abstain from rude or coarse behavior. It is precisely, as Smith remarked, because every person "becomes in some measure a merchant"[43] in commercial society that commerce leads increasing numbers of people to acquire habits of order and economy. In his lectures on jurisprudence, Smith commented that "When the greater part of people are merchants, they always bring probity and punctuality into fashion, and these therefore are the principal virtues of a commercial nation."[44] People experience a sense of what Tocqueville called "real sympathy"[45] with others in commercial society precisely because the set social roles of pre-commercial society have broken down. They may not be ready to sacrifice themselves quickly for each other, but people are careful with each other. "It makes no difference," Tocqueville wrote, "if strangers or enemies are in question."[46] The capacity to behave in a civilized fashion is regarded as something of which all people are capable. The idea of self-improvement thus looms powerfully throughout commercial society's understanding of civility. As the growth of commercial society breaks down structures of caste and inherited hierarchy, more people become capable—and understand themselves of being capable—not only of searching for knowledge, but also, Tocqueville envisaged, of receiving and assimilating knowledge.[47]

The spread of this desire for education in commercial society and the subsequent growth of access to education has in turn powerful civilizing effects. The importance of sound education begins to be recognized throughout all sectors of society, especially by those who perceive a certain utility in education for successful commercial enterprises. Examples include the development of skills such as accounting, not to mention the acquisition of languages. Moreover, the spread of high expectations for oneself and others in commercial society begins to undermine social, economic, and political practices that slowly became understood as unjust, unreasonable, and unworthy of civilized people. The idea that

one group is endowed with more political power than others by virtue of hereditary privilege, for example, becomes viewed as unacceptable. So too do barriers
to free exchange.

Another feature of civility in commercial society is the quality of self-
restraint. "Self-command," Smith wrote, "is not only itself a great virtue, but
from it all the other virtues seem to derive their principal lustre."[48] The emphasis
upon self-control flows, in part, from the realization that self-improvement in
commercial orders requires much delayed gratification. To exercise initiative in
any field, but especially in commerce, is not simply to select an object to pursue.
It means staying firm in our choices despite the obstacles, temptations, and adver-
sities encountered as we pursue certain objectives, and obeying an order that we
impose on ourselves and therefore to discipline our passions. In commercial society, the civilized person is distinguished from the uncivilized at least in part
because of the former's ability to suppress impulses for immediate pleasure in
order to achieve longer-term social and economic goals. These restraints are thus
found within rather than imposed from without.[49]

In commercial society, the self-restraint associated with civility is closely
linked to the pursuit of self-interest, self-improvement, and especially prosperity.
It extends, for example, from entrepreneurs deferring much satisfaction if they
are to accumulate the capital that they need for a loan, to those in a small business who need to work long and disciplined hours if their business is to grow significantly, to middle class property owners who voluntarily put aside considerable resources to fund their retirement or to help their children acquire the
expensive education they need if they are to enhance their chances of success in
a market order. The incentives for self-restraint in commercial society are thus
more considerable and also accessible to larger numbers of people than any previous social order. Thus while it is true that in commercial society, as Helmut
Kuzmics writes, "the society of the working bourgeois adopts the rituals of
courtly society,"[50] this is partly because manners and habits of politeness smooth
the process of market exchange and the daily intensity of business and often
become broadly associated with the achievement of prosperity.

But having attained a certain degree of wealth, many people in commercial
society find themselves able to spend time and energy on activities ranging from
patronage of the arts, philanthropy, and the pursuit of hobbies previously perceived as the preserve of aristocracy. The irony is that civility in commercial
society often begins as a means to the end of material prosperity, a prosperity
that in turn allows more people than ever before to engage in activities that,
while often bringing them little to no personal monetary gain, are regarded as
reflective of man's higher aspirations to truth, goodness, and beauty: the truly
civilized man. Commercial society alone, of course, will not make men moral—
no society can do that as long as people have free will. Yet, as Muller remarks,
commercial order does "hold out the potential of a society in which most men
would be decent, gentle, prudent, and free."[51] This is no small achievement.

Peace and Tolerance

Part of the vision of civility in commercial society involves people refraining from using violence to achieve their ends. In the pre-commercial world, war was perceived on the part of figures ranging from Alexander the Great to Napoleon as the path to greatness and glory. By contrast, commercial society thrives upon and inculcates the value of peace. Though it is true that commercial societies have engaged in war, they do tend to accord higher worth to peace more than their predecessors. This owes much to their commercial character. War is commercially beneficial for industries such as arms manufacturing, but generally disruptive to free trade, the forging of commercial links, and society's overall material well-being. As Archbishop François Fenélon of Cambrai (1651–1715) wrote to King Louis XIV toward the end of the Sun King's many wars:

> Your peoples die of hunger. Agriculture is almost stationary. Industry languishes everywhere, all commerce is destroyed … Your victories no longer cause rejoicing. There is only bitterness and despair … You relate everything to yourself as though you were God on earth.[52]

Commercial society's ability to promote peace is closely associated with its undermining of the false notion that one person's gain is always at another's expense. Part of Smith's critique of the mercantile practices of his time was their assumption that one's country's gain could only be at the expense of others. Such theories facilitated much aggressive behavior of nations against each other as they fought to secure colonies and exclusive trading rights. "Each nation," Smith wrote, "has been made to look with an invidious eye upon the prosperity of all the nations with which it trades, and to consider their gain as its own loss. Commerce, which ought naturally to be, among nations, as among individuals, a bond of union and friendship, has become the most fertile source of discord and animosity." In Smith's view, "a nation that would enrich itself by foreign trade is certainly most likely to do so when its neighbors are all rich, industrious, and commercial nations."[53]

Considerable incentives thus exist for commercial societies to avoid war. "Peace is the natural effect of trade," Montesquieu writes. "Two nations who traffic with each other become reciprocally dependent; for if one has an interest in buying, the other has an interest in selling; and thus their union is founded on their mutual necessities."[54] Tocqueville underscored the manner in which commerce undermined incentives for war when observing that "The ever-increasing number of men of property devoted to peace, the growth of personal property that war so rapidly devours, mildness of mores, gentleness of heart, that inclination to pity which equality inspires, that cold and calculating spirit which leaves little room for sensitivity to the poetic and violent emotions of wartime—all these causes act together to damp down warlike fervor."[55] The less-appreciated paradox is that commerce and trade allow nations to achieve many of the objectives they had previously pursued through war. This was apparent to the nine-teenth-century French liberal, Benjamin Constant:

> We have finally reached the age of commerce, an age which must necessarily replace that of war, as the age of war was bound to precede it. War and commerce are only two different means to achieve the same end, that of possessing what is desired. Commerce is ... an attempt to obtain by mutual agreement what one can no longer hope to obtain through violence....
>   War then comes before commerce. The former is all savage impulse, the latter civilized calculation. It is clear that the more the commercial tendency prevails, the weaker the tendency to war must become.[56]

Commercial society's reluctance to embark upon war is not simply a matter of resenting the financial restrictions and potential losses associated with the prosecution, winning, or losing of war. It also concerns protecting the fabric of freedoms upon which commercial societies depend. War has a reorganizing logic all of its own. Societies at war take on forms directed to the successful prosecution of war. The difficulty, as Tocqueville pointed out, is that "All those who seek to destroy the freedoms of the democratic nations ought to know that war is the surest and shortest means to accomplish this."[57] "Any long war," he wrote elsewhere, "always entails great hazards to liberty."[58] When nations go to war, governments are given the authority to do things that they are forbidden from undertaking in peacetime and often allowed to expand their powers in those realms where they already exercise considerable authority. This can include acquiring powers that diminish the protections afforded by private property and the rule of law, permitting the raising of taxes to exorbitant levels, and redirecting commercial society's creative energies into areas of a decidedly non-commercial character. Perhaps the greater long-term problem that war creates for commercial societies is that the state is often reluctant to relinquish its newly acquired powers, thereby reducing the sphere of freedom that underpins commercial society and allows it to flourish.

Commercial society's aversion to the use of force is not confined to the sphere of war and foreign relations. It also applies to relations between people within a commercial society and the desire to minimize conflict within this society. As Adam Smith explained, it was not a coincidence that as commercial relations developed between towns and rural areas, "order and good government, and with them, the liberty and security of individuals became more pronounced among the inhabitants of the country, who had before lived almost in a continual state of war with their neighbors, and of servile dependency upon their superiors. This, though it has been the least observed, is by far the most important of all their effects."[59] Few would question that the religious wars of the sixteenth and seventeenth centuries facilitated developments in the idea of tolerance, permeations that we find in the works of figures ranging from Locke to the seventeenth-century Huguenot (then Catholic, then Protestant again) theologian Pierre Bayle.

Though these wars often had more to do with the emergence of nation-states than religious differences per se, the devastation caused by these events caused many to become wary of the consequences of persecuting people for their religious beliefs.

At the same time, there is little question that the emergence of commercial society created particular incentives for the value that many began—albeit slowly and not without significant regressions—to attach to tolerance. Commercial society's emergence and continued growth is very dependent upon a high degree of openness to new ideas and endeavors. A society that closes itself to concepts and investment from people whose political and religious beliefs differ from the dominant culture places itself at a potential economic disadvantage from those communities open to such people. Moreover, many of the tools, institutions, and mechanisms of commercial society depend upon people distancing themselves from assuming hostile positions toward people with differing views. As modern commercial societies began to assume their present form during the seventeenth and eighteenth centuries, wealth became far more mobile, as did banking and trading practices. Businesses became less family-orientated and thus far less uniform in their linguistic, ethnic, and religious composition. Even the language of commercial society—capital, profit, loss, property, markets—though rooted in the Western tradition, has showed a remarkable capacity to transcend cultural and religious boundaries. The mediums of credit and money were able to communicate, as A. J. Conyers points out, certain human needs, wants, and desires across the very same boundaries. With the growth of joint-stock companies, there were increasing numbers of people who had financial interests in enterprises and organizations that engaged in commerce across a variety of areas with different cultural, political, and religious traditions. In short, the spread of markets brought people from very different backgrounds into contact with one another through their mutual pursuit of wealth. With good reason therefore, Montesquieu declared:

> Commerce is a cure for the most destructive prejudices; for it is almost a general rule, that wherever we find agreeable manners, there commerce flourishes; and that wherever there is commerce, there we meet with agreeable manners.
>
> Let us not be astonished, then, if our manners are now less savage than formerly. Commerce has everywhere diffused a knowledge of the manners of all nations: these are compared one with another, and from this comparison arise the greatest advantages.[60]

The desire for free trade necessitates links across regions, oceans, and national boundaries. Through engaging in trade, people are forced to encounter the traditions and habits of others, a process that often leads to people comparing and learning more about their respective customs and practices. Montesquieu suggests that this leads to people becoming more tolerant, less attached to obsolete traditions of the past, and less violent in their treatment of others and strangers. Tocqueville echoes these reflections:

> Trade is the natural enemy of all violent passions. Trade loves moderation, delights in compromise, and is most careful to avoid anger. It is patient, supple, and insinuating, only resorting to extreme means in cases of absolute necessity. Trade makes men independent of one another ... it leads them to want to manage their own affairs and teaches them how to succeed therein. Hence it makes them inclined to liberty but disinclined to revolution.[61]

The common desire to create wealth in ways that can be permanently sustained encourages people to soften the intensity of their cultural, political, and religious differences and conflicts, not least because the erection or persistence of such obstacles over time is likely to encourage people to trade elsewhere. This need not mean that they should consider their differences to be irrelevant. Nor does it suggest that tolerance implies that people ought to embrace a type of indifferentism or syncretism. Indeed, there are many things that no society, commercial or otherwise, can or should tolerate.

Neither peace, tolerance, nor civility is sufficient for commercial society. Nevertheless, taken together and integrated with trust, practical wisdom, creativity, and self-interest rightly understood, they are surely indispensable for societies that wish to move away from static or impoverished economic arrangements. They need not exclude other, more communal habits of choice and interaction. Altruism is not something foreign to commercial order. Commercial society has actually created the material basis for altruism to occur on a scale unprecedented in history. But this ought not blind us to the fact that a society that lacks trust, or disdains creativity, or is dismissive of the workings of rational self-interest is not a social order in which commerce can flourish, even if the very same societies possess some or all of the economic and legal institutions conducive to commercial order.

This becomes more evident when we turn to the economic foundations of commercial society and begin to see just how much features ranging from free exchange to the division of labor presuppose that people will, for instance, be able to pursue their self-interest, develop special forms of creativity, and possess the wisdom to organize people in practical ways. It soon becomes apparent that these habits require the existence of particular economic institutions if they are to realize their promise. Self-interest pursued in a market of free exchange is, all other things being equal, likely to lead to prosperity not for the few but the many. Self-interest that has no alternative but to be pursued in statist or collectivist arrangements normally produces the opposite.

Notes

1. A concise summary of this may be found in J. Norberg, *In Defense of Global Capitalism* (Sydney: Centre for Independent Studies, 2005).

2. Smith, *Wealth of Nations*, I.intro.4.

3. Michael Novak, *The Spirit of Democratic Capitalism* (London: IEA Health and Welfare Unit, 1991), 166.

4. Certainly utility and efficiency are—all things being equal—better than disutility and inefficiency. But the basic immorality of, for instance, a Communist labor camp is not diminished by the fact that it is less efficient at killing people than a Nazi concentration camp.

5. Pierre Manent, "Situation du libéralisme," *Les Libéraux*, vol. 1 (Paris: Hachette, 1986), 20.

6. Many theologians associated with the Jansenist movement in seventeenth- and eighteenth-century Catholicism spoke about a type of self-interest being integral to many acts of charity. The theologian Jean Domat insisted, for example, that: "The fall of man not having freed him from wants, and having on the contrary multiplied them, it has also augmented the necessity of labor and commerce, and of ties; for no man being sufficient of himself to procure the necessities and conveniences of life, the diversity of wants engages man in an infinite number of ties, without which they could not live.

This state of mankind induces those who are governed only by a principle of self-love, to subject themselves to labor, to commerce, and to ties which their wants render necessary. And that they may reap advantage from them, and persevere in them both their honor and the interest, they observe in all those intercourses, integrity, fidelity, sincerity .... We see, then, in self-love, that this principle of all the evils is, in the present state of society, a cause from whence it derives an infinite number of good effects ... And thus we may consider this venom of society as a remedy which God makes use of for supporting it ..." Jean Domat, *Lois Civil dans leur ordre naturel, le droit public, et legum delectus*, Nouv. éd. (Paris: 1713), xx.

7. Max Weber, *Gesammelte Aufsätze zur Religionssoziologie*, 2d ed. (Tübingen: 1922), 22.

8. See *ST*, II-II, q.44, a.8, ad.2, q.26, a.5. As John Finnis notes, if a person is truly a friend to himself, then he should want a superabundance of the goods of reason and virtue for himself. Moreover, Finnis adds, given that the goods of reason and virtue are goods for any human being, and that they include friendship and every form of harmony between persons, then this reasonable self-love helps to facilitate the realization of moral goods common to all. See John Finnis, *Aquinas: Moral, Political, and Legal Theory* (Oxford: OUP, 1998), 113.

9. See Alexis de Tocqueville, *Democracy in America*, vol. 2, ed. J. P. Mayer, trans. G. Lawrence (London: Fontana, 1994), 525.

10. Ibid., vol. 2, 525.

11. Ibid., 526.

12. Ibid., 526–27.

13. Ibid., 527.

14. Ibid.

15. Ibid.

16. See Kenneth Arrow, *Social Choice and Individual Values*, 2d ed. (New Haven: Yale University Press, 1963), 114–15, n. 26; and Amartya Sen, "Rational Fools: A

Critique of the Behavioral Foundations of Economic Theory," *Philosophy and Public Affairs*, 6 (1977): 317–44.

17. Tocqueville, *Democracy*, vol. 2, 526.

18. The key is the influence of reason upon each self's pursuit of its particular interests. Tocqueville, for one, was concerned about what would happen if people's pursuit of private interest was not shaped by reason. Cheryl Welch notes that Tocqueville "distrusted what he perceived as a tendency to confound wealth with happiness." See Cheryl Welch, *De Tocqueville* (Oxford: OUP, 2001), 69. Tocqueville also worried about the pursuit of self-interest by people who chose to remain "ignorant and coarse." Tocqueville, *Democracy*, vol. 2, 526. It would, he wrote, "be difficult to foresee any limit to the stupid excesses into which their selfishness might lead them, and no one could foretell into what shameful troubles they might plunge themselves for fear of sacrificing some of their own well-being for the prosperity of their fellow men." Tocqueville, *Democracy*, vol. 2, 526–27.

19. Alexis de Tocqueville, *Journeys to England and Ireland*, ed. J. P. Mayer, trans. G. Lawrence and J. P. Mayer (New Brunswick and London: Transaction Publishers, 2003), 115–16.

20. Tocqueville, *Journeys to England and Ireland*, 116.

21. Ibid., 116.

22. Ibid.

23. See William Doyle, *The Oxford History of the French Revolution* (Oxford: Clarendon Press, 1989).

24. Montesquieu, *Spirit*, bk.22, chap. 14.

25. Karl Marx, *The Communist Manifesto*, 19–20.

26. Passivity is not to be confused with contemplation. Contemplation involves the active use of the mind for purposes of reflection and renewal.

27. Bernardino of Siena, *Opera Omnia* (New York: Fordham University Press,1591/1928), 292; Raymond de Roover, "The Scholastic Attitude toward Trade and Entrepreneurship," *Explorations in Entrepreneurial History*, 2 (1963): 76–87.

28. Tocqueville, *Democracy*, vol. 1, 285.

29. Ibid., vol. 2, 459.

30. Ibid., 460.

31. Ibid, 462.

32. Ibid., vol. 1, 403.

33. See ibid., 402.

34. Roscoe Pound, *An Introduction to the Philosophy of Law* (New Haven: Yale University Press, 1954), 236.

35. Wolfgang Kasper, *Property Rights and Competition: An Essay on the Constitution of Capitalism* (Sydney: Centre for Independent Studies, 1998), 6.

36. Adam Smith, *Glasgow Edition of Works and Correspondence of Adam Smith*, vol. 5, *Lectures on Jurisprudence*, ed. Ronald L. Meek, D. D. Raphael, and Peter Stein, *Glasgow Edition of Works and Correspondence of Adam Smith* (Oxford: Oxford University Press, 1978), (B), 539.

37. This commentary on banking draws upon Samuel Gregg, *Banking, Justice, and the Common Good* (Grand Rapids, Mich.: Acton Institute, 2005), 39–45.

38. Walter Bagehot, *Lombard St: A Description of the Money Market* (Homewood, Ill.: Richard D. Irwin, Inc., 1962), 38.

39. For a more detailed treatment of this subject, see Samuel Gregg, *On Ordered Liberty: A Treatise on the Free Society* (Lanham, Md.: Lexington Books, 2003), 101.

40. See J. G. A. Pocock, "Virtues, Rights, and Manners: A Model for Historians of Political Thought," in *Virtue, Commerce, and History: Essays on Political Thought and History, Chiefly in the Eighteenth Century* (Cambridge: CUP, 1985), 50.

41. Adam Smith, *Glasgow Edition of Works and Correspondence of Adam Smith*, vol. 1, *A Theory of Moral Sentiments*, ed. A. L. Macfie and D. D. Raphael, rev. ed. (Oxford: Oxford University Press, 1979), V.2.13.

42. Tocqueville, *Democracy*, vol. 2, 561.

43. Smith, *Wealth of Nations*, I.iv.1.

44. Smith, *Lectures on Jurisprudence* (B), 539.

45. Tocqueville, *Democracy*, vol. 2, 562.

46. Ibid., 564.

47. See ibid., 459–68.

48. Smith, *Theory of Moral Sentiments*, VI.iii.11.

49. This is not to suggest that the emphasis upon self-restraint did not exist before the rise of commercial society. Evidently many of the rules of chivalry—not to mention the taking of monastic vows by thousands of men and women before the eighteenth century—involved the voluntary suppression of passions and appetites, sometimes for the entirety of one's life.

50. Helmut Kuzmics, "The Civilizing Process," in *Civil Society and the State: New European Perspectives*, ed. John Keane (London: Verso, 1988), 162.

51. Muller, *Adam Smith in His Time and Ours*, 137.

52. François Fenélon, "Lettre secrète à Louis XVI," *Correspondance de Fénelon*, vols. 16–17, *Les dernières années* (Paris: Droz, 1972–1999). Montesquieu was equally devastating in his critique of the effects of war upon society's economic well-being: "Great princes," he wrote, "not satisfied with the hiring or buying of troops of petty states, make it their business on all sides to pay subsidies for alliances, that is, generally to throw away their money. The consequence of such a situation is the perpetual augmentation of taxes; and the mischief which prevents all future remedy is, that they reckon no more upon their revenues, but in waging war against their whole capital. It is no unusual thing to see governments mortgage their funds even in time of peace, and to employ what they call extraordinary means to ruin themselves ..." Montesquieu, *Spirit*, bk. 13, chap. 17.

53. Smith, *Wealth of Nations*, IV.iii.c.9, 11.

54. Montesquieu, *Spirit*, bk. 20, chap. 2.

55. Tocqueville, *Democracy*, vol. 2, 646. Note that Tocqueville does not suggest that commerce rules out war. While it does diminish the incentives for war, we should acknowledge that some commercially orientated societies have employed war-like force in order to open up new trading opportunities. A good example is America's use of implied force to compel Japan to open up its markets in the mid-nineteenth century, as well as the intervention of European powers into China during the same century.

56. Benjamin Constant, "The Spirit of Conquest and Usurpation," in *Political Writings* (Cambridge: Cambridge University Press, 1988), 53.

57. Tocqueville, *Democracy*, vol. 2, 650.

58. Ibid., 649.

59. Smith, *Wealth of Nations*, III.iv.4. This is not to claim that the pre-commercial societies of the West did not possess an idea of toleration. When Christianity emerged in

the ancient world, it conducted a significant internal debate about whether there was anything worth preserving from the world of Greece and Rome. Some early Christian thinkers such as Tertullian famously wondered, "*Quid Athenae Hierlsolymis*"? What has Athens to do with Jerusalem? Others such as Clement of Alexandria (150–215 A.D.) labored to illustrate that there was much in Greco-Romano philosophy and literature that could be incorporated into orthodox Christian faith. Over the centuries, Christianity proved remarkably open to absorbing the thought of pagan philosophers such as Plato and Aristotle. During the Middle Ages, for example, the Christian world did not try to cut itself off from the rest of the world in a manner akin to the path taken by Japan and China. The period of the Crusades, for example, was marked by the influx of materials and trade from the East into Europe. The remarkable intellectual and economic creativity of the Christendom of the High Middle Ages, in which disciplines such as the sciences as we know them today first emerged, was due in part to Christianity's relative openness to the influx of Aristotelian ideas into the West via Islamic Spain through the work of Jewish philosophers in Cordoba such as Maimonides and Muslims such as Avicenna. Christian Europe did not, of course, accept every idea that entered its environment. Indeed, the secular arm was charged with suppressing, sometimes with violence, those ideas that directly contradicted Christian truth or, more often, the stability of the body politic. Nonetheless, it proved able to assimilate many ideas of non-Christian origin, precisely because they were understood to complement, even bolster, the claims of the Christian Church. In other words, a type of attitude and practice prevailed throughout Christian Europe that, as A. J. Conyers writes, "left the lines of communication open among believing and thinking communities." See A. J. Conyers, *The Long Truce: How Toleration Made the World Safe for Power and Profit* (Dallas, Tex.: Spence Publishing, 2001), 39.

60. Montesquieu, *Spirit*, bk. 20, chap. 1.

61. Tocqueville, *Democracy*, vol. 2, 637.

3

The System of Natural Liberty

The member of Parliament who supports every proposal for strengthening this monopoly is sure to acquire not only the reputation of understanding trade, but great popularity and influence with an order of men whose numbers and wealth render them of great importance. If he opposes them, neither the most acknowledged probity nor the highest rank, nor the greatest public services can protect him from the most infamous abuse and detraction, from personal insults, nor sometimes from real danger, arising from the insolent outrage of furious and disappointed monopolists.

—Adam Smith

It was perhaps the economic differences between commercial societies and their feudal, barter, agricultural, and subsistence predecessors that were most visible to those eighteenth-century Scots studying the rise of commercial society. In his analysis of Scotland's economic development, the geographer Ian Whyte illustrates that "From being one of the least urbanized countries in Europe in 1500, 1600, and even 1700, Scotland was by ... measure of people living in centers with over ten thousand inhabitants, fourth in Europe after England, the Netherlands and Belgium"[1] by the middle of the eighteenth century. For most Scottish Enlightenment figures, the changes were viewed as beneficial. By contrast, Marx was to take the visibility of the economic changes associated with the dawn of capitalism and invest them with demonic characteristics.

For those living in contemporary commercial societies, it is relatively easy to lose sight of the sheer scale of their economic achievements. The advent of commercial society involved the rapid diminishment of the number of people who were able, in Wilhelm Röpke's words, "to satisfy their wants independently of the outside world" and more people becoming completely dependent upon the "indirect method of want-satisfaction."[2] By the latter, Röpke means a situation by which almost everyone is provided daily with essential and luxury goods and services by millions of others. This is very different to the closed, small communities that proliferate in pre-commercial societies in which the basic necessities of life are usually made available on a very local basis—a consequence being that a sudden dearth in availability of goods usually resulted in sickness, destitution, and death for that community.

The beauty of the economic character of commercial society, expressed so clearly in Adam Smith's *Wealth of Nations*, is that no one person or committee is charged with meeting everyone's material needs and wants. As Röpke stresses, "No dictator rules the economy, deciding who shall perform the needed work and prescribing what goods and how much of each shall be produced and brought to market.... *Thus, the modern economic system, an extraordinarily complex mechanism, functions without conscious control by any agency whatever.*"[3] Röpke goes so far as to describe it as a type of "ordered anarchy", noting that while "political anarchy leads invariably to chaos," "anarchy in economics, strangely, produces an opposite: an orderly cosmos."[4]

Evidently the order that Röpke had in mind has nothing in common with the direction imposed by central planners of command economies or even the implementation of mercantile and Keynesian policies. By "order," he appears to mean certain rules and procedures that allow human needs and wants to be met indirectly. These rules and processes are primarily of an economic and legal nature. Some, such as private property, cannot be neatly categorized because their origins and implications lie in both realms. In this chapter, we identify and analyze those foundations of commercial society most adequately described as economic in character.

The Economic Dilemma

Before considering these fundamental economic foundations, it is worth recalling the nature and scale of what may called the "economic problem." Virtually all economists identify the dilemma as the issue of scarcity. Every society, including those communities that possess great aggregate wealth, has to confront scarcity: a scarcity of goods, time, and talent. The Australian economist Ian Harper neatly summarizes this when he writes:

We live in a world in which we do not have unlimited supplies of everything that we desire. Because goods, or the things we use to produce goods, are limited in supply, choices must be made; some things must be given up in order that we might enjoy the benefits of other things. The need to choose implies the need to sacrifice. The very act of choice implies that, while one thing is chosen, another is left behind. Economists are accused, like Jeremiah, of harping endlessly on the costs of people's actions. But they do neither more nor less than point to the self-evident fact of scarcity. The choice of option A implies the rejection of option B. It is not possible to have both.[5]

Even the hermit living in isolation from everyone else has to overcome the problem of scarcity by himself because the possibility of exchange with another person does not exist. As soon as more than one person exists in a given situation, overcoming scarcity acquires a social even collaborative character.

Röpke identifies three means through which the scarcity issue can be solved in a social way. The first is through the use of violence, as in the case of force, deception, or fraud. Leaving aside the moral evil of such acts, the use of violence as a means of overcoming scarcity eventually destroys social bonds such as trust, thereby undermining the ability of a group to overcome scarcity in a social way and over the long term. It is not surprising, then, that this way of addressing scarcity remains at the margin of most societies, save in catastrophic situations. A second social method of overcoming scarcity is that of altruism. Altruism means that people give goods and services to others without expecting anything in return. In most societies, this manifests itself in a range of situations and to a variety of degrees. It is characteristic of most families' typical internal interactions as well as many charitable organizations. The third social method of addressing scarcity does not lend itself to single word definitions such as violence or altruism. Röpke describes it as "a type of contractual reciprocity between the parties to an exchange" which results in "an increase of one's own well-being ... by means of an increase in the well-being of others."[6] The mutual increase in the well-being of the parties is not, incidentally, normally directly intended by the people involved; it is a by-product of the arrangement. In these circumstances, people do not normally obtain what they need and desire through fraud, violence, or charity but rather through individuals or companies buying and selling goods and services to each other.

In commercial society, all three ways of overcoming the scarcity problem are present and overlap in many instances. Stealing and theft exist, though there are constant efforts to minimize these activities. Exchanges characteristic of reciprocal family relationships as well as charitable work also exist in commercial orders. The normative means of overcoming scarcity in commercial society nevertheless remains the process of mutually beneficial exchange, sometimes broadly summarized as a market economy. Though, as we will see, the effectiveness of this activity is often compromised by excessive taxation, protectionism, subsidies, and the imposition of artificial monopolies, the market economy remains central to the way that commercial society addresses the problem of scarcity. Once the market economy is replaced as the primary method of dealing with scarcity, commercial society has ceased to exist. Commercial society's economic foundations do, however, embrace more than the process of exchange. Even before the process of exchange can occur, the goods and services to be exchanged must be discovered and created. Entrepreneurship is thus indispensable to the growth and long-term stability of commercial society.

Entrepreneurship

Entrepreneurship is not confined to economic life or commercial society. Max Weber's work on bureaucracy illustrates that entrepreneurial skills are regularly exhibited in building organizational empires within government departments and public services. This makes it even odder that many are oblivious to the pivotal role played by entrepreneurs in economic activity. Commenting upon the state of economic analysis in the mid-twentieth century, the twentieth-century German social philosopher Oswald von Nell-Breuning stated that most economists described businesses as made up of people who contribute labor or capital.[7] This, Nell-Breuning added, ignored the fact that "[w]ithout question, *intellectus* comes first, that is ... initiative and enterprise."[8]

There are many reasons for this absence of attention to the centrality of entrepreneurs to economic life in commercial society. The British economist Lord Griffiths has ventured the opinion that various strands of Enlightenment thought encouraged people to think of economics as a system that runs according to its own established mathematical principles.[9] Thus much of the formal study of economics evolved into a type of mathematical formalism adopted from Newtonian physics. Over time, another economist Israel Kirzner reminds us, "as economic theory became more sophisticated, as marginal analysis and market equilibrium theory came to be more carefully and more fully articulated, the entrepreneur receded more and more from theoretical view."[10] With entrepreneurship not fitting easily into the equilibrium model associated with the then-dominant economic paradigms, some economists found it easier to focus on discovering systematic economic regularities. As Malcolm Fisher remarks: "Mathematical model builders, whether constructors of general equilibrium or macro-economic structures, do not like untidiness and loose ends, and any loose ends get speedily swept up in stochastic residual terms, or ignored."[11] This did not bode well for sufficient attention being given to entrepreneurs.

If we want to understand economic life in commercial society, considerable attention must be devoted to those engaged in it: human persons. Unlike animals, human beings can understand and shape the reality around them through their choices and action. This in turn indicates that it is through the study of human intentionality and human acts that we can understand social realities, including human economic activity. Underlining this point, the legal philosopher John Finnis comments:

> Human actions, and the societies constituted by human action, cannot be adequately understood as if they were merely (1) natural occurrences, (2) contents of thoughts, or (3) products of techniques of mastering natural materials.... True, there are elements in human life and behaviour.... such as the workings of one's digestion, or one's instinct and emotions, which can and should be understood as objects (subject-matter) of natural science.... But human actions and societies cannot be adequately described, explained, justified, or criticised unless they are understood as also, and centrally, the carrying out of free choices.[12]

In Chapter 2, we saw that much of commercial society can be explained in terms of humans acting in ways that reflect their choice to pursue their self-interest. With regard to entrepreneurship, it is perhaps the Austrian school of economics that best explains why it is economically foundational to commercial society. The Austrian approach's distinctiveness lies in its insistence upon grounding any reflection about entrepreneurship not in a theory of equilibrium, but rather in a science of human action. One of its founders, the Viennese economist Carl Menger (1840–1921), advised that the best way to understand large-scale phenomena was to break them down into their component parts.[13] In 1871, Menger published his *Principles of Economics*, a book which placed the individual at the center of economic inquiry—not the hedonistic social atom of Benthamite utilitarianism, but rather the individual with all his diverse wishes and sentiments. Another Austrian economist Friedrich von Wieser (1851–1926) stressed that to understand economic life, "we must now, by decreasing abstraction, familiarize ourselves with typical conditions of reality."[14] Consistent with Menger's methodological individualism and Wieser's impatience with abstraction, Austrian economic theory[15] involves working out the economic implications of the primordial fact that individuals engage in conscious actions toward chosen goals.

What, then, are the implications of this axiom? First, human action tells us that each individual's behavior is purposive. The very fact of each human act implies that the individual has chosen certain means to reach particular goals. As the doyen of Austrian economics Ludwig von Mises (1880–1973) stated, "acting man chooses, determines, and tries to reach an end."[16] The key to the human act's role in affecting change is what Mises denotes as each individual's unique "ability to discover causal relations that determine change and becoming in the universe."[17] By positing that it is freely chosen human acts that change the existing state of affairs, Mises indicates that the future is not fixed as Marx and other determinists hold. Only a mind of perfect foresight, Mises states, would be able to discern precisely how the future unfolds.[18] Unfortunately, acting humans have only an imperfect knowledge. They cannot possibly know everything. This introduces an inescapable element of uncertainty into the process of thought and choice that precedes and accompanies every human act. Thus Mises proposes that "[t]he act of choosing is always a decision among various opportunities open to the choosing individual."[19] To this extent, there is always a speculative dimension to human action.

But what, we may ask, motivates people to act? One cause, according to Mises, is that lack of contentment that causes people to want to change themselves, others, and the world so as to live and be better.[20] From this proceeds another motive for action: that human eagerness to "substitute a more satisfactory state of affairs for a less satisfactory one."[21] This desire must be complemented by the expectation that action will indeed bring about the envisaged better state of affairs. The action is unlikely to occur unless there is a clear incentive to act as well as a strong possibility that the act will indeed bring about a more satisfactory state of affairs for its enactor. Hence the activation of entrepreneurship must offer some direct gain to the potential discoverer himself.

Now we begin to understand why entrepreneurship is so important to commercial society. It relies upon a number of people attempting to foresee others' needs and wants and the combination of productive factors most likely to satisfy those needs and wants and then acting in a speculative way in light of the uncertain conditions of the future. This is in sharp contrast to the relatively fixed future that is the lot of the overwhelming majority of people in pre-commercial orders. While it is true that everyone acts in light of one's imperfect knowledge of the future, many barriers to larger numbers of people acting entrepreneurially are diminished in the freer economic conditions of commercial society. Such a state of affairs is especially suitable for those who are, Mises explains, "especially eager to profit from adjusting production to the expected changes in conditions, those who have more initiative, more venturesomeness, and a quicker eye than the crowd, the pushing and promoting pioneers of economic improvement."[22]

In commercial society, it is often the case that those with entrepreneurial insights lack the necessary capital to realize their vision. Entrepreneurship in commercial society is thus not confined to the initiators of risky ventures. Providers of capital need to be persuaded to embrace the same entrepreneurial insight. Even established firms require some entrepreneurial abilities if they are to sustain and increase market share in addition to keeping their competitive edge in a world full of people looking to meet the same needs and wants in more innovative and less expensive ways. Provided the incentives remain sufficiently strong, entrepreneurship in commercial society is, over time, potentially limitless in terms of what it can create.

Subjective Value, Exchange Value, and the Division of Labor

Once we appreciate entrepreneurship's critical economic role in commercial society, it becomes obvious that the economy of such societies cannot be static. This becomes evident when we consider that economic life reflects and embodies literally millions of choices and actions that in turn rest upon millions of subjective valuations of the relative worth of millions of goods and services that occur each day in the minds of millions of individuals. They are subjective insofar as the value of goods and services in commercial society reflects their subjective valuation by people. Their value is not to be found within the goods and services themselves. Nor can it be determined by an official price agency or government department. In commercial society, two people may ascribe their own particular value to the same piece of property. One person may be willing to offer more money to buy the property than another precisely because the first person values it more. Yet his valuation of the property remains ultimately subjective insofar as he cannot identify its objective value outside his own valuation, even though this is influenced by the subjective valuation of others, many of whom are unknown to him.

One major factor shaping the subjective valuation of all goods and services by all individuals is what is often called their marginal utility. This utility differs from the importance of a particular good or service for, for instance, the preservation of human life. Water is indispensable for human life, yet its marginal utility is—in most circumstances—less than that of diamonds. Röpke explains this disparity in the following manner:

> The larger the supply of a good at our disposal, the smaller is the amount of satisfaction procured by its individual units, and hence the lower is such a good ranked on our scale of values ... with increasing satisfaction of a want, the utility (satisfaction or enjoyment) furnished by each successive dose diminishes.... It follows that the minimum utility of the last dose or increment determines the utility of every other unit of the supply and therefore the value of the whole supply. The value we attach to water is not determined by the infinite utility of the single glass of water needed to save us from perishing of thirst; it is determined by the utility of the last dose used to bathe ourselves or to sprinkle the flowers.[23]

The subjective value of goods and services assumes particular importance in commercial society because of its influence upon the process of exchange and the division of labor. These arise from the fact of human differences and the manner in which people capitalize on these differences. In any society there is almost always a division of labor. Even a hunter-gatherer economic order reflects a basic division of work between those who focus their activities on hunting and killing animals and those who collect the fruits of an untamed nature. The production of goods and services in commercial society is based upon the overwhelming majority of people working to create, refine, and sell goods they rarely use themselves or only in minimal quantities. Thus the cow farmer does not produce milk for his own use. The vast majority of his milk is intended for the use of others. Likewise, the computer factory worker does not create thousands of microchips for his own use, but rather for people assembling computers who in turn will use very few of the computers they create, hoping instead that people will buy the computers.

In commercial society, the division of labor assumes manifestations and forms that make human work far more productive in terms of the quality and quantity of goods produced than previous economic arrangements. The high degree of specialization allows people to become genuine experts in one particular area and to develop sophisticated knowledge of an area that can in turn be transmitted to others who further refine the amount of expertise that exists in the area. Specialization in this case need not apply simply to different industries, but also to different functions that are transferable across industries, such as management and financial skills. Specialization also tends to create circumstances whereby most people are able to work in areas to which they are naturally suited. Another effect of heavy specialization is the manner in which it concentrates particular industries in geographical areas that enhance their effectiveness and efficiency. Thus, while large areas of the Middle East might not be especially suitable for breeding cattle, their natural deposits of crude oil have encouraged the development of highly sophisticated oil refinery industries in the region. Finally, the division of labor encourages the use of technology on a vast and productive scale. On several occasions, Smith stressed that the division of labor allowed some people to focus their minds and energies upon enhancing technology so as to create "a great number of machines that facilitate and abridge labor, and enable one man to do the work of many." Time was saved, people became more proficient at particular skills, and the overall sum of human knowledge was consequently advanced.

The end result of the division of labor, as Smith noticed, was that almost everyone in commercial society has hundreds of people working to provide things for them in some way. Any given product possessed or used by any one person has been shaped and formed by a large number of individuals, most of whom are unknown to the product's owner. Marveling at the beauty of these arrangements, Smith wrote:

> How many merchants and carriers, besides, must have been employed in transporting the materials from some of those workmen to others who often live in a very distant part of the world? How much commerce and navigation, how many ship-builders, sailors, sail-makers, rope-makers, must have been employed in order to bring together the different drugs made use of by the dyer, which often come from the remotest corners of the world! ... If we examine, I say, all these things, and consider what a variety of labor is employed about each of them, we shall be sensible that without the assistance and co-operation of many thousands, the very meanest person in a civilized country could not be provided, even according to, what we very falsely imagine, the easy and simple manner in which he is commonly accommodated.[24]

The ensuing prosperity promoted by the division of labor does leave us squarely facing the fact that it presumes that human beings will be able to exchange goods and services. Moreover, with people in commercial society becoming more and more specialized in their work, it becomes clear that people's ability to exchange directly one good (such as milk) for another (such as bread) is increasingly limited. It is always possible to engage in a direct exchange of goods if people can and desire to do so. Such is the basis of a barter economy. With the highly specialized division of labor in commercial society, it becomes increasingly difficult to exchange one thing directly for another. The process of exchanging goods and services produced for use by others is thus facilitated by ascribing an exchange value to all such goods. This means that a farmer produces vast quantities of milk because he believes that he will be able to exchange this milk in return for something that he values in return (most likely, in this instance, a certain monetary sum). The farmer is thus primarily concerned with the milk's exchange value. He also hopes that this exchange value will be at a minimum the same as and preferably more than the subjective value placed upon milk by consumers. At this point, we begin to see why money as a symbol and store of value is so indispensable for commercial society.

Money, Credit, and Banking

Röpke once wrote that it is impossible to understand the history of civilizations if attention is not given to the way in which money has shaped human society.[25] Money as an indirect medium of exchange is present in all but the most primitive economic orders. Even Communist economic systems relied upon the use of money for exchange. It has not proved easy for either historians or monetary theorists to identify the origins of money in human history. But there is almost universal consensus that money came into existence because it was able to fulfill the most basic requirement of being generally acceptable and exchangeable as a means of payment for goods and services.

Commercial activity normally begins with some type of barter. In a barter system, it is not always possible to find someone who wants to change some of your goods with them. A horse dealer may not, for example, have much use for car engines. The evident limitations of bartering resulted in the introduction of coinage as the medium of exchange. This event truly merits the over-used adjective "revolutionary." In economies that used money, people no longer had to exchange directly one good for another. One commodity could now be exchanged against a sum of money and vice versa. The speed and convenience subsequently introduced into economic transactions swiftly led to money becoming the means of exchanging goods. So valuable was this service that it was not surprising that, in many cultures, money quickly assumed the form of highly valued metals such as gold and silver.

In the ancient world, the use of money as a means of exchange depended upon people's willingness to accept that the money was the correct weight. To reduce fraud, the material (gold, silver, etc) of the money on offer was commonly weighed before the transaction was completed. Unitary weights of these metals were introduced throughout much of the Mediterranean world, probably in the second century B.C. These metals were given official stamps that guaranteed their purity and weight, thereby allowing people engaged in transactions to dispense with weighing and rely primarily on counting. Many words used for money units today, such as "pound," evoke this past.

For some time these currencies were valued according to their material value. A currency-pound of gold was worth the value of an actual pound of gold. Within time, currency began to be issued in the form of "token money." A currency-pound of gold was no longer worth exactly the same as an actual pound of gold. There was no longer an exact correlation between the exchange value of the currency and their actual material value.[26] Paper money also originally had a material dimension. It was different from coin because it was originally treated as a receipt for a defined amount of metal held on deposit by a bank. Paper money was thus a claim held against a bank, but one that circulated.

Some aspects of money make it like any other commodity. Its value is settled by supply and demand. But some features also make money different from other economic goods. Strictly speaking, money cannot ultimately satisfy a want in the way that food, a house, or a vehicle satisfies a want.[27] Generally money provides what Röpke calls "circulatory satisfaction:" that is, "we do not derive satisfaction from money by eating it, but by spending it and making it circulate, intact, from hand to hand."[28] Another difference is that while some goods leave the process of exchange when they are consumed, money does not, precisely because of its circulatory qualities.

Money's functional dimension is crucial to its distinctiveness as this defines money's very utility. We know this from those periods when a money-currency has become useless. They are almost automatically replaced by some type of limited commodity, such as coffee or cigarettes in Germany after World War II, or by people using a foreign currency. To economists, "anything constitutes money which is generally accepted as a means of exchange."[29]

In modern commercial societies, money's functions are performed independently of its material value in the form of paper-currency or banknotes. Where this was once a claim on an identified institution to pay an amount of the commodity used as money (e.g., gold), money now represents, as the social philosopher Johannes Messner writes, "a claim to any goods of specified value out of the yield of socio-economic cooperation. Such money is simply 'purchasing power.'"[30]

People tend to value a currency in commercial society when it is capable of fulfilling certain functions. First, money will only act as a medium of exchange if it serves as a general means of payment.[31] From a legal standpoint, money is the final way by which a person liquidates his debts. In most of the world, this is true insofar as money is given the status of being "legal tender for all debts, public and private." This enables debtors (those obliged to pay) to do so by giving the creditor (those owed payment) something that legally frees him from that debt.[32]

Second, money must be capable of serving as a general measure of value. Whatever the currency, it must permit us to measure the value of one good or service against another, thereby allowing us to gauge whether the seller is in fact selling at market price. This capacity proceeds from money's unique ability to calibrate almost instantly to shifts in the supply and demand of goods and services. Businesses need to be able to evaluate how much value (income) they need to create if they are to be able to expend value (cost) while having enough value left over (profit) for future investment. This valuation of cost-factors and anticipated income is made in money-units. In this way, to cite Röpke, "money makes possible rational economic calculation in that it provides a device for comparing production and consumption, profits and costs, and ... reduces all economic quantities to a common denominator."[33] The pricing mechanism created by money thus helps to free us from ignorance and permits us to determine how much money is required to buy any one good.[34]

Third, money in commercial society must be capable of being a means of storing, moving, and investing value in the form of capital. Mises described this function in terms of money as a vehicle for conveying value through space and time. It was therefore only with the existence of money that people could begin to conceptualize the offering of credit and allowed them to engage in transactions such as capital loans. Not only does money allow people to transfer economic value between individuals and groups; it also permits the creation of the relationship of "creditor" and "debtor." The unprecedented and widespread provision of credit is especially important when it comes to distinguishing commercial society from previous economic orders. With the emergence and spread of new commercial wealth in twelfth-century Western Europe, there was a corresponding increase in the demand for money. This was not driven simply by increased consumption and the heightened processes of exchange. It was also based on the need for money as a measure and store of value.

Once money is seen as a depositary of value, it releases us from the necessity of being attached to particular elements of property or forms of work, such as laboring on the land. To this extent, money assists societies to transition from pre-commercial to commercially-orientated social arrangements. As long as exchanges are free and the money is sufficiently stable in terms of its value, a person can live off the process of buying and selling goods without having necessarily to create new things. Far from taking anything away from people, money-exchanges preserve value and even increase it by putting the money back into circulation as well as through investments. Once money begins to serve this purpose, more people start to realize that money can be used to create new and more wealth through investment. Not only does the potential acquisition of money become an incentive for economic activity, but money itself can be capital.

The emergence of banks, banking, and the financial industry on an unprecedented scale has made credit available to a degree unimaginable in pre-
commercial societies. The contemporary practice of banking emerged toward the
end of the eleventh century, most probably as a way for merchants to avoid having to carry large amounts of money with them while traveling. Italian merchants
led in this regard, opening up what amounted to branch offices in the cities where
they conducted major business. Those who had more coinage than they needed
for their immediate expenditures were not slow to take advantage of this opportunity to store their own coinage securely and safely. This eventually led to the
emergence of a number of "money holding" institutions throughout Europe. By
1150, Northern Italy had become Western Europe's banking center with Italian
banking houses having correspondents in every major city and town.

Continuing difficulties involved with securing the safety of money, especially with regard to its transfer, led to the appearance of particular tools of critical importance to modern banking. Those who placed their money in such institutions wanted at intervals to reduce or add to their monetary holdings, either
directly or by formally instructing the bank to pay some money to someone else.
Here we find the origin of banking devices such as checks, drawing accounts,
and bills of exchange.

Those merchants willing to place their vaults at the disposal of others wishing to deposit their coinage soon saw the possibility of making further profit by
lending out the money deposited into their vaults in return for interest payments.
Hence, by 1660, a large number of London merchants, for example, were
engaged in what we would today call banking activities. Apart from discounting
commercial bills, buying and selling bullion, and engaging in traditional money-
changing, these merchant-bankers were willing to accept deposits at interest.
They gave receipts to depositors, the presentation of which led to repayment.
These promises, in the form of receipts to pay the deposit, began to circulate
throughout society.[35] It was not long before banks discerned that the money
deposited and the money withdrawn from their vaults tended to offset each other.
Nor were they slow to detect that "drawn notes" or "banknotes" were beginning
to flow through the economy as money, backed by people's confidence in the
likelihood of redeeming them.

Banks also realized that, in normal circumstances, they only needed to retain
a certain ratio of reserves-to-liabilities that would allow the bank to meet the
expected demands for redemption in the normal business cycle.[36] The next step
was for banks to decide they were willing to introduce more banknotes into circulation than the equivalent of their precious metal reserves. Banks therefore
began to issue more promises of payment (i.e., banknotes) than they would have
been able to meet in the unlikely case of all such notes being simultaneously presented to the bank for payment. Banks commonly circulated these extra banknotes in the form of commercial credits.

Over time, the types of credit offered by banks have expanded considerably. The ability of modern banks to provide credit in commercial society derives partly from their capacity to provide deposit service; that is, they hold money in deposits for customers in deposit, savings, or current accounts from which their clients can withdraw, either by check or in cash. In legal terms, the bank is considered to own the money on deposit and owes a debt to the one who originally deposited the money.[37] The customer has a personal money claim against the bank rather than a specific property right over a particular set of banknotes. The lender (in this case, the depositor) loses ownership of the specific money he deposits, and the borrower (in this case, the bank) becomes the owner of that money and owes the creditor its equivalent.[38]

The granting of credit by banks occurs in two ways. First, banks *grant credit*, as Mises writes, through the issue of fiduciary media: that is, notes and bank balances that are not covered by money.[39] To create credit in this way is in effect to create money. Second, Mises states, banks act as *negotiators of credit*.[40] They effectively borrow money (be it in the form of deposits by individuals, business, or other banks, or loans from other banks) in order to lend it. Their profit on this type of transaction is, as Mises relates, "the difference between the rate of interest that is paid to them, and the rate that they pay, less their working expenses."[41] Banks thus create an intrinsic link between debit and credit transactions. They avoid insolvency by ensuring that the date on which a bank's obligations fall due does not precede the date on which its corresponding claims can be made. Plainly such activity involves risks and the willingness of banks to take such chances is one of the moral grounds upon which they justly claim their profit.

Banks and other financial institutions thus play a classic brokerage role between savers and investors. Until a savings is employed or invested, it exists only in the form of money. But when placed in a bank, it is swiftly employed to other purposes. If, for example, 100 million dollars is put in a bank and only 10 million needs to be held on reserve, then 90 million dollars is available for use. Much of the surplus capital lodged in banks is not employed by banks to assist in the creation of new enterprises or businesses. It is often lent to an existing and growing commercial activity. The injection of extra capital helps to develop that activity further and thereby stimulates other trade. In this way, loaned money, sound credit, and the profits gained from the ensuing prosperity act together to facilitate commercial prosperity (just as reduced available capital, bad credit, and diminishing profit drive societies toward recession and economic decline). To this extent, banks assist businesses to provide millions of people with the chance to satisfy their material needs. They thus help to create conditions that open up new possibilities for people to share in commercial society's fruits in a myriad of ways they otherwise would not.

Free Trade, Market Competition, and Prices

To varying degrees, features of economic life such as credit, entrepreneurship,
subjective value, the division of labor, and money as capital, credit, and incentive exist within pre-commercial orders, albeit in sometimes fragile forms.
Commercial society's emphasis on free trade and competition allows each of
these to assume a prominent place within market orders.

In the twenty-first century, it is easy to forget the sheer scale of the restrictions that existed upon trade in the world before the rise of commercial society.
Prior to the eighteenth century, the dominant economic framework of Western
Europe was essentially mercantilism, a form of political economy that positively
discouraged and often actively prohibited free trade and competition. Focused
primarily upon enriching a nation through encouraging exports and restricting
imports, mercantilism invariably involved a close relationship between trading
companies (such as the Dutch East Indies Company or the Hudson Bay
Company) and the governments of emerging nation-states in the early modern
period. Governments acted to protect merchants from competition (especially
foreign competition) through devices such as tariffs, granting monopolies, and
imposing quotas. Trade by sea, and thus potential competition from abroad, was
especially restricted under mercantile arrangements. While it was rare for states
to ban outright the importation of goods and services from abroad, governments
introduced a number of restrictions that served to minimize competition. In 1650
and 1651, for example, England introduced the Navigation Laws. These sought
to prevent foreign-owned ships from engaging in coastal trade within the English
realm. The same laws required any trade between English colonies and the
mother country to be conveyed on colonial or English ships. Those seeking to
break into these protected markets often found that their only recourse was to
engage in smuggling. Established merchants who benefited from these arrangements typically returned the governments favors by acquiescing in the raising of
taxes and the paying of customs dues that provided funding for, among other
things, wars undertaken by the state to make territorial acquisitions through conquest and establishing colonies around the globe.

The economic assumption underlying mercantilism was that one person's
commercial gain is another person's loss. In *Wealth of Nations*, Smith articulated
a forceful critique of this position. As Laura Lahaye summarizes:

> First, he demonstrated that trade, when freely initiated, benefits both parties. In
> modern jargon it is a positive-sum game. Second, he argued that specialization
> in production allows for economies of scale, which improves efficiency and
> growth. Finally, Smith argued that the collusive relationship between govern-
> ment and industry was harmful to the general population. While the mercantilist
> policies were designed to benefit the government and the commercial class, the
> doctrines of laissez-faire, or free markets, which originated with Smith, inter-
> preted economic welfare in a far wider sense of encompassing the entire popu-
> lation.[42]

Free trade within and between nations is a particularly effective way of increasing the wealth of all, in the sense that this implies consumer satisfaction. When two people freely agree to engage in a simple exchange of money for goods, the buyer does so because he believes that he will be better off with less money but possessing the goods. The seller believes that he will be better off with more money but fewer goods. Thus, in subjective terms, both emerge better off than they previously were. This also holds true for complex and large transactions.[43] Buying and selling ocean liners, for instance, often involves a large number of free transactions. Ocean liners are expensive to build, test, and transport. Fortunately, the gains from the existence and continued improvement of ocean liners are much more than the costs incurred—otherwise people would not engage in these transactions.

With many European governments dismantling the edifice of mercantilist policies from the late eighteenth century onwards, the ensuing trade freedom allowed prices to match the real supply-demand equilibrium across national boundaries. It also permitted credit to become more available on an international scale. Free trade and competition also heightened incentives for entrepreneurship, as established merchants could no longer rely on governments protecting them from domestic and foreign competition. Lastly, free trade allowed for the development of the division of labor across nations. People living in different countries discovered that their competitive edge lay in some areas rather than others and began to engage in more extensive specialization. As Smith stated:

> It is the maxim of every prudent master of a family, never to attempt to make at home what it will cost him more to make than to buy ... If a foreign country can supply us with a commodity cheaper than we ourselves can make it, better buy it of them with some part of the produce of our own industry, employed in a way in which we have some advantage.[44]

A critical effect of free trade is the manner in which it allows consumers rather than the state or a guild to determine the allocation of resources. As Smith informed the mercantilists of his time and ours, "The real and effectual discipline which is exercised over a workman, is not that of his corporation, but that of his customers. It is the fear of losing their employment which restrains their fraud and corrects his negligence."[45] In his study of contract law, P. S. Atiyah reminds his readers that free trade implies that consumers "determine, by choosing to buy one thing than another, in one place rather than another, by one means rather than another, what resources should be devoted to the production and distribution of what goods and services."[46] Commercial society thus relies upon the maxim that giving consumers the ability to choose freely and suppliers the freedom to respond to what consumers want, will result in free exchange providing people with what they want in the long term and at a price they are willing to pay.

An essential component of free trade in this regard is an implicit commitment to market competition. Free trade is heavily reliant upon the ability of individuals and companies to continue a relentless search for more effectiveness in their operational methods so that they can produce better quality products at lower costs. Competition creates incentives for maximizing the number of experiments demanded by such a search, and simultaneously limits the scope, potential losses, and genuine risks associated with each experiment. In a competitive environment, many different ideas occur at the same time. This makes it prudent to devote only a small amount of available resources to any one testing of a proposed efficiency or unproven entrepreneurial insight. This increases the chances of finding only very efficient alternatives to existing goods and services. At the same time, it is precisely because competition does not reward inefficiency that commercial society is relatively protected against the consequences of failure. This is borne out by what happens in those societies that unduly restrict or prohibit competition. Their economies lack the ability to detect failure of experiments or a basis for comparing the relative efficiency or inefficiency of different experiments. Moreover, because many experiments in such economies are driven by political decisions rather than people whose personal fortunes are at stake, there is considerably less concern about the possibility of failure and therefore less chance of early intervention to end bad experiments.[47]

This brings us to the heart of one of the great economic problems that commercial society, and more specifically free competition and the price mechanism, has proved remarkably effective in resolving. Sometimes called "the knowledge problem," it confronts any society possessing a relatively sophisticated economy. When millions of people engage in economic exchanges, it is simply impossible for any one person to know everything about the particulars of these exchanges, including their own. Knowledge of such details is beyond the capacity of any one human mind.

Market competition allows people to discover how, at any particular moment, they might be able to satisfy their changing needs and wants in light of the fact of scarcity and the necessity to exchange something of what they have to obtain something that they want but which is possessed by others. Market competition achieves this by enabling a variety of "signals" to be sent simultaneously to many people. This provides them with objective information on which to base decisions such as where to buy and sell goods and services, which businesses are profitable and which are not, and where entrepreneurial opportunities exist and where they do not. Competition thus indicates when a failure has occurred, either in terms of the inability of an individual or firm to compete, thereby encouraging people to invest their assets and entrepreneurial skills in other areas. Conversely, competition's ability to identify market success encourages others to attempt to replicate the product or service at a lower cost. Last, market competition encourages people to "turn on" their entrepreneurial alertness, thereby facilitating further innovation as they seek to gain an advantage that will make their products more attractive than their competitors' products.

An important component of competition's ability to send such signals is the price mechanism—more specifically, prices that reflect the subjective valuation of different products by producers and consumers rather than prices fixed by legislative or judicial fiat. The advantage of free prices is that, as long as free competition exists, there is no room for arbitrary pricing. They will be a true measure of the scarcities in question. Resources can only be utilized effectively on the basis of a calculation of value or price, which in turn depends upon a competitive market. Röpke considered this so important that he emphasized on many occasions that "the formation of prices is the regulator of our economic system and it cannot be tampered with without requiring, in the end, a reconstruction of the entire economic system."[48] Röpke's point is that it is only through allowing prices to reflect the available supply of and demand for different goods and services at any one time that consumers can compare the values of different goods and services and then make decisions concerning where, in light of their own resources, they want to spend or invest their money. Prices are equally important because of their ability to convey knowledge to potential entrepreneurs and investors as well as consumers. The high price of a good or service encourages others to explore alternative ways of producing the same or a better good at a lower price.

Statements of profits and losses in a free market perform a similar information function. Profits signal a firm's relative effectiveness and efficiency thereby helping it to attract investors and encouraging entrepreneurs and competitors to develop faster, more efficient ways of delivering the same good or service. Losses, by contrast, indicate that something is wrong with the firm, be it inefficient management, declining market share, inadequate investment, or technological ineptness. Such signals deter potential investors from making a mistake and provide the firm's leadership with an objective basis with which to persuade others that the company requires drastic changes if it wishes to remain viable.

Profits and losses thus act as incentive signals for people to increase their knowledge of a growing market, to expand their investment, or cut their losses by shifting their assets elsewhere. This means that any attempt to interfere with or manipulate the knowledge provided by such signals tends to lead to poorer-quality decisions by producers and consumers alike. Such meddling cannot help but distort the signaling process. A profit-loss statement supplied by a firm whose business is protected from free competition by tariffs or subsidies may be accurate in terms of what they reveal about the income and costs of the business. Such statements are nonetheless misleading in terms of what they reveal about the firm's long-term prospects. People investing in such a firm are thus acting on the basis of distorted knowledge, a fact that will become plainer to them as the company's profits begin to decline, for reasons ranging from the lack of incentives for the firm to innovate, to the domestic and foreign competition that normally wear away whatever advantage is temporarily conferred by anti-competitive policies.

An Interdependent Society

Our analysis of commercial society's economic foundations underlines once again the interdependence that explains so much about commercial society. Without, for example, a shift from mercantile to free trade policies, credit will remain limited in practice to those merchants who establish a privileged legal position for themselves. Likewise, the division of labor is not only facilitated by free trade, but the very efficacy of free trade assumes a heavy degree of specialization in the production of goods and services across and within nations. This interdependence is not confined to the economic institutions. Commercial society's economic foundations rely heavily upon the prevalence of the particular moral-cultural habits identified in Chapter 2. Entrepreneurship is underwritten by people attaching high value to the quality of creativity. Relatively easy access to credit and capital is dependent upon a society's reserves of trust. The division of labor requires a high degree of self-restraint and delayed gratification insofar as many people need to be willing to invest time and energy in acquiring often extremely specialized skills. A society that does not attach a high value to commercial liberty is less likely to be committed to free trade arrangements. The information conveyed by competition is only as useful as the degree of practical wisdom developed by the people assimilating this knowledge.

There is, however, another set of foundations required by commercial society. Broadly speaking, these constitute a range of legal principles and institutions that lend legal weight to commercial society's moral impulses and provide judicial support to many of its economic characteristics. As the following chapter illustrates, qualities such as self-restraint and practices such as free trade presuppose the existence of a corresponding juridical order.

Notes

1. Ian Whyte, "Urbanization in Eighteenth Century Scotland," in *Eighteenth Century Scotland: New Perspectives*, ed. T. M. Devine and J. R. Young (East Linston: Tuckwell Press, 1999), 181.

2. Wilhelm Röpke, *Economics of the Free Society*, trans. Patrick M. Boarman (Chicago: Henry Regnery Company, 1963), 2.

3. Ibid., 3–4.

4. Ibid., 4.

5. Samuel Gregg and Ian Harper, *Economics and Ethics: The Quarrel and the Dialogue* (Sydney: Centre for Independent Studies, 1999), 10.

6. Ibid., 20–21.

7. Oswald von Nell-Breuning, S.J., "Socio-Economic Life," in *Commentary on the Documents of Vatican II*, ed. H. Vorgrimler, vol. 5 (New York: Herder and Herder, 1969), 291.

8. Ibid., 299.

9. Brian Griffiths, *The Creation of Wealth* (London: Hodder and Stoughton, 1984), 107–8.

10. Israel Kirzner, *Discovery and the Capitalist Process* (Chicago: University of Chicago Press, 1985), 3. Harvey Leibenstein agrees, suggesting that it is one of the "curious aspects of the relationship of neo-classical theory to economic development" that "in the conventional theory, entrepreneurs, as they are usually perceived, play almost no role." Harvey Leibenstein, *General X-Efficiency Theory and Economic Development* (Oxford: Oxford University Press, 1978), 9.

11. Malcolm Fisher, "The Entrepreneur, the Economist and Public Policy," in *The Entrepreneur in Society* (Sydney: Centre for Independent Studies, 1983), 23.

12. Finnis, *Aquinas*, 22.

13. See J. R. Hicks, and W. Weber, eds. *Carl Menger and the Austrian School of Economics* (Oxford: Clarendon Press, 1973).

14. F. von Wieser, *Social Economics* (London: Allen and Unwin, 1927), 207.

15. There are many differences in emphasis and substance in the thinking of various Austrians. Given that our intention is to provide only a short and simplified introduction to their thought, we do not dwell upon these in detail.

16. Ludwig von Mises, *Human Action: A Treatise on Economics*, 3d rev. ed. (Chicago: Henry Regnery, 1966), 12.

17. Ibid., 22.

18. See ibid., 105.

19. Ibid., 45.

20. See ibid., 2.

21. Ibid., 13.

22. Ibid., 255.

23. Röpke, *Economics*, 8–9.

24. Smith, *Wealth of Nations*, I.i.11.

25. See Röpke, *Economics*, 79.

26. For the purposes of our discussion, we absent ourselves from the debate about whether the value of money ultimately depends upon a concrete material content, such as silver or gold. A de-linking of the two, it might be noted, does not seem to exclude the possibility of circulatory satisfaction. If money's value depends on what we think we can buy with it, then a currency with no material value of its own may be said to possess "value." What matters is what people value. Money can have a functional value that is not the same as its material value. Hence, it is money's functional value that gives money its material value.

27. Money can, Röpke declared, provide some "real" satisfaction to some people, such as those who like to collect coins. See Röpke, *Economics*, 82–83.

28. See ibid., 82–83.

29. F. H. Lawson and Bernard Rudden, *The Law of Property*, 3d ed. (Oxford: OUP, 2002), 31.

30. Johannes Messner, *Social Ethics: Natural Law in the Western World*, trans. J. J. Doherty (St. Louis & London: B. HerderBook, Co., 1964), 774.

31. This need not mean that an exchange always occurs. We can give someone a gift of money without expecting or wanting anything in return.

32. Money's legal character emerges when the law confers particular legal rights and duties upon its possessor. These include the duty not to destroy the money and the pos-

sessor's right to have his money accepted as payment for debt, as well as the right to convert money into other kinds of money. The legal character of money is not, however, its essence. There have been many times when money has managed to function successfully without a legal status conferred by the state.

33. Röpke, *Economics*, 84.

34. The purchasing power of money is determined by the level of prices. If prices fall, money can buy more. If prices rise, money will buy less. Money's purchasing power is also influenced by the quantity actually being spent in a given period.

35. See Giuseppi, *The Bank of England*, 8.

36. This ratio was later legally fixed in most countries.

37. This is recognized by most legal systems. See, for example, Lawson and Rudden, *Law of Property*, 36.

38. See Lawson and Rudden, *Law of Property*, 36 and 70. Some loans (such as renting out a house) involve the owner retaining the ownership and selling only the use of the thing. In the case of money, use cannot be separated from ownership. If A allows B to use A's money precisely as money, then A effectively transfers the ownership of the money to B, precisely because the grant of the use of money is the grant of the thing we call money. An exception might be when A lends his money to B in order that B might display the money. See Finnis, *Aquinas*, 204.

39. See Ludwig von Mises, *The Theory of Money and Credit*, trans. H. E. Batson (New Haven, Conn.: Yale University Press, 1953), 262.

40. See ibid., 261.

41. See ibid.

42. Laura LaHaye, "Mercantilism," in *The Concise Encyclopedia of Economics*, http://www.econlib.org/library/Enc/Mercantilism.html

43. This example draws from ibid.

44. Smith, *Wealth of Nations*, IV.ii.11–12.

45. Ibid., I.x.c.31.

46. P. S. Atiyah, *An Introduction to the Law of Contract*, 5 ed. (Oxford: Clarendon Press, 1995), 5.

47. This analysis of the connection between markets and experimentation draws upon Rojas, *Rise and Fall of the Swedish Model*, 10–19.

48. Röpke, *Economics*, 146.

4

The Liberty of Law

The inhabitants of these nations do have things, but they lack the process to represent their property and create capital. They have houses but not titles, crops but not deeds, businesses but not statutes of incorporation. It is the unavailability of these essential legal representations that explains why people who have adapted every other Western invention, from the paper clip to the nuclear reactor, have not been able to produce sufficient capital to make their domestic capitalism work.

—Hernando de Soto

A common perception of commercial society is that it relies upon the diminishment of laws that promote unnecessary regulation of free trade, competition, and the pursuit of self-interest. In itself, this claim enjoys validity. Yet it often obscures the extent to which commercial society's emergence, expansion, and prosperity relies upon the existence and preservation of certain legal principles and institutions. Commercial society is far from being a lawless entity. Legal protection for certain liberties such as freedom of association or certain procedural safeguards against arbitrary actions by individuals, associations or state authorities are so important for commercial society that it is scarcely possible to imagine a market order existing in their absence. Property, for example, is essentially prior to legal and political institutions because it proceeds so immediately from the need of all humans to survive. It is harder, however, to make a case that property arrangements can exist without legal order or without being invested with definitive legal characteristics.

Many living in relatively commercial societies often take these legal foundations for granted, precisely because they assume that private property will, in most circumstances, be protected: that judges will apply received law in a consistent manner and that there are certain things which, save in exceptional cases, governments are legally prohibited from doing when it comes to the free exchange of services and goods. Commercial peoples often take this for granted precisely because the law is working, virtually unnoticed in many cases, to realize these ends. The workings of something as vital to commercial society as credit illustrate the point. One person may wish to purchase something with credit, but no one is likely to advance such credit without some security. By means of the device of contract, the law enables creditors and debtors to reduce their potential risk via the provision of a conceptual apparatus that specifies what is expected and agreed by both parties while also providing legal remedies and sanctions in case of the unreasonable failure of either party to fulfill their promises. Some of the applicable law is provisional insofar as it depends upon the choices of individuals to make certain promises. Other parts of the same law of contract, however, exist by default (unless the transacting parties choose to construct their own particular arrangements), while others are mandatory, such as many of the provisions concerning the purchase, sale, or leasing of property.

In this chapter, we do not propose to examine matters such as the specific ways in which rule of law has manifested itself in different nations or the consequences of different legal systems for commercial society. We confine ourselves to exploring the significance of particular legal foundations—specifically, the right of private property, freedom of association, freedom of contract, the rule of law, and constitutional guarantees against arbitrary government—for commercial society. Before considering these matters in more detail, some attention to understanding the nature of law and its importance for human choice and decision-making is required.

The Significance of Law

While moral and political philosophy seeks to identify fair and reasonable principles for resolving various practical issues in human societies, law focuses on something different. Law and legal theory seek to explain, as one legal philosopher writes, "why, and on what conditions, principles and solutions once settled upon are to be given effect even when there is no consensus that the settlement was or is still correct, or that correct principles for arriving at such solutions were followed or are even available."[1]

From this perspective, law's function is to resolve what may be called "coordination problems." By this, we mean any situation where a *coordination* of choices and actions allows an otherwise unobtainable number of benefits to be attained by significant numbers who have sufficient interest in making such coordination workable and effective, and, second, where the *problem* is, as Finnis writes, "to select some appropriate pattern of coordination in such a way that coordination will actually occur."[2] Law deals with the related issues of how to select an appropriate solution, what makes this resolution count as *the* solution, and what is involved in preserving this resolution as the solution throughout its implementation. Law is thus instrumental in securing desirable forms of coordination that secure the creation and maintenance of activities that depend for their value on general support from society. Coordination means that there are substantial benefits that could be attained by significant numbers of people "in a way which other persons, even if harmed or at least not benefited by that option in that situation, could count as a 'good thing'."[3]

When it comes to securing the ongoing coordination of thousands, even millions, of human choices and actions, there are only two ways: the consensus of unanimity or the force of authority. Regardless of the method chosen, two subsequent issues have to be resolved. The first is how to select a pattern of coordination. The second is how to implement that pattern so that it produces the desired benefits. One might, for instance, determine that cooperation between persons in a particular area is best obtained by the exchange of legally binding promises, as in the case of contract. If the cooperation is to last, there must remain unanimity between the two parties that exchanged promises about what they have agreed to do. If unanimity breaks down at any point, someone or some institution needs to be charged with the necessary authority to resolve this new coordination problem, either by holding those involved to the promises that they have made and/or by providing authoritative guidance that resolves the dispute.

The situation is further complicated by the fact that any one exchange is only one of thousands, that the type of exchanges will vary greatly in their nature and duration, and that exchanges are only one of many ways that people seek to coordinate their actions. An associated problem is that many ways of resolving coordination problems are not just applicable to one case and need to be designed with many potential future cases in mind. The very idea of legal precedent and thus legal consistency depends upon widespread acceptance that the decision to resolve a coordination problem in the past in a particular way did not just authoritatively settle the case for that particular instance, but also for the present and future.

This suggests that if the resolution of the coordination problem is to be regarded as authoritative, there must be a consistency in its application or, at a minimum, noncontradiction with previous decisions. Different individuals may be displeased with the particular result yielded by the agreed-upon framework. It is more important, however, that they agree upon the desirability of both the framework for decision-making and the need to conform, save in exceptional circumstances, to the decision made through the procedures set out in the framework. The quality of the framework that exists for resolving coordination problems is therefore important, especially what one legal scholar calls "its general salience."

> By holding itself out as a public and privileged identification of a solution for the case of every coordination problem, and by offering grounds for acknowledging that privileged status, the law achieves the salience it seeks in particular coordination problems. The grounds for acknowledging that privileged status are several. The law ... offers the prospect of combining speed with clarity in generating practical solutions to constantly emerging and changing coordination problems, and in suggesting devices by which such solutions can be generated. Its institutions for devising and maintaining solutions secure fairness by the stability, the practicality and the generality or non-discriminatory character of the solutions, and by the imposition of those solutions on free-riders and other deviants by processes which minimize arbitrariness and self-interested or partisan deviance in the very processes themselves. In short, it is the values of the *Rule of Law* that give the legal system its distinctive entitlement to be treated as the source of authoritative solutions.[4]

A legal system's capacity to persuade people that it is worth adhering to its authoritative solutions is especially important in light of the many temptations experienced by people who may wish to act in an illegal manner, either occasionally or on a regular basis. Here we see that law is especially significant precisely because of the authority—backed by its unique ability to engage in legitimate coercion—it lends to one way of resolving things over others. People may disagree about how to deal with a particular problem in society such as prostitution. Some may be opposed to a general campaign against prostitution for reasons ranging from apathy, concerns over the likely financial cost, or a desire to avail themselves of prostitutes. They may even acknowledge the moral and health problems generated by prostitution, but fail to find these sufficiently convincing reasons to overcome their apathy, their desire to use prostitutes, or their worries about the unforeseen effects of an anti-prostitution campaign. If, however, a law is passed that prohibits prostitution and allows the use of legal coercion against the managers and users of prostitutes, a new element enters into the reasoning of those opposed to an anti-prostitution campaign. They may well decide that while they oppose the anti-prostitution law as much as they opposed the anti-prostitution campaign, there are compelling reasons for them to obey the law. These reasons are the many benefits that people receive from the legal system in which they live, such as the protection that law accords to their lives and possessions.

Given the potential benefits bestowed by law, people tend to be willing to accept the burdens imposed by law. To continue with the example above, some people may consider not complying with the anti-prostitution law. They may well, however, decide to obey the law precisely because they want to be regarded as just, decent and law-abiding citizens who want others to behave in a just, decent, and law-abiding manner. They may also choose to obey the law against prostitution because it has been made in a just and equitable manner that reflects the state's commitment to, and procedures for, the making of law in a fair and reasonable manner. These people may judge that it is the regular and impartial administration of the law itself in the midst of complex and ever-changing circumstances that gives them an interest in cooperating with the law. While they may be displeased with this particular law, there are likely to be many more laws which they believe are just and reasonable. Since they expect these laws to be obeyed, they may be willing to conform to the requirements of this particular prostitution law.

The preceding observations underline the fact that law must be seamless insofar as its very nature as law means that those subject to the law are not permitted to pick and choose among its various stipulations and prescriptions. This seamlessness extends to the fact that law links together people's interests, concerns, transactions, and well-being, grounding them in the past, shaping them in the present, and orientating them to the future. This is not to overestimate law's ability to achieve such an end. Law cannot, for example, enhance every single condition affecting every human interaction in the past, present, and future. Yet awareness of the coercion that may be legitimately exercised through the law in some circumstances often persuades those insufficiently motivated by the duties that they owe in general to others (such as refraining from killing, stealing, defrauding, torturing, or enslaving others) or the specific obligations that they have freely taken upon themselves through agreement such as contracts.

As the previous chapter illustrated, many coordination problems in commercial societies are resolved through nonlegal means. Competition and the price mechanism, for example, are ways in which commercial society coordinates the creation, selling, and purchase of thousands of goods by millions of people over time. Yet even these devices rely to some degree upon law for their efficacy. Suppose, for instance, that there was no prohibition or punishment of fraudulent profit statements or if the law did not protect the wealth legitimately acquired through competition from arbitrary seizure by stronger individuals or the state. In such circumstances, the functionality of particular economic foundations of commercial society would be severely impaired. Also relevant for commercial society is the fact that the coordination achieved in a society ruled by law differs sharply from collectivism or statism. By definition, law-as-coordination leaves tremendous scope for people to pursue their individual initiatives precisely because this is part of its objective. By contrast, neither collectivism nor statism is concerned with assisting people to exercise their freedom in the midst of others also making free choices.

Private Property and Private Property Rights

Law has always been intimately concerned with property use and ownership. The precise structure of property institutions, laws, and regulations usually reveals much about what a society considers to be important. A common feature

of collectivist or statist systems is their implicit hostility to private property and
their attempts to diminish laws protecting private ownership. While many such
regimes allow a certain degree of private ownership, they invariably attempt to
supplement this with substantial public ownership and limit dramatically what
people are allowed to do with what they own. Although the Nazi regime did not
embrace the type of economic collectivism found in the Soviet Union, this did
not stop it from directly expropriating private property owned by particular
groups such as Jews, Catholic religious orders, and opponents of the regime. The
Nazi government also placed significant restrictions on the flow of foreign capital
into Germany and did not look kindly on German industries that invested in
enterprises located in other countries.[5] During the Second World War, rationing,
price controls, and the compulsory redirection of much of German industry
toward the production of military munitions completed the most significant dilu-
tion of the protections associated with private property since German reunifica-
tion in 1871.

By contrast, societies that purport to value human freedom, especially economic liberty, tend to ascribe high importance to private property and invest it
with significant legal value. It follows that private property constitutes one of the
primary legal institutions of commercial society. It is not just the unique ability
of private property to identify the ownership of goods and services that makes it
essential to commercial society. Private property is indispensable for the coordination of billions of individual and group investments, purchases, and exchanges
in the present and with an eye to the future. This becomes evident when we try to
conceive of a world without property. It might be possible that contemporary
societies lacking the legal form of property would create things as complex as
computers. Without property, however, no one would be able to situate themselves with regard to these objects as we do with property. In a property-less
world, Stephen Munzer notes, "Persons might possess artifacts in the sense of
having physical contact with or control over them. But they would have no right
to exclude others and no normative power to transfer artifacts to others."
Moreover, Munzer adds, people would not be able to exercise the same claims
or normative powers over things that are not artifacts, such as land, plants, and
minerals.[6]

In one sense, property reflects the fact that different parts of the material
world are morally tied in a special way to a particular person, persons, or organizations. It seems doubtful, however, that property could exist without law or at
least legal recognition.[7] Law provides commercial society with the conceptual
apparatus that tells us, for instance, what is and is not property. As the property
law theorists F. H. Lawson and Bernard Rudden point out:

> We cannot ... effectively give, sell, lease, or bequeath our reputation, or our
> surname ... these may be ours, and may be valuable, but they do not count as
> property so as to form the subject matter of disposition. The law of property
> also determines the types of interests that will be treated as proprietary, that is

as being more than merely personal, familial, or contractual, and it spells out the consequences of a finding that a particular interest is proprietary.[8]

While property is commonly regarded as referring to tangible things that can be possessed by people, ranging from land to buildings, it also includes more intangible goods such as patents. The very idea of copyright is impossible without a prior notion of property.

In commercial society, property is generally defined and protected by a legal system that emphasizes and protects people's ability to pursue their own projects. Measures such as taxation are justified, in part, by the need to finance particular state institutions such as courts that protect, among other things, property rights and arbitrate property disputes. One might imagine that the legal institution of private property simply protects people from having their private possessions being confiscated by others who do not have a just claim on that property, or, we should add, expropriated by the state without due process, a proven claim of legitimate public use, and just compensation. Though this is part of property's importance for commercial society, property additionally embraces a range of legal relationships between people with respect to tangible and intangible things, and a range of legal expectations with regard to different people's possession and use of these things.

Perhaps the most significant concept embodied by private property is excludability: the notion that an owner can legally exclude people from using or expropriating his property.[9] On a very basic level, excludability establishes the relationship of different people to different objects and ideas. Without being able to identify the ownership of goods, free trade is impossible. If we cannot identify a good, idea, or service as belonging to this person rather than another, we cannot know who may legitimately exchange, offer, or deed particular objects, services, and ideas. Excludability thus facilitates various forms of control of things by private individuals and companies. One is the direct control exercised over something by its owner. Within the limits established by the coordinating function of the law, the owner of something can do with it as he wishes. Another form of control is the ability to exclude the state from interfering directly with our use of our property. A third control is a type of authority exercised over those whom one allows to use one's property.[10] A person who is a guest in another's house is expected to act in certain ways that he might otherwise not.

Why are these types of control essential for commercial society? In the first place, excludability entitles a person to sell, give, or deed the things and ideas he owns to others. It also restricts the use, possession, and benefits of things, labor, and ideas to particular persons, unless the owner chooses to allow others to use, possess, or benefit from a particular good. These forms of control are especially important for commercial society if people are to be entrepreneurial and create wealth. People tend not to take risks with things they own unless they are highly confident of a substantial degree of control over the use and disposition of much of the wealth created through such risk-taking.[11] As Adam Smith understood, when people "are secure of enjoying the fruits of their industry, they naturally exert it to better their condition, and to acquire not only the necessaries, but the conveniences and elegancies of life."[12] The experience of Communism and Socialism reminded humanity that people are less inclined to work, let alone be entrepreneurial, if they see little prospect of keeping a considerable if not the majority of the gain for themselves. The English philosopher Jeremy Bentham articulated this in terms of expectations. In his view, property was "a basis of expectation; the expectation of deriving certain advantages from a thing which we are said to possess, in consequence of the relation in which we stand toward it."[13] Here we should recognize that property can be assigned a subjective value measurable by the price signals conveyed by money. The value of property is thus calculable. People can therefore make prudent choices about matters such as the degree of risk they can afford when using their property, ascertain how much they need to keep in reserve, and determine how long they can persist in pursuing a particular exercise. To this extent, the secure possession of property, be it our own or loaned by another, provides people with a basis for planning future commercial enterprises.

This is especially important because excludability makes an important contribution to what Wolfgang Kasper calls property's enhanced divisibility and tradability in commercial society.[14] By divisibility of property, Kasper means that "the value of an asset can ... often be greatly enhanced by making institutional provision for the separation of the various rights"[15] associated with a piece of property. Excludability is not the same as exclusiveness. Several people can have legal interests in the same piece of property, as in the cases of joint ownership, the holding of shares in a publicly traded company, or the relationship between landlords and tenants.[16] A landowner, Kasper demonstrates, can lease part of his land to another for farming, to another for fishing in the stream that runs through his property, and to yet others for recreational uses. Property law begins, for example, to develop rules for sharing ownership, for distinguishing between owners and users of property (e.g., landlord and tenant), and establishing what might be called various forms of limited property (such as franchises). The advantage of these arrangements, Kasper stresses, is that different people with different knowledge and motivations can make different and yet simultaneous use of the same privately-owned asset.

Loans are a concrete example of this divisibility. In commercial society, few individuals who, having satisfied their needs and wants, allow their property to remain static. Invariably they choose to invest it, sometimes in businesses that employ people and create more wealth that is further invested, and sometimes in banks and financial markets which in turn provide others with access to the capital that they need to finance new enterprises and initiatives. Without property being tradable or divisible, it would be exceedingly difficult for people with a new insight, but without assets, to give substance to their idea. As noted by Antoine de Salins and François Villeroy de Galhau, "the savings of some are used to finance the investment needs of others, in the hope that this financial circuit will play its part in attaining an optimal financial growth."[17] Hence, as Kasper comments, when property can be traded, its value increases, and the discovery of new knowledge is facilitated.[18]

Freedom of Association, Contract, and Contract Law

The benefits flowing from the legal protection of private property and the growing sophistication of property law in commercial society are themselves highly dependent upon legal protections being conferred upon the freedom to associate and the mediation of such association through the legal device of contracts. In the absence of freedom of association, it would be impossible for property to be created, exchanged, or divided. All such actions depend upon people being free to choose when and with whom they want to exchange things. Without freedom of association, the capacity of individuals to pursue their self-interest and respond to available incentives is undermined. It may not, for example, be in a person's self-interest to be forced to associate with others when it comes to negotiating contractual or employment arrangements. Freedom of association also allows people to establish commercial enterprises with other like-minded individuals and organizations under their own volition. Even something as individualistic as entrepreneurship is difficult without the freedom to associate. The insights of an entrepreneur cannot be brought to fruition if he is prohibited from associating with those who may be able to provide capital. Nor would commercial society function if people were unreasonably restricted from choosing to end one economic association in favor of beginning another. People would not, for instance, be able to move from purchasing goods from one provider to another vendor able to supply the same goods at a lesser price.

The significance of freedom of association for commercial society is better appreciated when we consider the powerful legal limits placed on this liberty in precommercial societies. In the eighteenth-century Prussia of Frederick the Great, both peasant and lord were strictly limited in their mobility.[19] Nobles were forbidden from traveling abroad without the king's permission. Peasants were often not free to decide where they wanted to work. Until the late eighteenth century, the vast majority of Europe's rural population was legally limited in their ability to choose where they worked and with whom. In this world, relationships between people were often fixed, sometimes in a hereditary sense. It was not a coincidence that these barriers only tended to break down in those cities with powerful commercial orientations such as Milan, Venice, Cadiz, Amsterdam, and London.

In commercial society, economic relationships are no longer mediated through feudal or semi-feudal legal arrangements. Instead, the freedom of association underlying commercial relationships is often organized through the legal medium of contract. In Chapter 2, the quality of trust was underlined as an especially important moral foundation of commercial society. Although trust is indispensable for free exchange and association, the productivity of commercial society is enhanced through contract laws that protect people's ability to contract freely with each other. Such law usually covers, among other things, the lending and borrowing of money, employment, and the leasing, hiring, buying, and selling of objects and services.

So important is contract law for commerce that Adam Smith was convinced that contracts arose almost inevitably from the spread of commerce.[20] Contract law provided greater guarantees that agreements would be honored in commercial conditions and, in Smith's view, reflected the increasing seriousness with which people viewed the unreasonable breaking of freely-made promises. In relatively primitive societies, there was little need for contracts. Life tended to follow certain relatively fixed patterns; there was often little need for people to enter into free economic exchanges with those belonging to other families and groups. Basic necessities such as food were often found and cultivated in a person's immediate environment. The vast majority of families tended to live in the same vicinity for many generations.

The development of commerce and the spread of economic interdependency beyond the frontiers of village, region, and nation invariably results in a corresponding decline in the relative self-sufficiency described above. The customs that enable relatively homogenous groups located in particular areas to arrange their internal economic affairs no longer suffice because of the sheer diversity of customs likely to be found in even a small number of villages, many of which may have little in common with each other. In such circumstances, societies often seek to identify uniform methods of ordering economic relations between people accustomed to different cultural mores. The method typically employed in commercial society is free agreements between individuals and groups, the reasonable provisions of which are guaranteed and, if necessary, upheld by law.

This theory of the emergence of contract appears to match the historical record. In the Hellenic world, laws of contract expanded as several Greek city-states gradually abandoned tribal-like organization and began trading among themselves and throughout the Mediterranean in the fifth century B.C.[21] A corresponding development occurred in the Jewish treatment of contract when commerce became more characteristic of Palestine's Jewish community in the first century B.C. and throughout the Jewish Diaspora.[22] The greatest expansion of contract law occurred with the rapid spread of commerce in seventeenth and eighteenth-century Western Europe. With the growth of trade between cultures and even continents, there was a growing need for laws that protected and upheld the increasing number of private commercial agreements.[23]

A particularly strict definition of contract may be found in the American Restatement of Contracts which identifies a contract as "a promise or a set of promises for the breach of which the law gives a remedy, or the performance of which the law in some way recognizes as a duty." This definition should be supplemented by the observation that it is doubtful whether some contracts embody more than an implied promise. A person who buys a newspaper has certainly entered into some type of contract with the seller. It would be an exaggeration, however, to imagine that the newspaper seller and buyer only entered into the contract after reaching agreement on a promise or set of promises. In this instance, the exchange of promises is not only implied but occurs simultaneously.

How then do contracts facilitate free exchange? In his book on contract, Atiyah outlines several essential functions.[24] First, contracts are a device for enforcing promises and protecting the reasonable expectations generated by these promises and associated conduct. To the extent that contracts embody enforceable legal sanctions against those who refuse or fail to do what they promised, they actually encourage free exchange and thereby allow people greater certainty in the way that they coordinate their present and future exchanges with a range of other people. Contract law is therefore fundamental to everyone's life in commercial society. Atiyah notes, for example, that "A consumer's bank account, his right to occupy his house if rented or mortgaged, his employment, his insurance, his shareholdings, and many other matters of vital importance to him—all depend for their value on the fact that, in the final analysis, the law of contract will enable him to realize his rights."[25]

Second, contracts reinforce the wrongness of unjust enrichment insofar as they do not recognize or protect the transfer of property without free exchange. While the law of restitution is the means by which such unjust acts are normally addressed, contracts remind us that there are just ways of exchanging property, goods, or services. Without the legal device of contracts, people would be forced to find other, less desirable and perhaps unjust ways of resolving disputed agreements and promises.

Third, contract law is designed to prevent a range of harms and to compensate those who suffer from harms. It is especially attentive to those who have relied reasonably upon others' promised actions and behavior and have found themselves or their interests damaged in some way as a result of others not acting or behaving as they promised. Contract law tends to intersect here with tort law to varying degrees in different jurisdictions insofar as tort law tries to provide redress against those who harm others.[26] Contract law is not therefore exclusively concerned with private promises and obligations. It also embodies a strong notion of justice insofar as the law subjects contracts to the test of reasonableness.

The precise modes of justice embodied in contracts and contract law are primarily commutative and corrective justice. Commutative justice concerns fairness in the freely chosen interactions and interrelationships between two or more individual parties, usually with reference to standards such as legal equity and fulfillment of contractual duties.[27] It regulates exchanges between persons in accordance with a strict respect for their rights rather than issues of distributive justice. It involves, for instance, safeguarding property rights, paying debts, and fulfilling obligations freely contracted. The element of corrective justice in contracts involves the application of legal remedies to unreasonable failures to perform contract agreements.

Careful study of the rules and principles of nineteenth- and twentieth-century contract law indicates that they tend to be articulated in very general terms, with, as one legal commentator remarks, "no distinction being made between types of party (such as trader, consumer, friend, relative) or of transaction (in corresponding terms)."[28] A basic assumption of legal equality thus underlines the law of contract. This was stressed by the United States Supreme Court in 1908, when Justice Harlan wrote:

> The right of a person to sell his labor upon such terms as he deems proper, is in its essence, the same as the right of the purchaser of labor to prescribe the conditions upon which he will accept the labor from the person offering to sell it. So the right of the employee to quit the service of the employer, for whatever reason, is the same as the right of the employer, for whatever reason, to dispense with the services of the employee ... In such particulars the employer and the employee have equality of right, and any legislation that disturbs that equality is an arbitrary interference with the liberty of contract, which no government can justify in a free land.[29]

Harlan's words underline the point that contracts and contract law in commercial society are not and cannot be primarily concerned with issues of distributive justice. Distributive justice is focused upon outcomes, which involves consideration of matters of merit, need, desert, and contribution. By contrast, contract law involves rectifying matters that have gone wrong between individuals as a result of a breach of contract. Contract law is not therefore in itself concerned with the rectification of social and economic inequalities. As becomes apparent in Chapter 5, the very essence of contract is undermined when attempts are made to subject contract law to such considerations. Contract law that prioritizes freedom of contract attaches great value to the notion that people should be relatively free to make their own decisions about what they want to sell and buy. It is thus orientated to providing for the enforcement of private agreements agreed upon by the contracting parties. The fairness of the transaction's outcome is not central to the workings of contract law. The primary objective of contract law is, as Atiyah states, to "assist one of the contracting parties when the other broke the rules of the game and defaulted in the performance of their actual duties."[30]

In conceptual terms, two ideas are at work in freedom of contract and its associated laws. One is that contracts are created through the workings of the participants' free choices. In this schema, justice largely consists of enforcing reasonable promises made in contract, not least because it is in the interests of the common good that people are reasonably held to their contractual promises. Whenever a person freely chooses to enter a contract and accepts the terms of the agreement, he is generally forbidden by law from unilaterally repudiating the contract. People entering contracts thus freely choose to inhibit their own scope for action to the extent that the contract obliges them to do so. These agreements will not be second-guessed by a court, save in exceptional circumstances, provided they remain within the ground rules that define a free contract. Such is the importance attached to free choice by contract law. Indeed, a sound contract law must embody the notion of freedom of contract; that is, the parties engaged in a contract must be free to choose the terms of their agreement. A person forced at gunpoint to agree to certain conditions cannot be said to be contracting freely.

The second axiom is that mutual agreement to the specified terms establishes a contract.[31] This sounds self-evident, but the judicial workings of much contract law involve testing whether the mutual agreement is objective rather than subjective. This does not mean determining what the contracting parties "really meant" or intended in their innermost minds. Contract law involves assessing whether the conduct and language of the parties involved are such that they would lead reasonable people to assume they have in fact promised to do something.[32] Hence the choice of an insane person to enter into a contract would not be regarded as binding the person once they have regained their sanity. No reasonable person would regard any promise made while insane as being legally binding. Likewise a contract entered into by a child would not be held as valid.

Contract law also plays a role in determining the actual meaning of various phrases in contracts. No matter how clear a contract, there is always a possibility of different interpretations, some of which may have implications for what the contracting parties believe that they have promised to do. Though the printed words of a contract are considered binding, the actual meaning of the printed words can sometimes be a legitimate matter for dispute. The role of the courts in these instances is to determine the reasonable meaning of the words that bind. In many cases, it is a question of courts discerning the implications of what the contracting parties promise, both in terms of the meaning of the specific terms but from the perspective of what is *implied* by the wording of the contract.

In commercial society, people engage in contractual relationships more often than they imagine. Whenever a person freely purchases something from another, we can affirm that he has entered into a contract with another person, be it an individual shopkeeper or a legal person such as a business or corporation. Whether it is buying food or purchasing entertainment, all such activities involve people in consensual transactions that have legal implications defined under the law of contract. In commercial society, however, the greatest economic benefit of freedom of contract and contract law is that they allow free exchange to become particularly sophisticated. This becomes more evident when we realize that no exchange involving any significant degree of complexity can normally occur simultaneously. Many free exchanges in market orders involve at least one person carrying out his side of the bargain in the future, or people agreeing to perform their role in a particular way and at a certain time. By specifying these details, contract law can provide a higher degree of certainty and creates accountability for what parties to a complex exchange have formally agreed to do, thereby generating efficiencies over the long term. This is underlined by the fact that the need to enter into formal contracts facilitates a great deal of pre-contractual exploration and negotiation. People need to find out who are in a position to provide the service, consider their historical record of doing so in previous transactions, and assess the capacity of different people to do what they say they can do. While the negotiating and finalization of a contract normally involves expenditure of time and resources, the agreements attained help to reduce the degree of uncertainty surrounding any free exchange or entrepreneurial opportunity. Then there is the follow-up to contract agreements, such as ensuring that all parties are abiding by the contract, resolving any ensuing disagreements or misunderstandings, sometimes with the assistance of the legal system. This process is long, complex, and occasionally difficult. It is, however, a medium through which free persons in a market economy can resolve acute coordination problems.

The Rule of Law

On many occasions, the enforcement of contracts requires legal intervention and judicial adjudication. The efficacy of contracts thus depends upon the law embodying a range of characteristics often grouped under the collective heading of "rule of law." Given that laws deal with coordination problems, they are by definition focused on the activities of millions of people. They therefore need to be drafted in ways that accurately state what should occur in order for the necessary coordination to be achieved. The same laws need to be easily comprehendible and should avoid providing people with opportunities for corruption and other forms of arbitrary behavior on the part of court and government officials. When laws fail to embody these characteristics, or when these principles are widely ignored or flouted, then we may say that a society embodies the rule of men rather than the rule of law.

Rule of law describes a range of requirements in the application of law that must be met if such an application is to be considered just. Such principles of natural justice normally include the following characteristics.[33] First, rules are promulgated, and are clear and coherent with respect to each other. Second, rules are prospective rather than retroactive and not impossible to comply with. Third, there is a recognized division of responsibility in administering the law. No one can, for example, be simultaneously judge, witness, public prosecutor and public defender. Fourth, laws are sufficiently stable to allow people to be guided by their knowledge of the content of the rules. Fifth, those charged with the authority to make and administer law are accountable for their own compliance with the laws and administer the law consistently. By conforming to these principles, law makes a vital contribution to freedom from unjust coercion. When people are subject to the same law, their obedience to the law means that they are not formally subject to the arbitrary will of those wielding legitimate coercive power. The focal issue of law here is not, "Is this the right decision in these circumstances?" In fact, there are good reasons to think that there is often no uniquely correct solution to a problem. Instead, maintenance of liberty under the rule of law requires lawmakers to ensure that laws are applied reasonably, generally, and equally to everyone.

The importance of rule of law as a legal foundation for commercial society is not difficult to understand. In his *Constitution of Liberty*, Friedrich von Hayek wrote that "the importance which the certainty of law has for the smooth and efficient running of a free society can hardly be exaggerated. There is probably no single factor which has contributed more to the prosperity of the West than the relative certainty of the law which has prevailed here."[34] It was through upholding the rule of law that figures such as Hayek believed that the state made its most important contribution to commercial society. Rule of law, Hayek insisted, did not amount to unreasonable government interference in the economy. Figures such as Adam Smith, Hayek believed, conceived of "interference" as "the exercise of the coercive power of government which was not regular enforcement of the general law and which was designed to achieve some specific purpose."[35]

How, then, does rule of law contribute to the growth and preservation of commercial society? First, rule of law normally means that the laws concerning what one may not do remain relatively stable and coherent. This enhances our ability to make informed economic choices because it decreases the chance that we will find ourselves being second-guessed or having certain operating assumptions suddenly changed in an unpredictable manner. It is not surprising that an absence of this certainty created by rule of law often encourages entrepreneurs and other agents and institutions of wealth-creation to choose to remove themselves to other jurisdictions or simply decide in light of the uncertainty not to try to create the wealth in the first place.

A second benefit of rule of law for commercial society is the manner in which it reduces the state's ability to interfere directly with the exercise of economic liberty by pursuing aims inimical to the long-term stability and prosperity of commercial society. Rule of law forbids, as we have seen, the arbitrary treatment of people. This being the case, it limits the capacity of state officials, as Hayek remarks, to interfere with decisions about who provides, buys, and sells most goods and services, not to mention the prices at which goods and services are sold. The scale of the knowledge problem confronted by legislators or judges seeking to influence such matters in commercial society means that they must inevitably decide to privilege one individual or group over others. Prices in commercial society, as we have seen, are shaped by the buying and selling choices of individuals and groups, decisions that are in turn affected by continuing innovations and events. It follows that any interference with prices by government organizations could not be determined by an all-embracing rule; it could only be shaped by the same organizations making judgments about who ought to sell and buy what goods, in what quantities, and with what frequency. In the end, the scale and size of economic life force us to conclude that such judgments could only be arbitrary. By contrast, Hayek points out, "A government which cannot use coercion except in the enforcement of general rules has no power to achieve particular aims that require means other than those explicitly entrusted to its care and, in particular, cannot determine the material position of particular people."[36] Adherence to rule of law thus drastically limits the state's ability to engage in the type of extensive economic planning that undermines many of commercial society's foundations. The use of legislation, for example, to engage in the widespread redistribution of wealth means that one engages in using law to discriminate in favor of particular individuals in order to attain a certain goal, such as "equality of result" or "equality of opportunity." As Chapter 5 demonstrates, achieving these ends in commercial society (indeed, any society) is not only impossible, but the very pursuit of such ends, be they as concrete as equality of result or as vague as equality of opportunity, cannot but lead to laws becoming unstable, lacking coherence with respect to each other, potentially retroactive, difficult to comprehend, and an incentive for public officials to apply law in an arbitrary manner: in short, the very antithesis of rule of law.

It is not, however, simply that rule of law prohibits the state from doing certain things that makes rule of law so important to commercial societies. A third function of rule of law is that it establishes very clearly in the minds of the population what the state needs to do in commercial society. The preservation of commercial societies requires the state to act to enforce contracts, to protect private property, to maintain peace, to punish fraud, and to uphold people's freedom to trade, buy, and sell. The state's ability to perform these functions in a stable, coherent, consistent, non-discriminatory manner depends upon its adherence to the rule of law. A state that protects some people's property from arbitrary seizure but not others, or that punishes some people's fraud but not others, not only contributes to a disintegration of rule of law, but also undermines basic assumptions upon which commercial society's vitality is heavily dependent.

Constitutional Government and Constitutionalism

In commercial society, the concern to limit the government's capacity to engage in arbitrary behavior extends beyond an emphasis upon rule of law. Since the emergence of modern commercial societies during the eighteenth century, it has become clearer that such societies rely heavily upon a commitment to constitutionalism for their preservation. By the twentieth century's conclusion, almost all nations had a written document or set of texts that delineated the respective powers of their national political and legal institutions, such as parliaments, courts, and governments. Some of these documents also list a number of fundamental rights, such as the right to religious liberty or the right to a fair trial by one's peers. Usually the provisions of these documents are not easily changed, and the texts themselves normally specify how this must occur if change is to meet the test of legitimacy. Constitutions also typically restrain all government institutions from engaging in particular actions. Likewise, legislative and executive bodies are formally prohibited from doing certain things. Defining the character and extent of these limits are normally the responsibility of courts whose decisions constitute part of constitutional law.

In the case of some countries, it is relatively easy to identify such a document, such as the Basic Law of the Federal Republic of Germany. In other instances, finding such a definitive document is more difficult. There is, for example, no document or text in the United Kingdom that meets the criteria specified above. Yet this does not mean that Britain lacks a constitution. As outlined by the constitutional scholar Eric Barendt, the word constitution refers to "the collection of legal and nonlegal rules which compose the system of government ... Legal rules are those which are interpreted and enforced by the courts, while non-legal rules are the customs and conventions regarded as imposing obligations, although they are not enforceable by judges."[37]

Different constitutions have arisen throughout history for different reasons. The constitution of the United States was created in the aftermath of a political revolution and with the purpose of establishing and limiting the authority of a range of new government, legislative, and judicial institutions. Other constitutions are drafted to outline the fundamental principles of a new political order established following its predecessor's collapse. This was the case with the various French constitutions established after the fall of successive regimes. Other constitutions have surfaced following the defeat of totalitarian systems such as the Soviet Union and Nazi Germany as part of an effort to ensure that strong legal constraints exist to inhibit the re-emergence of such tyrannies.

Older constitutions associated with emerging commercial societies in countries such as Great Britain and the United States tended to protect a very small number of entitlements and freedoms such as the right to property (including patent protections) and freedom of association. Few of these entitlements were absolute.[38] The fifth amendment to the United States Constitution, for instance, states: "... nor may private property be taken for public use without just compensation." Though this does not deny that there are circumstances in which private property may be expropriated, the very wording of this "takings clause" intimates a powerful limit on the government's ability to expropriate private property by stressing that the taking must be for "public use" and that "just compensation" must be paid. While the constitution appears to have left it to courts and legislatures to decide what constitutes "public use" and "just compensation," the very fact that these are mentioned suggests that serious reasons have to exist before the state may act in such a way. Interestingly, the original state constitutions of the American rebellious colonies listed the various freedoms that were not to be unreasonably interfered with by the government. Though the constitution drafted in Philadelphia in 1787 did not originally list or express these freedoms, ten amendments were added in 1791 (otherwise known as the Bill of Rights) and other amendments added at later dates (such as the Thirteenth and Fourteenth Amendments), partly to provide precisely such protections. The Fourteenth Amendment, added in 1868, specifies that no state shall "deprive any person of life, liberty, or property without due process of law." Thus it is not unthinkable that the government may circumscribe a person's liberty (by sending him to jail for crimes committed), life (capital punishment), or property (taxation). The point is that the government cannot *arbitrarily* do such things.

Constitutionalism's attentiveness to curbing arbitrariness is especially important for commercial society. While commercial societies are often concerned with ensuring that their constitutions protect many of the aforementioned practices and institutions, commercial societies are especially concerned that constitutions provide what Barendt describes as a "power-map" that accurately describes the specific powers allocated to different office holders and institutions. Knowing, for example, who is and is not authorized to employ legal coercion in different areas is essential to reducing the political uncertainty that may discourage private individuals and companies from pursuing trade in one country rather than another.

Yet commercial society demands more than this from the political order. It specifically requires what has been described as "simple and liberal constitutions" and a formal commitment to constitutionalism. The full import of this becomes apparent when we consider that even tyrannical regimes often have constitutions that formally delineate which institutions are allowed to do what. This may reduce the degree of arbitrary behavior on the part of despotic regimes in the sense that one arm of the tyranny may appeal to formal constitutional documents to exclude another institution from interfering with its particular activities. But such a constitution is not likely to prevent a despotic regime from interfering with essential institutions of commercial society. Article 17 of France's 1789 Declaration of the Rights of Man and the Citizen stated that property was an "inviolable and sacred right." The fact that this did nothing to prevent the mass appropriation of property by successive revolutionary regimes underlines that such declarations are devoid of significance unless a sincere attachment to constitutionalism prevails.

Constitutionalism in commercial society thus embodies more than a commitment to abstract impersonal rules. Barendt defines constitutionalism as "a belief in the imposition of restraints on government by means of a constitution."[39] This means that the moral and legal authority of the constitution must be lent to certain specific principles. This authority protects these principles and freedoms precisely because undue interference with them by the state would result in significant, perhaps irreparable, damage to commercial society. It is also important that the same protections must not be diluted by granting constitutional authority to a range of other entitlements, real or purported.

Barendt correctly states that this idea of constitutionalism is strongly linked to the doctrine of the separation of powers as formulated by Montesquieu in his *Spirit of the Laws*. "When the legislative and executive powers are united in the same person, or in the same body of magistrates," Montesquieu wrote, "there can be no liberty."[40] "Constant experience," he added, "shows us that every man invested with power is apt to abuse it."[41] Given that power is based in institutions, there is a need to check such institutions. Hence, Montesquieu contended that "there is no liberty, if the judiciary power be not separated from the legislature and executive. Were it joined with the legislative, the life and liberty of the subject would be exposed to arbitrary control. Were it joined to the executive power, the judge might behave with violence and oppression."[42]

Adam Smith certainly understood the importance of the separation of powers for commercial society. With trade and economic life becoming more sophisticated, people tend to look to the courts for legal remedy on a more regular basis. If justice is to be administered impartially in such circumstances, Smith reasoned, then the separation of executive and judicial power is essential and the judicial authorities need to enjoy a high degree of independence from the legislature. Such a situation, Smith continued, could be said to exist in the Britain of his own time. Executive power lay with the king and his ministers, while the House of Commons was the repository of legislative power. Judges were appointed for life by the Crown, but their lifetime appointment meant that they were relatively autonomous.[43]

This attention to the separation of powers is mirrored in the thinking of the framers of the United States Constitution as well as the highly influential *Federalist Papers*. Their common theme is that by separating the powers of the judicial, executive, and legislative wings of government, it becomes difficult for government officials to accumulate enough power to act arbitrarily precisely because they are checked by other wings of government, either by being involved in each other's functions (such as the executive and the legislative) or through powers of review, as exercised by the judiciary. This need not require total separation of these functions. The United Kingdom's constitutional arrangements, for example, do not formally embody a separation of persons between the legislative and the executive. The Prime Minister and most of the ministry are members of the House of Commons, and, until 2006, the head of the judiciary was a member of the executive branch, sitting in the Cabinet.[44] Separation of powers nevertheless prevails because the separation of powers is not concerned with the complete divorce of executive, legislative, and judicial branches of government from each other. Instead it is focused upon preventing the concentration of power. In the United States, for instance, the president can veto the acts of the legislature. Given enough votes, the legislature can override presidential vetoes and even impeach the president. The Supreme Court may rule on the constitutionality of executive and legislative decisions, but its members are nominated by the president and subject to legislative approval.

Another key element of constitutionalism is the idea of judicial review. This concept is a relatively new development. Until World War II, only a small number of constitutions formally expressed this concept. It was only in 1971 that the French Constitutional Council began to identify laws found to violate the 1791 Declaration of the Rights of Man as unconstitutional. In the contemporary United Kingdom, courts cannot invalidate legislation, precisely because this would conflict with the principle of Parliament's sovereignty and supremacy. Prior to the Revolution of 1688, judges such as Sir Edward Coke stated that any act of parliament contrary to common law and right reason was invalid.[45] We should, however, recall that the doctrine of the Supremacy of Parliament was itself determined and shaped by the courts.[46] Other constitutional systems specifically mandate judicial review. The Basic Law of Germany, for example, provides for the judicial review by the Constitutional Court of legislation and executive actions deemed to violate certain basic rights.[47]

Commercial society's interest in judicial review is that it gives effect to a key premise of constitutionalism. Judicial review allows the identification of arbitrary acts by any branch of government (including all but the highest of courts) and provides a means of redressing such acts through law rather than force. As Chief Justice Marshall of the United States Supreme Court stated in *Marbury v. Madison* (1803):

> If an act of the legislature, repugnant to the constitution, is void, does it, notwithstanding its invalidity, bind the courts and oblige them to give it effect? Or, in other words, though it be not law, does it constitute a rule as operative as if it was a law? This would be to overthrow in fact what was established in theory; and would seem, at first view, an absurdity too gross to be insisted on. It shall, however, receive a more attentive consideration. It is emphatically the province and duty of the judicial department to say what the law is. Those who apply the rule to particular cases, must of necessity expound and interpret that rule. If two laws conflict with each other, the courts must decide on the operation of each.[48]

Judicial review is not a simple exercise. One question regularly subject to judicial review is the question of the limits of various entitlements that are crucial for commercial society. Under what circumstances should freedom of association, for example, be limited? What constitutes legitimate public appropriation of private property? But no matter how potentially complex are such matters, commercial societies should always prefer such questions to be resolved through the coordinating medium of law rather than arbitrary acts of government or the force of populist impulses.

Judicial review is often critiqued as sitting uneasily with the aspirations of commercial societies that have embraced democratic forms of government. The legal philosopher Jeremy Waldron proposes, for instance, that judicial review does not respect the democratic principle that all citizens have the right to participate in the determination of political decision-making, no matter how complex the issue.[49] The protections and entitlements contained within a constitution are, he suggests, more aptly determined by legislatures or popular referenda. One objection to Waldron's argument is, as Barendt states, that the same right of participation can be ensured "in the course of litigation before a constitutional court, in discussion of its decisions, and in campaigns for the reversal of a decision or a constitutional amendment."[50] Another objection, especially relevant for commercial society, is that judicial review is one way that some of the foundations of commercial society can be protected from majoritarian tendencies, be they emanating from a branch of government, political movements, or the population as a whole.

In the 1930s, for example, the United States Supreme Court played a critical role in protecting such foundations from a range of measures adopted by the Roosevelt administration as part of its New Deal program. The 1933 Agricultural Adjustment Act (AAA), sponsored by the Roosevelt administration, attempted to stabilize farm prices by levying a tax on the processing of agricultural commodities with which to pay subsidies to farmers who would agree to reduce the acreage sown to crops. In 1936, Justice Roberts wrote in *United States v. Butler et al.* that the levy of the tax was not a legitimate use of the taxing power but the "expropriation of money from one group for the benefit of another." The court also found the AAA unconstitutional as "a statutory plan to regulate and control agricultural production, a matter beyond the powers delegated to the federal government." Likewise, in a unanimous 9-0 decision, the Supreme Court struck down the "National Industrial Recovery Act" (NIRA) in *Schecter Poultry Corp. v. United States (1935)*. In 1934, the Schecter corporation was convicted of violating the NIRA's Live Poultry code, including the code's wage and hour stipulations. On two separate grounds, the Court declared the prosecution of the corporation unconstitutional. First, the NIRA represented an indiscriminate delegation of legislative power. It was, according to Justice Cardozo, "delegation running riot." The court also established that the corporation's business was in intrastate commerce. This being the case, the court ruled that the federal government had no authority to regulate working conditions in the firm. Finally, in *Carter v. Carter Coal Co. (1936)* the court stated that congress lacked power to legislate concerning wages and hours of bituminous coal miners, even though coal mining was a major national industry. "[P]roduction," it held, "is a purely local activity. It follows that none of these essential antecedents of production constitutes a transaction in or forms any part of interstate commerce."

In these instances, the process of judicial review protected the free flow of prices, prevented the unjust expropriation of private property, stopped the payment of subsidies, and limited the federal government's ability to control private businesses or intervene directly in their internal affairs. We can safely assume that the Roosevelt Administration's measures enjoyed the support of most of the American Congress and a majority of the population. Judicial review nonetheless provided a commercial society in crisis with some protections against such policies. Though the constitutions of federations like the United States, Canada, and Australia typically stress that interstate commerce is subject to the provisions of federal law rather than individual states, judicial review was the means by which it was established that the federal government in the United States could not do whatever it wanted in this realm.

Politics and Commercial Society

Despite their role in protecting commercial society, neither judicial review nor constitutionalism has a perfect record when it comes to protecting commercial society's foundations. Much New Deal legislation, for example, was eventually validated by the United States Supreme Court, especially following the retirement of judges who regarded such protections as implicit to the United States Constitution.

However strong or weak, commercial society has never been able to escape the influence of political pressures seeking to limit or eliminate the effects of free trade and competition. While such pressures accelerated after the First World War, they have always been present wherever commercial society has existed. The guilds that inhibited the growth of commerce during its first widespread flourishing in the Middle Ages are one example, as were the socialist movements that began to exert significant political influence in the middle of the nineteenth century. It is also notable that political efforts to limit the impact of such movements have themselves negatively impacted upon commercial society. Confronting the emergence of a mass-scale Social Democratic movement, for example, Germany's Iron Chancellor Otto von Bismarck exclaimed, "The action of the state is the only means of arresting the Socialist movement. We must carry out what seems justified in the socialist program and can be realized within the present framework of state and society."[51] The result was the creation of the German welfare state, a system that continued to grow long after Bismarck had departed the German political scene and to proportions unimaginable even to many socialists of Bismarck's time. There have been attempts to strengthen the foundations of commercial society through political action, figures such as Margaret Thatcher and Ronald Reagan being good examples. But by and large, much political activity in commercial orders has been directed toward ends such as constraining free markets, limiting freedom of contract, and a range of measures that diminish the incentives for economic creativity, often in the name of greater equality.

Commercial society, then, has not been without its challenges, some of which have succeeded in substantially reducing its scope, such as Keynesianism, or virtually obliterating its existence as in the case of Communism. Not all the contemporary challenges are as blatant as the aspirations of Karl Marx or I. V. Lenin. In our own time, the threats to commercial society are far more nuanced in nature.

Notes

1. John Finnis, "The Authority of Law in the Predicament of Contemporary Social Theory," in *Natural Law*, ed. John Finnis, vol. 2 (New York: New York University Press, 1991), 259.

2. Finnis, "The Authority of Law," 277.

3. John Finnis, "Law as Coordination," *Ratio Juris*, 2, no. 1 (1989): 100.

4. Finnis, "The Authority of Law," 280. Emphasis added.

5. See, for example, Harold James, *The Nazi Dictatorship and the Deutsche Bank* (Cambridge: CUP, 2004).

6. Stephen R. Munzer, *A Theory of Property* (Cambridge: Cambridge University Press, 1990), 15.

7. Taking issue with John Locke, Immanuel Kant held that full private property rights did not exist in the state of nature and that society simply secures those rights. Instead, Kant claimed that the law legitimizes private property protections and entitlements by giving them a name. See Immanuel Kant, *The Philosophy of Law*, trans. W. Hastie (Edinburgh: T&T Clark, 1887), 182–88. One need not agree with the entirety of Kant's critique of Locke to recognize that Kant's attention to the role of law in establishing property underscores a gap in Locke's theory of property.

8. Lawson and Rudden, *The Law of Property*, 4.

9. See Munzer, *Theory of Property*, 89–90.

10. For the relationship between control and property, see Morris Cohen, "Property and Sovereignty," *Cornell Law Quarterly* 13 (1927): 8–30; and Munzer, *Theory of Property*, 91–92.

11. See Munzer, *Theory of Property*, 16.

12. Smith, *Wealth of Nations*, III.iii.12.

13. Jeremy Bentham, *The Theory of Legislation*, ed. C. K. Ogden (London: Routledge & Kegan, 1931), 111–12.

14. Kasper, *Property Rights and Competition*, 74–75.

15. Ibid., 74.

16. See Munzer, *Theory of Property*, 16.

17. Antoine de Salins and François Villeroy de Galhau, *The Modern Development of Financial Activities in the Light of the Ethical Demands of Christianity* (Vatican City: Libreria Editrice Vaticana, 1994), 18.

18. Kasper, *Property Rights and Competition*, 75.

19. See Asprey, *Frederick the Great*, 202–13.

20. See Smith, *Lectures on Jurisprudence* (A), 91–94.

21. See Harold F. McNiece, "Freedom and the Law," in *Concept of Freedom*, ed. Carl W. Grindel (Chicago: Henry Regnery Company, 1955), 181.

22. See Morris R. Cohen, "The Basis of Contract," *Harvard Law Review*, 46 (1933): 553–56.

23. See McNiece, "Freedom and the Law," 181–83.

24. See Atiyah, *Introduction to the Law of Contract*, 35.

25. Atiyah, *Introduction to the Law of Contract*, 7.

26. Other bodies of law such as tort law and restitution law are treated by the law as applicable—and, in some instances, primarily applicable—to the world of commerce.

27. See *ST*, II-II, q.61, a.1.

28. John Finnis, "On 'The Critical Legal Studies Movement'," *American Journal of Jurisprudence*, 30 (1985), 29.

29. *Adair v. United States*, 208 U.S. 161, 174, 175 (1908).

30. Atiyah, *Introduction to the Law of Contract*, 9.

31. This is not to suggest that all contracts, however freely made, ought to be enforced. Few individuals were as committed to freedom of contract as Friedrich von Hayek. He suggested, however, that "No modern state has tried to enforce all contracts, nor is it desirable that it should. Contracts for criminal or immoral purpose, gambling contracts, contracts in restraint of trade, contracts permanently binding the services of a person, or even some contracts for specific performances are not enforced." Friedrich von Hayek, *The Constitution of Liberty* (London: Routledge and Kegan Paul, 1960), 230.

32. See Atiyah, *Introduction to the Law of Contract*, 9.

33. See John Finnis, *Natural Law and Natural Rights* (Oxford: Clarendon Press, 1980), 270–273.

34. Hayek, *Constitution*, 208.

35. Ibid., 221.

36. Ibid., 231.

37. Eric Barendt, *An Introduction to Constitutional Law* (Oxford: Oxford University Press, 1998), 2.

38. Nowhere is it stated in the American Constitution that the Supreme Court may invalidate executive decisions or legislative enactments that exceed the powers conferred by the constitution onto the executive or legislative. This power was determined by the U.S. Supreme Court itself in *Marbury v. Madison (1803)*. This maintains that judicial review was implicit to written constitutions and, it might be added, constitutionalism. While the objective of a written constitution is to state and thereby limit the powers of different government organs, *Marbury* holds that courts have the responsibility to resolve conflicts between constitutional provisions and pieces of legislation or executive acts deemed by some as violating those provisions. If the court determines that a violation has occurred, then it could rule such legislation or executive action to be invalid.

39. Barendt, *Introduction to Constitutional Law*, 14.

40. Montesquieu, *Spirit*, bk. 9, chap. 6.

41. Ibid., bk. 11, chap. 4.

42. Ibid., bk. 9, chap. 6.

43. See Smith, *Lectures on Jurisprudence* (A), 269–75.

44. See http://www.dca.gov.uk/

45. *Dr. Bonham's Case* (1610) 8 Co. Rep. 114, 118.

46. Barendt, *Introduction to Constitutional Law*, 86–88.

47. *Basic Law*, Art. 93 (1), par. 4a.

48. An obvious and as yet unresolved concern is what occurs when the most authoritative interpretative court decides to interpret constitutional law in an arbitrary manner.

49. See J. Waldron, "A Rights-Based Critique of Constitutional Rights," *Oxford Journal of Legal Studies*, 13 (1993): 36–45.

50. Barendt, *Introduction to Constitutional Law*, 23.

51. Otto von Bismarck cited in A. J. P. Taylor, *Bismarck: The Man and the Statesman* (New York: Vintage, 1967), 162.

Part 2

CHALLENGES

5

The Temptation of Politics

Of all things, an indiscreet tampering with the trade of provi-
sions is the most dangerous, and it is always worst in the time
when men are most disposed to it; that is, in the time of
scarcity. Because there is nothing on which the passions of
men are so violent, and their judgment so weak, and on which
there exists such a multitude of ill-founded popular prejudices.

—Edmund Burke

While usually regarded as the intellectual founder of modern conservatism, the
economic thought of Edmund Burke closely parallels the views of his contemporary, Adam Smith, commonly viewed as a father of classical liberalism. Though
Burke was firmly of the view that "charity to the poor is a direct and obligatory
duty upon all Christians,"[1] he was equally vehement that government intervention in the market place amounts to defying "the laws of commerce, which are
the laws of nature, and consequently the laws of God."[2]

Today the expression of such ideas generates, as it did in Burke's time, loud
assent, qualified approval, and passionate disagreement. The intensity of these
debates reminds us that the place of politics and the state in modern commercial
societies remains a complex and controversial subject. In historical terms, commercial society owes its emergence both to the progressive breakdown of a variety of quasi-political organizations such as guilds and the promotion of alternative political ideas about society's proper ordering. Certain forms of political

order appear more compatible with commercial society than others. Political arrangements that limit the state's capacity to engage in arbitrary behavior seem indispensable if many of the moral, economic, and legal foundations of commercial society are to fulfill their promise. Yet the very same foundations also depend upon the state authorities performing certain tasks in a coherent and consistent manner.

Some political systems are less congenial than others to the growth and flourishing of commercial societies. By the very fact of their totalitarian impulses and ambitions, deeply collectivist systems are antithetical to commercial society. The hostility of Marxist ideologies to the institution of private property, the practice of free exchange, and the pursuit of rational self-interest render commercial life impossible within these political systems, save in the form of the black market. But even political movements ostensibly devoted to liberty have had devastating effects upon key institutions of commercial society. In 1789, the French Revolution began with the ostensive goal of protecting not only individual freedom but also private property through the use of sovereign power. By 1793, revolutionary leaders were using the same sovereign power to destroy individual liberty and to confiscate property, all in the name of popular sovereignty.

Nevertheless, it would be a mistake to imagine that the collapse of command economies across the globe somehow resolved the political questions facing commercial societies. The outright antipathy of Communist systems to the foundations of commercial orders simplified matters insofar as it was easy to identify the nature of their animus against commercial society. In a post-Communist world, the challenges are less immediately obvious and often more subtle in design and effects. These range from the persistence of various forms of protectionism throughout much of the world (even in countries as ostensibly commercial as the United States), to the apparent inability (and often unwillingness) of many Western nations to diminish the state's share of gross national product, to more specific phenomenon such as the persistence of anti-commercial populism in Latin America. Then there are even broader issues that Communism's downfall does not resolve for commercial society, such as whether the growth and viability of commercial societies is ultimately facilitated or corroded by democratic political arrangements.

Writing in 1984, the legal philosopher Joseph Raz commented that governments had achieved the capacity to make people do many things without necessarily invoking their legal authority to do so. "It is," he wrote, "an important fact about the modern state that to an ever greater extent it affects our fortunes by means other than exercising, or claiming to exercise, authority over us. In many states the government, or public authorities generally, are the largest employers in the country, control much of the infrastructure through a state monopoly on the provision of mail, telephone, airport and seaport services and the like. The armed forces are the largest clients for many high technology industries and so on. The details vary from state to state, but the overall picture is rather similar."[3]

With the implementation of privatization schemes throughout much of the world, some of these conditions have changed. And yet many people continue to believe that governments should still exert a major influence over features of economic life such as employment levels and wealth distribution in relatively commercial societies. This in turn raises questions concerning the adequacy of existing constitutional means for limiting government power, something vital for commercial society's continued growth. While the state has always engaged in public works and employed people, the scale on which it does so today—in addition to the vast array of other programs it manages—would have been beyond the comprehension of a Burke or Smith.

When Burke penned his defense of free trade and commercial liberty, he was responding to pressures being brought upon William Pitt's government to alleviate food shortages that afflicted Britain in the 1790s as it waged war against Revolutionary France. Burke was reacting against a perennial problem encountered in commercial society: if a considerable number of people become dissatisfied with their lot, they become tempted to view politics as a means for obtaining a range of material compensations for their discontent, regardless of the economic, political, and moral-cultural costs. The *philosophe* Jean-Jacques Rousseau gave voice to such sentiments when asserting that in commercial societies, "the privileged few ... gorge themselves with superfluities, while the starving multitude lacks the necessities of life."[4] Then there are those who regard politics as the best way to address apparent injustices engendered by commercial activity. The economist P. J. Hill captures the motivations underlying such efforts when he writes: "An oft-expressed sentiment is that though markets are efficient, they are unjust, since market processes create significant economic inequality. Therefore, modern egalitarians believe, a legitimate role for government is to equalize the distribution of wealth or income in society."[5] The end result is the evolution of politics into a type of redistributive machine that those holding political office begin to use with less and less restraint, even as the risks involved, the goals pursued, and the efforts required begin to exceed all measure of reason.

In this chapter, we limit ourselves to examining some of the more powerful contemporary ideas that often underlie this turn to politics. The first is the persistent strength of particular understandings of equality and the associated emphasis upon interventionist policies that seek to redistribute wealth. The second is the continuing influence of a set of ideas about the political ordering of economic life often referred to as "corporatism."

The Conundrum of Equality

That certain forms of inequality exist in commercial society is a given. Though it is indisputable that the medium standard of living for everyone, including the poorest, continues to rise in commercial society, some people will always possess more wealth than others. Gaps in wealth between different income segments of the population often increase in commercial society, even though very few people become poorer.[6]

Despite the overall increase in almost everyone's living standards, the economic inequalities that exist in commercial society are a source of considerable angst for many. Western civilization, for instance, has been profoundly influenced by the teaching of Judaism and Christianity that everyone has an obligation to help one's neighbor in need. While some suggest that there is no such obligation, contemporary debates tend to be orientated around questions concerning the most efficacious means of helping those in genuine need. In Tocqueville's view, the intensity of these discussions in commercial society is heightened by democracy's emergence. The equalizing tendencies of democracy were not something that he regarded with unequivocal appreciation, especially in terms of its impact upon liberty.

> Democratic peoples always like equality, but there are times when their passion for it turns to delirium.... It is no use pointing out that freedom is slipping from their grasp while they look the other way; they are blind, or rather they can see but one thing to covet in the whole world.[7]

Though Tocqueville held that democracy's emergence was underpinned by the effects of the Judeo-Christian belief in the equality of all people in God's sight, he perceived a type of communal angst in democratic majorities that drove them to attempt to equalize all things, even if this meant behaving despotically. This has particular implications for commercial society, given that several of its foundations are jarring to aspirations to equality. While market orders promote the notion that people have an equal right to compete, some object that this is unfair because people start competing in different positions and possess varying talents that receive dissimilar valuing from the market. To rectify this state of affairs, the argument goes, efforts need to be made to bring everyone down to the same starting level, thereby allowing the competition to be truly between equals.

None of this is to intimate that the concept of equality has no place in commercial society. Not only are various forms of equality—such as the equality in dignity (understood as the equal worth of each human being *qua* human beings)—compatible with commercial society, but some of commercial society's foundations depend on particular understandings of equality for their rational consistency. One obvious such equity is equality before the law: laws are applied to people according to the specifics of the law without any particular regard for the person or persons involved. The legal scholar Lloyd Weinreb specifies that this is grounded in the principle that "no person is altogether above the law and exempt from its requirements, or beneath it and deprived of its protection."[8] This reflects the very nature of rules, a point underlined by Sir Isaiah Berlin in his famous essay on equality:

All rules, by definition, entail a measure of equality. Insofar as rules are general instructions to act or refrain from acting in certain ways, in specified circumstances, enjoined upon persons of a specified kind, they enjoin uniform behavior in identical cases. To fall under a rule is *pro tanto* to be assimilated to a single pattern. To enforce a rule is to promote equality of behavior or treatment ... This type of equality derives from the conception of rules as such—namely, that they allow of no exceptions.[9]

Such assumptions of equality are integral to the importance attached by commercial society to the very concept of rule of law as well as the equal protection accorded by the law to parties to a contract. Equality before the law thus reflects commercial society's animus against arbitrary use of state power and the privileging of particular groups by the law.

Equality of Result

Few theorists of commercial society suggest that the political order should completely refrain from attempting to assist those in material need. But generally this is regarded primarily as the responsibility of noncommercial voluntary associations. One reason for this reluctance to have the state too closely involved in direct poverty alleviation is an awareness of the negative implications of using the state to promote economic equality. The pursuit of any particular predetermined pattern of wealth distribution through state power in the name of equality of result or opportunity inevitably undermines key institutions of commercial society.

The basic philosophical claim underlying the notion of equality of result is that if one person has something, then others are entitled to have the same thing. Leaving aside obvious objections to such an argument (such as its arbitrary dismissal of the claims of merit, ability, desert, contribution, etc.), we should note that equality of result does not concern itself with other ends: productivity, entrepreneurial creativity, even human flourishing. The goal is, Berlin once wrote, "the maximum similarity of a body of all but indiscernible human beings." It is, he added, "not merely ... an end in itself, but ... *the* end, the principal goal of human life."[10] Anything constituting an obstacle to such an end—such as competition, rule of law, limited government, economic liberty, even civility and tolerance—are subordinated to this objective. This alone makes "equality of result" antithetical to the very existence of commercial society. Pursuit of such policies has led not only to exorbitant taxation rates but also the Killing Fields of Cambodia. Less appreciated is the unfeasibility of such an end in a world where it is impossible to be self-sufficient. Unless one is prepared to simply freeze people in a state of complete equality (which implies the use of omnipresent coercion), the necessity of trade means that while free exchange increases the well-being of all, some will have more than others. Equality of result thus implies the prohibition of trade. But, as Montesquieu sagely remarks, "The total privation of trade ... produces robbery."[11]

The quest for result-equality differs from "equality of opportunity" policies insofar as equality of opportunity does not deny the fact, and therefore relevance, of differences in individual ability. Equality of result regards such matters as irrelevant. In an equality-of-result orientated world, the state must subordinate human liberty to the end of ensuring that everyone, regardless of one's actual abilities and characteristics, is a recipient or contributor to an equal outcome of the distribution of things. To the extent that the state single-mindedly focuses on such an end, it must embody the ambition of omnipotence. Lord Acton indicated as much when he wrote:

> Whenever a single definite object is made the supreme end of the state, be it the advantage of a class, the safety or the power of the country, the greatest happiness of the greatest number, or the support of any speculative idea, the state becomes for a time inevitably absolute. Liberty alone demands for its realization the limitation of the public authority, for liberty is the only object that benefits all alike, and provokes no sincere opposition.[12]

Equality of Opportunity

While equality of result is focused upon what people have with respect to each other, equality of opportunity is concerned with what people are able to do with respect to each other. The two are interlinked insofar as what a person has often determines what he can do. After Communism's defeat, equality of opportunity has become a more common policy goal in most societies. As a rhetorical device, equal opportunity is very powerful. Yet, as Weinreb notes, it is very difficult to ascertain precisely what this phrase means. While equality of opportunity recognizes that the end result need not be equal, it attempts to affirm human equality beyond equity before the law while simultaneously acknowledging differences in abilities, talents, and effort.

This presents innumerable complications. First, we must wonder if it is possible to arrange matters through law and public policy so that comparative advantages are distributed equally, thereby producing equal opportunity. This presumes that there is some schema available for actually measuring such differences. Thus far, no one has identified such a schema. Second, defining the minimal resources that everyone must possess if equal opportunity is to prevail is a notoriously difficult exercise. It begs the question, minimal for what? Different requirements and costs are associated, for example, in trying to ensure everyone's basic survival or everyone's all-round human flourishing. Stephen Munzer proposes that minimal ought to be understood in terms of "a decent life in society." This, he adds, involves basic needs such as food, clothing, shelter, and health care as well as basic capacities such as being able to appear in public without shame, to read, write, and do arithmetic at a rudimentary level, and to work at a job.[13] Yet even this seemingly minimal proposal is problematic. Being equipped with the minimal requirements to do a job, for example, surely depends on the nature of the work. Munzer himself concedes that it is impossible to establish a universal minimum (understood as the same minimal level of property) for all within a society,[14] not least because our definition of what constitutes a minimum amount of property changes as standards of living rise over time.

Then there are questions concerning when and how redistributist policies associated with equal opportunity policies, such as high progressive taxation rates and tariffs, ought to be applied and if and when they should be phased out. If people are successful in the initial first round of equalized competition, does equal opportunity mean that they should be disqualified from using the fruits of their success during the next round of competition? It should also be recognized that equal opportunity policies and programs are unlikely to be of any real assistance to significant proportions of the population of any given society. John Schaar puts this somewhat bluntly when observing that under a regime of equal opportunity, "a man with, say, an Intelligence Quotient of ninety, is given equal opportunity to go as far as his native ability will take him. That is to say, it lets him go as far as he could have gone without the aid of the doctrine—to the bottom rung of the social ladder."[15]

Those committed to redistributionist policies might well say that such considerations are unimportant. Those who are materially less well off, it has been suggested, will tend to judge their economic position based upon comparing their situation with those who possess more. Hence any reductions in material inequalities will, from their standpoint, have improved their lot. Unfortunately, such viewpoints assume, as Hill stresses, that envy is somehow a morally legitimate attitude.[16] The same argument also says nothing about whether the objective material well-being of those who are poorer has actually been improved. It seems more concerned with highly subjective matters such as psychological mind-sets rather than actual results. Here we encounter one of those paradoxes of commercial society. It produces what Hayek called "an increasing awareness of facts which before had passed unnoticed. The very increase in wealth and well-being which had been achieved raised standards and aspirations. What for ages had seemed a natural and inevitable situation, or even an improvement on the past, came to be regarded as incongruous with the opportunities which the new age appeared to offer. Economic suffering both became more conspicuous and seemed less justified, because general wealth was increasing faster than ever before."[17] This is despite the fact that, as Smith pointed out to his contemporaries, relatively poor people in wealthy societies are usually better off than many wealthy people in poorer societies:

> Observe the accommodation of the most common artificer or day laborer in a civilized and thriving country.... Compared, indeed, with the more extravagant luxury of the great, his accommodation must no doubt appear extremely simple and easy; and yet it may be true, perhaps, that the accommodation of a European

prince does not always so much exceed that of an industrious and frugal peasant, as the accommodation of the latter exceeds that of many an African king,
the absolute master of the lives and liberties of ten thousand naked savages.[18]

Unforeseen Consequences and Redistribution

Redistribution schemes inspired by the goals of equality of result or equality of
opportunity have certainly resulted in some people acquiring resources that they
might otherwise lack. This boon should not distract us from recognizing the
many negative consequences for commercial society that proceed from such
policies. In his short book, *The Ethics of Redistribution*, the French philosopher
Bertrand de Jouvenel underlines the fundamental incompatibility between what
he calls the redistributionist and anti-redistributionist mentalities. "The redistributionist," de Jouvenel comments, "thinks of income essentially as a means to
consumer-satisfaction, and he puts forward a case for equating satisfactions. To
the anti-redistributionist, income is primarily a reward for productive services,
and he is eager to scale rewards in such a way as to encourage a maximum flow
of services."[19]

De Jouvenel's analysis underlines the importance of incentives for understanding the workings, successes, and problems of any society. Once governments begin to engage in redistribution programs, people in commercial society
become orientated towards securing the maximum amount of resources from the
redistributing state instead of seeking employment in the market economy or
pursuing entrepreneurial opportunities. Many of the same characteristics and
habits that facilitate wealth-creation become directed towards the appropriation,
especially through political means, of as much redistributed wealth as possible. It
follows that the greater the proportion of the economy subject to redistribution,
the more people will shun commercial society in favor of seeking to maximize
their advantages in what might be called "redistributist society." For why should
people choose to enter the marketplace when they can obtain the majority of
their material needs and wants through successfully qualifying for government
programs or lobbying for a bigger share of government largesse?

The distortion of incentives following from government redistribution programs has particular implications for entrepreneurship. If it becomes the case
that the more one earns, the more one pays in direct and indirect taxes, we can be
sure there will be a corresponding decrease in the incentives for entrepreneurs to
grow the size of their enterprises and thereby create more wealth and employ
more people. Leaving aside the fact that progressive taxation, when conceived as
part of an income-redistribution policy, is difficult to reconcile with the idea that
all people are to be treated equally by the law, Israel Kirzner warns us that "To
announce in advance to potential entrepreneurs that 'lucky' profits will be taxed
away is to convert open ended situations into situations more and more approxi-
mating those of a given, closed character."[20] The incentive for entrepreneurs to

pay attention to anything save that which is already known is removed. There is, Kirzner adds, a corresponding decline in the wellsprings of alertness to potential entrepreneurial opportunities to create new wealth. A less visible, though equally damaging, effect on entrepreneurship proceeds from regulatory measures that seek to establish certain forms of equality in society. Tariffs and various forms of labor legislation do not, as Kirzner demonstrates, "merely limit numbers in particular markets. These kinds of regulatory activity tend to bar entrepreneurs who believe that they have discovered profit opportunities in barred areas of the market."[21]

Being gifted with creativity and insight, humans have proved adept at discovering ways to avoid the impact of redistribution programs such as high taxation rates. The very wealthy can afford to hire professionals adept at significantly reducing the tax burden in ways that often teeter on the very edge of legality. They can also afford to exercise the option of simply exiting a high-tax society, taking their resources and abilities to other countries. This results in a considerable loss of human skills and capital resources to the home country while other people, usually the less-wealthy, shoulder a higher proportion of the overall tax burden. A less obvious but equally damaging effect of high taxation on commercial society is the marginalizing effects on the middle class. Often insufficiently wealthy to exercise exit options or acquire superior technical advice that allows them to reduce their tax-burden legally, but also too wealthy to qualify for government assistance, many in the middle class find themselves having to work longer and harder just to preserve their socioeconomic status while continuing to shoulder the costs of redistribution.[22]

Perhaps an even more damaging effect of such redistributist programs is their impact upon the civility and philanthropic activities typical of commercial society. If the state assumes the prime responsibility for helping those in need, it is little wonder that the philanthropic impulse with commercial society begins to diminish.[23] A vicious circle is created insofar as the waning of the philanthropic instinct effectively necessitates increased spending on the state's part and therefore increased taxation, which in turn further reduces incentives to create wealth. De Jouvenel was thus correct to profess that political exercises in redistribution always move beyond what he called pure redistribution: that is, the simple transfer of income from those who are richer to those who have less. The ongoing undermining of incentives necessitates further exercises in redistribution. The damage is compounded by political pressures to extend services and benefits associated with redistribution upwards so that they become available to increasing numbers of people throughout society. The habits of commercial society are thus slowly supplanted by a politically orientated redistributist ethic.

Though few governments in a post-Communist era seek an absolute equality of result, the persistent prioritizing of some form of economic equality provides governments a license to engage in endless wealth redistribution as it pursues a goal that can never be realized: the perfect redistributist equilibrium. The imperative of constantly seeking to move closer to such a goal makes it essential that the state engage in some form of redistribution in almost every transaction. This inevitably facilitates the unceasing expansion of government activity in the economic sphere which means that very few forms of exchange are free of such intervention. As P. J. Hill explains:

> Assume that government intervention creates a desirable distribution of income at one point in time. If people are allowed to engage in voluntary transactions, there will be an immediate move away from this distribution.... Therefore, state intervention to achieve a particular distribution must be a perpetual activity. The government must continually restrict human freedom and take resources from one group if the distribution is to meet the social objective of equality. Advocates of income redistribution through government must recognize that they are advocating a permanent and large presence of that government in the lives of its citizens.[24]

The expansion of state power is not limited to involvement in these exchanges. The administration of state-organized redistribution requires the creation and maintenance of large and complex bureaucracies, a process that generates its own costs thereby reducing the available resources and thus necessitating more taxation.

Then there is the significant harm inflicted by politically inspired equality redistributions to freedom of contract. In tracing the history of contract law throughout the twentieth century, Atiyah associates the decline of contract freedom to several causes, including a reduction in the political importance attached to free choice. He links this to the emergence of restrictive trade practices ranging from official monopolies, protectionism, heavy regulatory environments, and restrictive employment practices,[25] especially in those situations where trade unions have established a monopoly over the labor supply. All these measures, Atiyah states, were encouraged by the emergence of skepticism about commercial society's ability to provide people with what they need, especially those believed to be in a disadvantageous position when it comes to negotiating contracts. The widespread nationalization of different services after the Second World War effectively removed entire spheres of economic life from the area of contract by placing them entirely within the state's purview. Everyone was thus forced to contract with a single provider of monopolized services. The state's virtual monopoly over these services, Atiyah argues, meant that people had limited redress when the service was poor. It also drastically reduced the opportunities to contract freely with other providers of the same service. In some instances, the provision of such services by private contractors remains legally prohibited.

Other more subtle limitations on contractual freedom influenced by the political pursuit of equal opportunity have been implemented though antidiscrimination legislation related to sex and race, or affirmative action programs obliging people to contract with people of particular backgrounds, especially in employment matters. The political inhibition of contractual freedom has been further exacerbated by the rise of what might be called a jurisprudence of externalities. In the 1960s, several courts began ruling that certain types of contracts could be invalidated if their side effects—what economists and legal scholars often call externalities—negatively affected the interests of third parties.[26] As noted, there are many positive externalities to free exchanges such as the prevalence of peace among trading nations. More commonly, courts have invoked the concept of externalities to invalidate or stop the performance of free contracts because of perceived negative externalities (such as environmental damage), or because courts were convinced that allowing a contract to proceed would facilitate certain social and economic inequalities.

Over the long term, much of this political interference with the workings of a basic legal foundation of commercial society has negatively impacted many of the people whom such changes were supposed to assist. In the first place, they have helped to undermine the economic efficiencies provided by contracts. Protecting monopolies of labor and services from the competitive effects of free contracts has allowed numerous industries to remain highly inefficient. This augments consumer costs and denies the benefits of new technology to vast numbers of middle and low-income people. To take a fictional example, the typewriter industry might plead and lobby for protection from competition from the computer industry because of the likelihood of unemployment among typewriter repairmen as more people start using computers. Unfortunately, the resulting restraints on free exchange between consumers and the computer industry not only encourages people to continue working in an industry that will eventually be surpassed by technological development, but also means that computers are affordable only by the very wealthy.

Analogous developments are discernible in the area of employment. Political restrictions on freedom of contract in the name of equality in this sphere have made employers reluctant to hire people if they know that it is extremely difficult to discharge inefficient employees. This produces the odd phenomenon of labor shortages and high unemployment and a tendency to fill shortages by employing people living in a state of illegality such as clandestine immigrants. Likewise, severe restrictions on freedom of contract in certain rental markets greatly reduce the amount of property available for rent. When tenants are protected by legislation and other devices that restrict what landlords may reasonably do with the property or how much rent they may charge, people become reluctant to put their property on the rental market. The result is a shortage of rental properties.

Upholding commercial society means accepting that the equal treatment of people by the same laws will not produce equality in terms of sameness. People are different in their abilities, intelligence, and education. Our futures are determined by many other things including our culture and family. Much of this is simply beyond the control of individuals and even the state. This make it virtually inevitable that there will always be differences and inequalities in society, the implication being that pursuing equality of result or opportunity requires the endless adjustment and interference in people's working and living conditions in an attempt to realize the unrealizable. While we ought not to be inhibited from removing obstacles that arise from unjust legal discrimination, such as prohibiting people of particular racial origins from attending certain schools, those favoring the growth of commercial society are right to be skeptical of political efforts to facilitate greater equity in a society's wealth distribution.

Throughout the nineteenth and twentieth centuries, the egalitarian impulse found its primary political expressions in a range of left-wing movements, ranging from militant Communism to relatively mild social democratic and labor parties. It also manifested itself in the promotion of mixed economies by governments of both the right and left more or less along the lines articulated by John Maynard Keynes and his followers. While some intellectuals, scholars, and activists continue to promote these or related ideas, Communism's defeat as well as the high unemployment levels and "stagflation" that afflicted Keynesian economies in the 1970s brought many such policies and movements into serious disrepute. Despite these developments, there remains one trend of thought associated with the egalitarian impulse that continues to be posed as an alternative to—or at least a way of seriously modifying—commercial society throughout much of the world, especially Latin America and the European Union.

The Third Way

One response to the emergence of market-orientated societies in the late eighteenth century was what is often called "corporatism." Just as there were different schools of socialism, a variety of theories are associated with corporatism. Leading contributors to corporatist thinking of the late nineteenth and early twentieth centuries included the Frenchmen Albert de Mun (1841–1914) and Emile Durkheim (1858–1917) as well as Germans such as Karl Marlo (1810–1865), Heinrich Pesch (1854–1926), and Oswald von Nell-Breuning (1890–1991). As an expression, corporatism owes its origins to the Latin word *corpus* meaning "body." It was commonly used to refer to any organization that was incorporated, usually in a legal sense. Its usage reflects medieval concepts of a whole society in which the various components were each viewed as playing a part in the life of the society, just as the various parts of the body fulfill specific roles in the life of a whole person.[27] Early corporatism consequently involved the exposition of an organic vision of society in which the whole consists of parts into which an integration of individuals has already occurred.

What then are the basic characteristics of corporatist thought? One emphasis of early modern corporatist thinkers was upon normalizing the division of labor through attempting to mandate particular forms of group life within a given society beyond natural categories such as the family. They shared the basic tenet that all economic sectors should be enveloped by organizations that embrace everyone working in them. These associations would be responsible for deciding wages, establishing working conditions, resolving industrial disputes, often via special work councils, and even determining economic policy in collaboration with government officials. Durkheim went so far as to venture that as market exchanges spread beyond the level of locality to the national and international arena, so too should corporatist arrangements be extended to national institutions.[28] He advocated merging workers' and employers' associations into single corporations, endowing these corporations with legal authority (and even the power to impose sanctions upon malcontents), and creating special tribunals to adjudicate industrial disputes. Corporations themselves would be governed by their own elected councils, with the division of electoral power between employees and employers corresponding to "the relative importance given by opinion to these two factors of production."[29] This, Durkheim hoped, would reduce conflict by assuring a continuity of employment and high wages and conditions and giving employees a powerful voice in what happens in their industry.

The underlying objective of such policies was to create communities of people within the economic sphere as opposed to the looser and freer forms of association characteristic of commercial society. Early corporatists saw little reason why the community idea of sociability found in families and other forms of noneconomic association could not be applied to economic life. In the words of the British guild thinker G. D. H. Cole, "We ... see such associations as natural expressions and instruments of the purposes which certain groups of individuals have in common."[30] The English philosopher John Stuart Mill went so far as to describe corporatist-like arrangements as inevitable. "The form of association," he wrote, "which if mankind continues to improve must be expected in the end to predominate is not that which can exist between a capitalist as Chief, and work people without a voice in the management, but the association of laborers themselves on forms of equality, collectively owning the capital with which they carry on their operations and working under managers elected and removable by themselves."[31]

Though nineteenth-century corporatist thinkers typically distinguished themselves from socialists by generally rejecting direct government ownership of industry, they invariably took the view that corporative organizations should operate alongside and under the state in shaping economic life. Close cooperation with the state was, in the view of some of its advocates, integral to corporatism's success. Some went so far as to venture that the state needed to ensure that these types of relations prevail in the economic sphere, usually through politically enforcing functional representation throughout the economic sphere. Durkheim asserted that the corporate functional bodies should play a political role and even declared that their functional representation as units should replace geography as the basis of electoral units.[32] The "organized profession or corporation" would become "the essential organ of public life" and society would thus evolve into "a vast system of national corporations."[33] In a similar vein, Cole was adamant that there should be chambers representing different segments of the economy, with all chambers being united into one cohesive whole with specific powers. "I conceive," he wrote, "that the various Guilds will be unified in a central Guild Congress, which will be the supreme industrial body, standing to the people as producers in the same relation as parliament will stand to the people as consumers."[34] In this light, it is hardly surprising that Cole spoke of the "co-sovereignty of the Guilds and the State."[35] While corporatism has some specific features, its similarity to the objectives and character of the medieval guilds is not coincidental. In his *Guild and Civil Society*, Antony Black convincingly establishes powerful thematic and historical continuities between ideas associated with the guilds and modern corporatist theories.

One twentieth-century manifestation of corporatism was what may be called state corporatism. To varying degrees, there were attempts to implement this in Fascist Italy, National Socialist Germany, Vichy France, Salazar's Portugal, Franco's Spain, and Dollfuss' Austria. Similar policies were pursued by some South American countries and associated with the emergence of nationalism and, in some instances, militarism.[36] Juan Perón's Argentina provides a case study of how state corporatism manifests itself.

Upon coming to power in Argentina in 1946, Perón pursued corporatist policies and used classic corporatist language such as "organized community." In his instructive study of Argentina's economic rise and fall in the nineteenth and twentieth century, Mauricio Roja observes that Perón's policies were based on "state-controlled cooperation between different groups in society."[37] Through a system of rewards and punishments, unions were co-opted into this system as a result of the state assuming the role of industrial conciliator, its refusal to deal with any union not recognized by the state, and its mandated conciliation packages. The result was the dominance of one set of compliant trade union leaders over more independent-minded figures. Corporatism in Argentina was accompanied by heavy state-directed industrialization, nationalization of key industries, and a radical redistribution of income in favor of employees. Another element of Argentine corporatism was a policy of minimizing the amount of foreign capital invested in Argentina, a strategy primarily pursued through nationalization of service industries, infrastructure, and banking. By 1949, Roja comments, Argentina had adopted a new corporatist-inclined constitution, the universities and the press had been organizationally integrated into the corporatist state, and Argentina's Supreme Court had lost its autonomy.

In the 1950s, Perón's government extended these policies by organizing other sectors of society into state-controlled associations. This included employers, public sector employees, university students, freelancing professionals, and even high school students. The state and its client trade unions also began to assume more direct control over social security.[38] The associated doubling of the number of public sector employees, Roja stresses, "triggered a development that was to lead to one of Argentina's severest problems, namely growing political corruption and a contest for privilege."[39] Not surprisingly, business activity ceased to be directed by market signals and became orientated by political priorities and the need to survive nationalization or semi-control by the state. As a consequence, Roja concludes:

> People were forced to commit heavy resources to a game which had very little to do with efficient resource utilization but was ideal for promoting corruption in both great things and small. Lawyers and political contacts were strategic facilitators to the corporations. Large departments were built up to deal with the endless paper work and lobbying activity which opened the way to vital import licenses, juicy public contracts, much sought-after start-up permits, cheap credits, special prices, lower exchange rates and so on. This was a colossal waste of resources, engendering abnormal corporate structures and a mercantilist entrepreneur mentality.[40]

Debates continue concerning the extent to which different regimes truly embodied corporatist principles and theories.[41] What is not in doubt is that many governments did seek to implement many of the ideas described above—partly, one suspects, to distinguish themselves philosophically from both Marxists and advocates of commercial society, and partly because such policies assisted these regimes in their efforts to control society. In state-corporatist systems, the state generally recognized one organization such as a national business group, agricultural body, or trade union as the only official representative of the people and associations that constituted the constituency of that organization. Alternative organizations were officially discouraged, harassed, or forbidden. Theoretically, state corporatism involved giving actual legislative power to "corporations" or "corporate bodies" that represented the officially recognized economic, industrial and professional groups. In Fascist Italy, for instance, business owners, employees, tradesmen, professionals, and other economic groups were organized into twenty-two corporations according to their industries. Each corporation was then permitted representation in a quasi-legislative organization called the *Camera dei Fasci e delle Corporazioni.*

State corporatism is not therefore a question of the state simply licensing or officially recognizing the existence of different organized interest groups. Rather, the groups are created or subsumed by the state and incorporated into the state's own centralized hierarchical system of regulation as instruments to pursue and legitimize their policies. In the case of Nazi Germany and Fascist Italy, trade unions that had hitherto enjoyed autonomy from the state were either dissolved or merged into a single labor organization controlled by the state. State corporatism effectively involved co-opting the leadership of these formerly independent associations (or simply replacing them with party officials) thereby circumscribing their ability to challenge state authority by establishing the one-party state as the very source of their legitimacy.

While state corporatism tended to be relatively respectful of private property, it also expected private enterprise to work primarily toward the national good, as defined by the corporatist state, rather than profit maximization. The detailed study of Deutsche Bank under the Nazi dictatorship by the economic historian Harold James underscores the reality that while businesses were expected to be profitable, this had to occur in a manner that the state deemed not detrimental to the nation.[42] Thus it became difficult for many firms in Spain, Germany, Argentina, and Italy to move any part of their operations to a foreign country, precisely because such decisions were considered to cause job losses in the firm's home country (unless, of course, such operations were regarded by such regimes as facilitating their political interests in foreign countries).[43] Nor were these arrangements necessarily limited to economically orientated organizations such as unions or business associations. State corporatism often involved supplanting voluntary associations with nonprofit corporations supported with corporate and state finances. Even religious groups often found it difficult to avoid co-option. In Nazi Germany, the main Protestant community became divided between that group which accepted a "Reich bishop" and thus subordination to the Nazi regime while the other half led by figures such as Dietrich Bonhoeffer remained independent.

The distinction, then, between state corporatism and the drive for totalitarianism is very fine. No doubt, many early corporatist thinkers would have been distraught at the association of their ideas with fascist and semi-fascist regimes. The question is whether corporatist ideas by their very nature tend to facilitate authoritarian arrangements. Here it is striking to read the observations of no less an impeccably anti-fascist than John Maynard Keynes when he reflected upon possible paths for economic reform in 1926:

> I believe that in many cases the ideal size for the unit of control and organization lies somewhere between the individual and the modern state. I suggest, however, that progress lies in the growth and the recognition of semi-autonomous bodies within the State: bodies whose criterion of action within their own field is solely the public good as they understand it, and from whose deliberations motives of private advantage are excluded, though some place it may still be necessary to leave, until the ambit of men's altruism grows wider, to the separate advantage of particular groups, classes, or faculties; bodies which in the ordinary course of affairs are mainly autonomous within their prescribed limitations, but are subject in the last resort to the sovereignty of the democracy expressed through Parliament. I propose a return, it may be said, towards the medieval conception of separate autonomies.[44]

It is difficult to distinguish here any significant difference between Keynes' vision and many of state corporatism's guiding principles.

The experience of fascism did not completely discredit corporatist thinking in the post-World War II era. A number of corporatist principles were adopted, to varying degrees and with different emphases, by several European democratic states in the post-war era, and were advocated by parties ranging from Christian Democrats to moderate socialists. This was especially true of the German-speaking nations of Austria, Switzerland, and West Germany, as well as successive governments of both the left and right in countries including Belgium, the Netherlands, Norway, and Sweden.[45]

Neo-corporatism commonly manifests itself in a range of policies. One is that of codetermination whereby it is legally mandated (as in contemporary Germany) that employees or workers' representatives (i.e., union officials) must be integrated into the governing bodies of any business with more than five employees.[46] The former Social Democrat Chancellor of Germany Gerhard Schroeder once served on the board of the Volkswagen corporation for precisely this reason. As late as 2006, German businesses with more than two thousand employees were still obliged by law to give fully half the seats on supervisory boards to company employees.[47] Not only do workers' representatives (*Betrieb-srat*) have the right to participate in certain management decisions within firms,[48] but they also wield considerable influence over performance bonuses and employee assignments. In mid–2006, codetermination structures existed in eighteen of the European Union's then-twenty-five member states.[49]

Another common expression of neo-corporatism is a compulsory process of bargaining between labor, capital, and government that is often presented as an alternative to the manner in which wage claims and disputes are resolved in socialist or free economies. These arrangements, it is held, allow employers and employees to assist the state in managing the economy by helping to control the business cycle, underpin social stability, and ensure regular economic growth.[50] To this extent, neo-corporatism is less concerned with the creation of specific corporate organizations and more interested in providing a specific juridical structure that regulates the relationship between the state, employers, and employees. It therefore often mandates negotiating between peak bodies that represent the different groups in a process supervised by state bodies invested with legal powers over the negotiated outcome. In guiding such discussions and shaping the eventual outcome, these courts and administrative tribunals are expected to link the negotiations with a direct concern for macroeconomic policies that focus on sustaining high wages and full employment, though with some attention to the demands of market competition. Typically, such negotiations are supposed to induce wage restraint in recessionary or inflationary periods, to split any productivity gains fairly among employers and employees, and to help ensure that the state can continue to provide generous welfare services. When negotiations fail, affected groups of employers and employees assume the role of litigants before the relevant courts. Examples of such systems are the collective bargaining arrangements that prevail in the Scandinavian countries, the Dutch "Polder-model" consensus system, Ireland's Social Partnership system, or Australia's now largely defunct Arbitration and Conciliation tribunals and industrial relations courts. There have been several attempts to implement similar arrangements in Italy, such as the Ciampi government's 1993 effort to mandate the peaceful negotiation of salary between the three main trade unions and the employers' federation under the state's supervision.

A third manifestation of neo-corporatism is the creation of quasi-legislative chambers to represent employers and employees. This system exists, for example, in contemporary Austria. These chambers are accorded what amounts to an extra-parliamentary status and are deemed to be the official representatives of employers and employees. They are regularly consulted by governments of all political shades[51] on matters ranging from legislation and government appointments, to the determination of economic and social policy. It is assumed that the chambers speak with a certain authority on behalf of those that they are held to represent. And thus, as Philippe Schmitter writes, "They influence the process of government directly, bypassing [parliament]. They are agents of authority. They deputize for the state in whole areas of public life."[52] In Belgium, for example, unemployment benefits have been administered by trade unions since the First World War.

Corporatist Fallacies

One might ask, at this point, how typically corporatist policies such as collective bargaining processes and *a priori* commitments to full employment and equal pay for equal work are supposed to be reconciled with market competition, commercial profitability and rule of law, not to mention the open-ended economy created and required by entrepreneurship. Careful reflection upon corporatist ideas, principles, and practices soon indicates that far from moderating commercial society's effects, they have the potential to undermine many of its foundations. The danger lies precisely in the fact that the prescriptions of corporatism seem far less antithetical to commercial society than those of socialism and communism. More careful analysis reveals, however, that Röpke had good reason to describe corporatism as *ersatz-socialism*.

The type of neo-corporatist arrangements described above is only possible in societies in which membership of trade unions is high and various labor unions are hierarchically organized in a single labor federation. This requires labor unions to be granted a privileged legal status not accorded to other groups and their effective exemption from many prohibitions—especially those concerning the illegality of private coercion—that apply to the rest of society. Given that there are good reasons why some employees may not wish to belong to a trade union, a society pursuing a neo-corporatist path must choose between mandating union membership, creating legal and monetary disincentives for those who wish to opt out, or allowing trade unions to pressure people into joining their ranks. The only alternative is to abandon neo-corporatist policies.

Any one of these three ways of ensuring a high degree of non-voluntary organized labor has grave implications for the freedom of association and liberty of contract integral to commercial society. They also have grievous effects upon free competition, most notably in labor markets. For the corporatist corralling of millions of employees into mass labor organizations amounts to creating monopolies of labor. Numerous economists have pointed out that the establishment of an effective monopoly on labor by trade union movements in many countries following World War II resulted in wages being determined largely outside the market disciplines of competition and prices.[53] The focus of wage determination thus shifted from the market price for the labor to the principle of equal pay for different work. In the absence of competition in the labor market, there were no incentives for monopoly labor organizations to adjust their wage requirements. Profound distortions were thus created in the price of labor, leading to wage levels that could only be sustained through inflationary monetary policies.

It is not, however, neo-corporatism's creation of labor monopolies that necessarily has the most negative impact upon commercial societies. Rather it is the tendency of neo-corporatist policies to institutionalize inertia within the economy. The neo-corporatist requirement for extensive and continuing consultation creates major obstacles for individuals and companies wishing to seize and develop new entrepreneurial opportunities that come their way. It becomes easier simply to proceed according to arrangements already in place. The same powerful protections against dismissal that neo-corporatist arrangements invariably guarantee to employees make it almost impossible for commercial enterprises to remove unproductive or problem employees.

Another difficulty created by corporatist arrangements for commercial society is that of the installation of an entire class of bureaucrats wielding considerable authority throughout the political and economic order and whose interests do not necessarily coincide with those of the individuals and groups that they ostensibly represent. The unspoken assumption of many corporatist supporters is that those who work in, for instance, chambers of industry and labor will have the public interest at heart. Leaving aside the problem of the vagueness of objectives such as "general welfare" oft cited by corporatist scholars, it is precisely such elusiveness that allows these expressions to be interpreted as whatever is in the best interest of those working within corporatist or neo-corporatist organizations or those who seek to co-opt such organizations for particular political ends. For once the type of structures required by corporatism are created—be they quasi-legislative chambers or quasi-judicial industrial tribunals—those staffing these organizations have little interest in seeing their power and influence diminished, no matter how deleterious the economic effects of their activities might be. As public choice economists have stressed, it is wrong to assume that the pursuit of self-interest is not confined by nature to private enterprise and economic life. The tendency of bureaucracies to associate the promotion of their own interests with those of the state is neatly captured in Montesquieu's observations about taxation:

> The public revenues are a portion that each subject gives of his property, in order to secure or enjoy the remainder. To fix these revenues in a proper manner, regard should be had both to the necessities of the state and to those of the subject. The real wants of the people ought never to give way to the imaginary

wants to the state. Imaginary wants are those which flow from the passions and
the weakness of the governors, from the vain conceit of some extraordinary
project, from the inordinate desire of glory, and from a certain impotence of
mind incapable of withstanding the impulse of fancy. Often have ministers of a
restless disposition imagined that the wants of their own mean and ignoble souls
were those of the state.[54]

It follows that those who head an employers' federation or a peak labor organization will often have considerable incentives to resist anything that might diminish their immediate relevance or power. This might include labor and business
competition from abroad, the importation of new technology that allows certain
tasks to be done faster and with less direct human input, not to mention new
ideas that have the potential to replace an industry (such as typewriter manufacturing) or entire group of workers (such as typewriter repairmen) with another
(such as computers and computer technicians). All such innovation and change
is integral to the value that commercial society attaches to creativity and liberty
of commerce. By contrast, neo-corporatist organizations tend to view such developments as a threat to their own existence. Nor, it should be added, do those who
work in neo-corporatist organizations have any incentive to assist the unemployed. Under neo-corporatist arrangements, the unemployed are disenfran-
chised. The very nature of corporate representation means that they have no
voice in workers' councils, chambers of industry, or trade unions.

A more insidious distortion introduced by neo-corporatist arrangements for
the workings of commercial society is that of accountability. In commercial society, market competition and the need to make profits creates accountability at
every level insofar as employers and employees who fail to perform are priced
out of the market. By contrast, corporatism is very weak when it comes to the
question of accountability. Instead of stressing accountability for performance,
corporatism emphasizes avoidance of conflict and the delegation of power to
decision-making bodies focused upon building consensus rather than doing what
is necessary for those they purportedly represent. Under such arrangements, both
trade union and business leaders can avoid accountability by stressing to their
members and shareholders that they have a responsibility to the national interest,
or that they have no choice but to agree to the demands of the state authorities, or
no option but to abide by arrangements negotiated by business, union, and government leaders without consulting their respective constituencies.

Corporatism's accountability deficit points to another problem facilitated by
corporatist tendencies: corruption. The public choice economist Gordon Tullock
has concluded that corruption usually amounts to the state "taking action, not for
its ostensible reason [i.e., the common good], but for the secret reason of private
benefit—i.e., one pretends to favor the public interest but is in fact favoring his
own pocketbook."[55] Though corruption will exist in every economic system as
long as human beings are capable of choosing evil, corporatism creates tremendous opportunities for corruption. In economic and legal terms, corruption may

be defined as the performance of illegal, voluntary transactions between two parties (the agent and his customer) with a detrimental effect on a third party (the principal) whom the agent was legally obliged to serve. By violating this obligation, the corrupt agent exercises the power received from his principal (e.g., the state) in a way different from his legal commitment to the principal. In so doing, the corrupt agent disposes of the principal's wealth or powers to his own benefit.[56]

Given their compulsory introduction of third parties into so many economic transactions, it is to be expected that neo-corporatist structures and procedures provide many opportunities for corruption. Corporatist arrangements create numerous intersections where political, bureaucratic and economic interests coincide and come into conflict. This gives rise to numerous opportunities for those who lead corporatist bodies, be they of employers or employees, to do deals with each other that resolve such conflicts while simultaneously furthering their own interests. The imposing of literally thousands of regulations on private economic activities via corporatist structures creates perverse incentives for people in the private sector to enter into corrupt arrangements with those who enjoyed decision-making powers by corporatist arrangements in order to buy their way around these restrictions. Such incentives are facilitated by the state legislating, for example, that contracts are not valid until they have been approved by a trade union council, workers' representatives on company boards, an employers' federation, or an industrial relations court. Some people will try to circumvent these barriers through bribes and favors. It is little wonder, for instance, that mandated codetermination arrangements in Germany are increasingly associated with corruption scandals, as employers, desperate to ensure that the official workers' representatives do not hinder any decisions that might involve staff reductions, have resorted to bribery and other illegalities to gain the approval of the *Betriebsrat* sitting on company boards and committees.[57]

Commercial Politics?

Many of the redistributist and corporatist policies and ideas identified in this chapter have been implemented by authoritarian and totalitarian regimes. As noted, this often reflects the desire of such governments to extend their control throughout the economic sphere, thereby reducing the potential for individuals and groups to exercise their liberty in this realm. This being the case, it seems reasonable to suggest that commercial society and liberty in general is facilitated by prudently minimizing the influence of the political sphere.

This should not be misinterpreted as an advocacy of apolitical tendencies. Rather it involves the cultivation of a political order that moderates and limits the effects of political power upon commercial society. Adam Smith seems to have understood this when he pointed out that, although commercial society is based on the presumption that there are limits to most people's capacity for being other-regarding, some of its members need to develop what Smith called a "superior prudence" as well as other "greater and splendid virtues, with valor, with extensive and strong benevolence, and with a sacred regard to the rules of justice, and all these supported by a proper degree of self-command."[58] These, he says, are what "accompany the more splendid actions of the hero, the statesman, or the legislator."[59]

A long-term challenge for legislators in commercial society is to identify and protect what Hayek called those "objective rules of just conduct independent of particular interests" rather than excessively concerning themselves with "the particular results of such conduct on the position of the different individuals and groups."[60] The more immediate challenge for politicians concerned for commercial society's long-term well-being is to eliminate those regulations designed to promote particular interests, and to ensure that businesses and entrepreneurs invest more time competing in the market place rather than lobbying politicians for favors. Private businesses have always understood that one way of insulating themselves from market competition and consumer demand is to establish legal monopolies that effectively limit a trade or economic activity to one company or group of businesses. Though invariably described as being in the public interest, such barriers are designed to benefit one group by excluding others from the marketplace or making it harder for them to compete. There will always be those who regard it as in their self-interest to avoid free competition and inhibit free trade so that they can obtain high prices for their goods without having to take risks, innovate, or work more efficiently. As Smith famously wrote, "People of the same trade seldom meet together, even for merriment and diversion, but the conversation ends in a conspiracy against the public, or in some contrivance to raise prices."[61]

Regrettably, the conversation rarely stops among themselves. It invariably results in efforts to persuade others, especially political and government leaders, that lending their support to such a conspiracy is in fact the just policy to pursue. There are always a good number of people who will attempt to restrict competition or limit entrepreneurship by persuading politicians that their particular sectional interest is identical to society's general welfare. In one of his best known economic fables, "The Petition of the Candle-makers against the Competition of the Sun," the nineteenth-century French economist Frederic Bastiat satirized such claims through his story of the candle-makers demanding the prohibition of windows because of the benefit conferred by the prosperity of candle-makers upon everyone else. Trade barriers are not created without substantial lobbying from businesses and trade unions wishing to avoid or reduce competition. The problem with these policies is, as Smith and others have illustrated, that they encourage labor and capital to move towards industries where these types of restrictions kept profits artificially high and the price of consumer goods artificially inflated.[62] "But in the mercantile system," Smith wrote, "the interest of the consumer is constantly sacrificed to that of the producer; and it seems to consider production, and not consumption, as the ultimate end and object of all industry and commerce."[63]

In the final analysis, it can only be legislators who prevent lobby groups from pushing government policies in directions that undermine commercial society. This requires considerable courage on the part of political leaders willing to place the interests of commercial society before the specific agendas pursued by those seeking exemption from market disciplines. It also involves being willing to show electorates how the very issues that drive many to want to regulate the market or to dilute commercial society are more adequately addressed through the workings of commercial society. This is especially true of those societies long disfigured by corporatist policies or decades-long redistribution schemes. Adam Smith offered particular advice to political leaders determined to reform such economic orders:

> When he cannot conquer the rooted prejudices of the people by reason and per-
> suasion, he will not attempt to subdue them by force.... He will accommodate,
> as well as he can, his public arrangements to the confirmed habits and preju-
> dices of the people.... When he cannot establish the right, he will not disdain to
> ameliorate the wrong; but like Solon, when he cannot establish the best system
> of laws, he will endeavor to establish the best that the people can bear.[64]

Not all governments pursuing redistributist and corporatist policies do so with the explicit intention of maximizing the power of the political realm over society. Yet the ease with which even freely elected governments wander down this path may reflect a failure on the part of some political leaders to appreciate that economic liberty must be real if freedom is to be anything else but nominal, and that their political office can be used to educate people about the nature and benefits of commercial society. But the challenges created by politics for commercial society do not cease here. Though democracy embodies some attention to freedom, democracy's long-term compatibility with commercial society is arguably open to question. This issue is especially relevant for those nations that have or are embracing market economic orders but have not yet opened themselves to democratic principles and structures. At first glance, the typical emphasis of democracy upon ideas such as liberty and widespread participation seems to parallel many of the dominant themes of commercial societies. Closer attention to the phenomenon of modern democracy suggests, however, that the relationship between democracy and commercial order is more ambiguous than often supposed.

Notes

1. Edmund Burke, "Thoughts and Details on Scarcity," in *The Portable Edmund Burke*, ed. Isaac Kraminick (Harmondsworth: Penguin Books, 1999), 203.

2. Ibid., 211.

3. Joseph Raz, "The Obligation to Obey: Revision and Tradition," in *Natural Law*, 288.

4. Jean Jacques Rousseau, *Discourse on the Origin of Inequality* (Indianapolis, Ind.: Hackett Publishing Company, 1992), 27.

5. Peter J. Hill, "Creating and Distributing Wealth: Whose Responsibility?" in *Wealth, Poverty, and Human Destiny*, eds. Doug Bandow and David Schindler (Wilmington, Del.: ISI Books, 2003), 1.

6. Readers would do well to consult the seminal studies by the Oxford economic historian R.M. Hartwell which illustrate the rapid growth of overall living standards in England as commercial society took root and flourished. See, for example, R. M. Hartwell, *The Industrial Revolution and Economic Growth* (London: Methuen, 1971); and *The Long Debate on Poverty: Eight Essays on Industrialisation and "the condition of England"* (London: Institute for Economic Affairs, 1972).

7. Tocqueville, *Democracy*, vol. 2, 505.

8. Lloyd Weinreb, *Natural Law and Justice* (Cambridge, Mass.: Harvard University Press, 1987), 166.

9. Isaiah Berlin, "Equality," *Proceedings of the Aristotelian Society*, 56 (1955–1956): 305–6.

10. Ibid., 315.

11. Montesquieu, *Spirit*, bk. 20, chap. 2.

12. Lord Acton, "Nationality," in *Selected Writings of Lord Acton*, vol. 1, *Essays in the History of Liberty*, ed. J. Rufus Fears (Indianapolis: Liberty Classics, 1985–1988), 424.

13. Munzer, *Theory of Property*, 241.

14. Ibid., 243.

15. John H. Schaar, "Equality of Opportunity, and Beyond," *Nomos*, 9 (1967), 234.

16. See Hill, "Creating and Distributing Wealth: Whose Responsibility?" 4.

17. F. A. Hayek, "History and Politics," in *The Collected Works of F. A. Hayek*, vol. 3, *The Trend of Economic Thinking—Essays on Political Economists and Economic History*, ed. W. W. Bartley III and Stephen Kresge (Chicago: University of Chicago, 1991), 65.

18. Adam Smith, *Wealth of Nations*, I.i.11.

19. Bertrand de Jouvenel, *The Ethics of Redistribution* (Indianapolis: Liberty Fund, 1990), 51.

20. Kirzner, *Discovery*, 111.

21. Israel Kirzner, "The Primacy of Entrepreneurial Discovery," *The Entrepreneur in Society*, 78.

22. Sweden provides an example of how mass redistribution policies in the name of equality actually achieved the opposite of what was intended. In 1960, Sweden's public sector spending amounted to 31 percent of GNP. In 1993, it was 74 percent. By the 1990s, Sweden's full employment had disappeared and was replaced by mass unemployment. Over 500,000 jobs disappeared between 1990 and 1994. The economic recovery of the

mid–1990s did little to resolve the situation. Sweden's overall economic decline has steadily continued. See Rojas, *Rise and Fall of the Swedish Model*, 86.

23. Even the creation of a predominately state-provided safety net leads to a type of redistribution. Very few people would oppose such a safety net. Yet once it is established, it is almost impossible to stop the net's growth. One solution, suggested by Hayek, would be to allow such safety nets to be provided by the state, on the condition that there was no restriction on what could be offered by the market as alternatives (e.g., unemployment insurance) and, second, it was not forbidden for non-state groups to devise other methods for dealing with unemployment. Practical experience of the modern welfare state, however, indicates that, with the notable exception of the United States, it quickly undermines and marginalizes private charity.

24. Hill, "Creating and Distributing Wealth: Whose Responsibility?" 10.

25. See Atiyah, *Introduction to the Law of Contract*, 18.

26. See ibid., 19.

27. See J. Canning, "The Corporation in the Political Thought of the Italian jurists of the thirteenth and fourteenth centuries," *History of Political Thought*, no. 1 (1980): 9–32; and Susan Reynolds, "The History of the Idea of Incorporation or Legal Personality: A Case of Fallacious Terminology," in *Ideas and Solidarities of the Medieval Laity: England and Western Europe* (Aldershot: Variorum, 1995).

28. See Emile Durkheim, *De la division du travail social* (Paris: Presses universitaires de France, 1973), xxvii–xxviii. Durkheim never indicated how corporatism would adapt to the international market.

29. Emile Durkheim, *Leçons de sociologie: physique des mœurs et du droit*, 2d ed. (Paris, 1969), 74.

30. G. D. H. Cole, *Self-Government in Industry* (London: Hutchinson Educational, 1971), 129.

31. John Stuart Mill, *Principles of Political Economy* (Amherst, N.Y.: Prometheus Books, 2004), 133.

32. See Durkheim, *De la division du travail social*, xxxi.

33. Ibid., xxxi–xxxii.

34. Cole, *Self-Government in Industry*, 154.

35. Ibid., 6.

36. See Mauricio Roja. *The Sorrows of Carmencita: Argentina's Crisis in a Historical Perspective* (Kristianstad: Timbro, 2002), 56.

37. See ibid., 59.

38. See ibid., 72.

39. Ibid.

40. Ibid., 84–85.

41. R. H. Bowen avows that the Nazi regime did not even come close to reflecting corporatist principles. See R. H. Bowen, *German Theories of the Corporate State with Special Reference to the Period 1870–1919* (New York: Whittlesey House, 1947).

42. See James, *The Nazi Dictatorship and the Deutsche Bank*, 1–10.

43. Deutsche Bank's operations during World War II in German-occupied territories, for example, were encouraged by the Nazi regime insofar as they assisted in the subjugation of Germany's real and imagined foes, especially when it came to appropriating Jewish assets throughout occupied Europe. See ibid., 108–218.

44. J. M. Keynes, *The End of Laissez-faire* (London: Hogarth Press, 1926), 288–89.

45. See P. C. Schmitter, "Still the Century of Corporatism?" *Review of Politics*, 36 (1974): 85–131.

46. West Germany's economic miracle of the late 1940s was the result of a small group of free-market economists successfully implementing currency reform, allowing prices to follow the process of supply and demand, and abandoning wartime economic regulations. These policies were opposed by a number of advocates of codetermination and neo-corporatist arrangements including Oswald von Nell-Breuning. The same neo-corporatists were, however, successful in having characteristically corporatist arrangements such as codetermination mandated by law. Such measures significantly blur the division of labor upon which commercial society depends. Moreover, as early as the 1950s, figures such as Röpke were noting that the ability of German firms to adjust to shifts in demand and supply in goods, services, and labor was being undermined by the legal requirements for endless consultation and the effective establishment of a trade union monopoly of labor.

47. Hugh Williamson, "Merkel Defends Labour Market Reforms," *Financial Times*, 25 May 2006, 6.

48. See J. Boswell, *Community and the Economy: The Theory of Public Cooperation* (London: Routledge, 1990); and L. Panitch, "The Development of Corporatism in Liberal Democracies," in *Trends towards Corporatist Intermediation*, eds. P. Schmitter and G. Lehmbruch (London: Sage, 1979): 119–46.

49. See Williamson, "Merkel Defends Labour Market Reforms," 6.

50. See G. Lehmbruch, "Consociational Democracy, Class Conflict and the New Corporatism," in *Trends towards Corporatist Intermediation*, 53–62.

51. In some cases, different shades of political opinion are built into the chambers. A chamber of employees may therefore have Marxist, Social Democrat, and Christian Democrat factions.

52. Schmitter, "Still the Century of Corporatism?" 99.

53. See, for example, Friedrich von Hayek, *1980s Unemployment and the Unions: Essays on the Impotent Price Structure of Britain and Monopoly in the Labour Market* (London: IEA, 1980).

54. Montesquieu, *Spirit*, bk. 11, chap. 1.

55. Gordon Tullock, "Corruption Theory and Practice," *Contemporary Economic Policy*, 14, no. 3 (1996): 11. This is not to deny that corruption may arise in the private sector. It is entirely possible for two agents of a private company to defraud an unsuspecting principal of the company (i.e., the shareholders). But private companies have an incentive to make every effort to prevent dishonest employees from striking deals with customers or suppliers for their own benefit and against the interests of the company. The incentive is reduced profit. An employee may perhaps be able to take advantage of a faulty procedure for his own benefit. Nonetheless, privately owned companies have strong incentives for prohibiting and exorcising such behavior.

56. This definition of corruption excludes nepotism, understood as the hiring of relatives irrespective of their merits. It includes, however, the sale of appointments to friends or strangers. It may also embrace what some call "revolving-door agreements" whereby public officials and politicians become employees or consultants in businesses with whom they have previously interacted in a public capacity.

57. See, for example, http://news.bbc.co.uk/2/hi/business/4429460.stm

58. Smith, *Theory of Moral Sentiments*, VI.i.15.
59. Ibid., VI.iii.13.
60. Hayek, "Liberalism," 139.
61. Smith, *Wealth of Nations*, I.x.c.27.
62. Ibid., IV.ii.2–3.
63. Ibid., IV.viii.49.
64. Smith, *Theory of Moral Sentiments*, VI.ii.2.16.

6

The Dilemma of Democracy

*The dogma, that absolute power may, by the hypothesis of pop-
ular power, be as legitimate as constitutional freedom, began
... to darken the air.*

—Lord Acton

It is tempting to believe that democracy is man's natural political state. Yet systems described as democratic have not been the norm of political organization
for most of human history. There are also significant differences between the
democracy of Pericles' Athens and the many forms of democracy scattered
around the globe in the twenty-first century. Even among these latter systems,
we find considerable variances between those with a strong emphasis on representative institutions and those that encourage more regular popular participation
in political decision-making.

While many studies have assessed the variance between different forms of
democracy and their effects, less attention has been given to the manner in which
democratic aspirations and institutions shape a society's culture, including those
with strong commercial impulses. Like other forms of government, democratic
political culture shapes human beings, sometimes without people even being
aware of it. Tocqueville even proposed that the difference between the monarchical and aristocratic regimes of the past and the democratic systems of the
present amounted to a distinction between two humanities.

125

Democratic man is a creature who lives according to a certain theory about humanity: that all people are born and live free and are equal in terms of a certain number of rights. This has many implications including the steady disassociation of questions of obedience from one's hereditary status and an emphasis upon the idea that a person need not obey anyone, save in those ways to which he has previously consented. This is not necessarily a recipe for anarchy. *Homo democraticus* is above all subject to the sovereignty of the people. Where they have spoken, he must obey.

Historically speaking, the rise of contemporary democracy appears to be associated with the emergence of modern forms of commercial society in the latter half of the eighteenth century. Nations with strong commercial orientations such as the United States and Great Britain experienced a gradual evolution toward more democratic political arrangements, not always without trauma such as England's Glorious Revolution of 1688 and America's revolutionary war. Those nations with less pronounced commercial tendencies, such as Russia and most Eastern European states, took much longer to embrace, at least formally, democratic methods of government.

As we have seen, commercial society is characterized by a strong animus against the legal privileging of different groups. This is one reason why the spread of commerce is often linked to the advent of democracy. But it is arguable that the priorities of commercial society and democracy do not always coincide. Many of the political liberties commonly associated with democratic forms of government, such as universal suffrage, are not essential to commercial society. Societies with powerful trading orientations have existed without a wide distribution of voting rights.

Commercial society is concerned with limiting state power so that it does not unduly interfere with the workings of the foundations of market orders. It thus seeks to confine government to the performance of certain specific tasks. Democracy is not concerned per se with limiting government power. It is focused on the question of who is directing government power and ensuring that as many people as possible are involved in this process, consistent with the demands of public order. Democracy also tends to regard the majority opinion as the primary source of legitimacy. Commercial society does not.

In his *Spirit of the Laws*, Montesquieu spent much time explaining that if we want to understand any political order or society, we must grasp what he called the "general spirit" animating it. In the case of eighteenth-century Britain, Montesquieu indicated that a commercial spirit informed much of the country's culture. Looking at another commercially orientated society, Tocqueville identified the democratic impulse as being at least as powerful as the commercial spirit that permeated early nineteenth-century America. In the second volume of *Democracy in America*, it becomes clearer that Tocqueville grew increasingly uncertain about the ultimate compatibility of the commercial and democratic spirits. Pierre Manent captures the essence of this unease when he states that "Love of liberty ... has a foundation that is clearly and emphatically inegalitarian and thus anti-democratic."[1] If the democratic state is all-sovereign—freed from all constraints created by natural law, tradition, reason, and religion—then fewer protections exist for commercial society's foundations. Democratic states do not have a good record of upholding these protections when faced with choosing between, for instance, greater economic liberty and greater economic equality.

This is not to claim that Tocqueville perceived no connection between various social and political tendencies associated with the rise of democracy and the spread of the commercial spirit. Despite this, serious questions remain about whether a range of social trends and expectations associated with modern democracy, especially its unending drive for a greater equality of conditions, necessarily results in the slow corrosion of some of commercial society's foundations. Before such matters can be examined in detail, a word on the most relevant elements of modern democracy is required.

The Spirit of Democracy

Democracy is commonly associated with the broadening of participation in political affairs. This was the case of ancient Athens which distinguished itself from the monarchical and aristocratic arrangements of other Greek city-states by virtue of the fact that a large number of political decisions in Athens were made by all the citizenry. Athenian citizenship was, we should recall, confined to men descended from other Athenian citizens and denied to women, slaves, and those with non-Athenian ancestry. In more contemporary times, democracy's spread has involved the enfranchisement of all adult citizens above a certain age, increased use of direct democracy mechanisms, and the cessation of a monopoly of power being accorded to one official political party or movement.

In themselves, these changes do not reflect the essence of what Montesquieu and Tocqueville regarded as democracy's essential spirit. Montesquieu was especially attentive to the place of *equality* in democracies. In a section of *Spirit of the Laws* entitled, "Of the Spirit of Extreme Equality," Montesquieu presented extreme equality as the antithesis of an ordered democracy. No doubt he regarded such equality as a potential threat to the fledgling representative system emerging in the eighteenth-century Britain that was his model of political order and highly restrictive in its voting base. By contrast, Tocqueville identified the spirit of equality as integral to American democracy. The passion for equality, he claimed, penetrated everything else—the economy, the law, religion—that non-democratic regimes had not penetrated or tried to change.

For Tocqueville, democracy is more than just another political system. It is rather the organizing and—to use Manent's expression—"comprehensive principle of a new society."[2] On several occasions, Tocqueville describes equality of conditions as "generative," by which he means that it shapes and influences everything. This, he adds, is partly due to the power of public opinion in democracies. In America, Tocqueville advises, public opinion is "the dominant power," especially common opinion, and its power lies in the fact that it is the only source of knowledge which carries authority. Throughout *Democracy in America*, Tocqueville presents public opinion as a form of the sovereignty of the people. This contrasts with the world of Christendom in which revelation is regarded as authoritative by everyone because it comes from God and all recognize and obey God, or at least want to be perceived as doing so. In Tocqueville's view, as Manent summarizes, "It is not dogma that comprises shared opinion [in democracy]; it is shared opinion that is dogma."[3]

The fact that most people hold an opinion does not make it true or prudent. Not surprisingly, this observation has led many over the centuries to devote much attention to the question of how we temper and guide the formation of public opinion in democracy. Numerous political and constitutional theorists have proposed devices such as the separation of powers and representative institutions. In his famous speech to the electors of Bristol in 1780, Edmund Burke went so far as to tell his constituents that his role was not simply to be their mouthpiece but rather to support what he believed to be in the nation's best interests. Burke's electoral defeat suggests that his constituents arrived at different conclusions.

Writing fifty years after Burke's Bristol speech, Tocqueville concluded that it was a mistake to overestimate the effect of representative institutions in moderating democracy's drives. "The people," he wrote about America, "take part in the making of the laws by choosing the lawgivers, and they share in their application by electing the agents of the executive power; one might say that they govern themselves, so feebler and restricted is the part left to the administration, so vividly is that administration aware of its popular origin, and so obedient it is to the font of power. The people reign over the American political world as God rules over the universe."[4] Significantly, Tocqueville associated the expanding drive for an equality of conditions and the growing power of public opinion with a weakening of the influence of individuals, even when expressed through representative forums. While representative democracy can often act as a buffer against populist pressures, representation still implies that things can be done as long as it acquires the consent of the representatives of the governed. To this extent, anything regarded as unrepresentative or which emerges from the interaction of other forces—such as market exchange or free contracts—does not have the same level of protection or authority accorded to it. Gradually, all legitimate power becomes focused upon the one legitimate political representative institution: the democratic state. Explaining this phenomenon, Manent writes:

> The modern idea of representation leads naturally to a continuous increase of the state's power over society, because it continually erodes the intrasocial powers that ensure the independence and solidity of this society. This is the paradox of representation: representative power tends necessarily to dominate the civil society that it claims to represent.[5]

Though Tocqueville regarded democracy as the path that would be taken by most nations, his *Democracy in America*, especially the second volume, is not entirely sanguine about its implications. While he did not consider in detail the consequences for commercial society, his insights into key cultural features and developments associated with democracy indicate that its spirit is capable of simultaneously facilitating and suffocating commercial society. Certainly commercial society is likely to benefit from democratically elected representatives willing to maintain a careful watch on key foundations of commercial order. Regrettably, if democratically elected representatives adopt a different attitude toward these foundations, the consequences for commercial society are less than benign.

Democracy as Liberation

In aristocratic societies, it was presumed that certain people were entitled to rule by virtue of their membership of a hereditary ruling class, and that others were not. Another characteristic of these societies, Tocqueville writes, was that each person knew only a particular man whom he was obligated to obey.[6] It was also the case that in the European world that existed from the fall of Rome until the late eighteenth century, the overwhelming majority of people lived and died in the same occupation, region, and country as their ancestors. Each person's existence was thus associated with a certain heritage to which he was expected to conform and into which he was expected to grow. Upward or downward mobility was uncommon. The weight of convention was heavy upon everyone, noble or peasant.

One prominent feature of democracy is that it treats everyone as an equal, even if they are not. It affirms that no one person enjoys a natural right to rule over others. Thus, as societies shift toward a more democratic political order, various modifications to the relationship between servant and master begin to occur. In aristocratic society, the relationship is almost organic; "the same families of valets," Tocqueville writes, "are settled for generations with the same families of masters."[7] Masters grow to view servants almost as appendages to themselves, while servants invest their identity in that of the master. Everyone is bound to a certain place. Even among the servants, there exists a distinct hierarchy.

Democracy changes this by introducing social mobility, a type of movement that is indispensable for commercial society. In democracies, people are much less inhibited from changing their occupation by familial or generational loyalty. Continuing with the same example, Tocqueville states "There is still a class of valets and a class of masters, but they are not forever composed of the same individuals, and more especially, not of the same families. Those who give the orders are no more permanent that those who obey."[8] While basic inequalities remain in democratic society between master and servant, democracy's equalizing tendencies undermine the previous links and change the relationship. Masters and servants become used to viewing each other less through the lens of heredi-tary relationships and more from the perspective of freely contracted relation-ships. The identity of masters and servants thus constantly changes and is never fixed. At some point, everyone is a master or servant in a never-ending change of relationships and associations. There is at once equality in terms of freedom to contract, and yet inequality insofar as everyone commands and obeys different people in a variety of contexts. People are at once above, below, and alongside everyone else.

Democracy does, it would seem, break down old associations and barriers that constrict and inhibit commercial relations by pronouncing that all people are equally free. Not for idle reasons did Montesquieu designate commerce as the profession of equals. It is also true that an equality of conditions tends to encour-age people to be their own judge of other people, things, and ideas. By giving each adult person an equal share, at least theoretically, in government, democ-racy encourages people to use their judgment and to recognize themselves as, again in theory, capable of doing things for themselves.

Democracy, it is often remarked, is silent on the ends of human action. While this creates a range of dilemmas in many areas of human life, it has the potential to open people's minds to the vast possibilities that may be realized through human creativity, free trade and the exercise of economic liberty. In the equality of conditions, there is room for competition of all against everyone. The possi-bility of changing one's future seems much more real. With the leveling of ranks in democratic society, and tradition and custom exerting much less influence, there is more scope and incentive for change. It is much harder for things simply to stay still. This is surely a boon for increased competition and entrepreneur-ship.

Democracy's emphasis upon the formal equality of human beings and an associated wariness of granting legal privileges to any one group (as exists in pre-commercial, aristocratic societies) may also assist in realizing some of the legal conditions that we associate with the rule of law. In commercial society, people see each other as fundamentally equal. While they generally want to improve their social and economic position, they do so according to the rules of economic competition and within a framework of property, contract, rule of law, and constitutional order. Though these rules do not guarantee equality of result or opportunity, the resulting inequalities are seen as fair. Willingness to accept the economic inequality associated with commercial society is highly dependent upon a widespread diffusion of the quality of self-restraint. The same moral habit is intrinsic to the long-term sustainability of democratic societies. Democracy relies heavily upon people accepting that there will be many occasions when they must restrain themselves, sometimes in the ways by which they try to per-suade sufficient numbers to support their position, and often by deferring to deci-sions with which they do not agree but whose democratic legitimacy is clear. Without self-restraint, even strong constitutionally legitimate procedures and institutions will only prevent a democracy from sliding toward anarchy or tyranny for so long. Self-restraint is, as we have seen, a habit upon which the workings of many commercial activities and institutions rely strongly.

But while these features of democracy may complement, and in some instances accelerate, the rise of commercial society, democratic society appears to embody an increasing intolerance for the types of inequality typical of commercial society and a corresponding willingness to use the state to try to diminish them.[9] People living in democracies cannot escape democracy's emphasis on equality. Yet they cannot help seeing that they are not equal in many ways, no matter what the law says. Some people are more intelligent, wealthier, and possess greater power. Being cognizant of these facts, many people may start to want more than just formal equality. They become anxious to make the reality in which they live conform to the equality of conditions, and begin viewing politics and state power as the means for realizing this end. This can result in a desire to abolish features of commercial society such as competition and the rule of law, precisely because to accept these things is to acknowledge that there will always be a certain degree of inequality in society.

Faced with a situation of inequality, people have two options in democratic society. The reaction of the American merchant, according to Tocqueville, was not to be overcome by feelings of envy, but to try to reduce his inequality by working to raise himself to the level of his competitor and even surpass him. This is the ambition and goal of many in commercial society and involves accepting the rules of the market order. The second option is to bring those who are more fortunate or enterprising down to our own level, not least by changing the rules governing economic life. To Manent's mind, while democracy can coexist with either approach, it tends to favor the second. To accept competition is to live in a fragile state. It means simultaneously accepting and refusing inequality. "In a democratic society," he writes, "public opinion, imbued with the feeling of human resemblance, and regarding inequalities as essentially accidental, naturally leans in the direction of denying them.... to regard inequalities as 'essentially accidental' is already to deny them in principle."[10]

Democracy as Bondage

Concerns about democracy's long term effects upon commercial society are not new. In 1943, the economist Joseph Schumpeter asserted there was an irresolvable conflict between democracy and capitalism.[11] Part of the problem is the pervasive belief that democracy normally means that the power of the majority is unlimited. A more practical issue is that if people want to gain and retain government power in democracies, they must cobble together large enough support based on a range of often incompatible promises made to often very different groups. Having attained this end, such governments are expected to use their political powers to favor their various supporters if they want to avoid having their erstwhile followers turn against them. The bartering of privileges and grants to different groups is almost thus inevitable in a democratic state if a party or group wants to retain majority support.

If one of the justifications for coercion by law in commercial society is that it is applied equally to all, then the business of gaining and retaining political power in democracy necessarily undermines this principle. Thus if a democratic government decides that it will accord economic privileges to any one group over others, then the law is no longer being applied equally to all people. A common defense of such discrimination in democracies is that the state is merely following the majority's desire to make provision for such privileges in the interests of some wider or more equal distribution of goods. Underlying these developments is the basic impatience that democracy tends to engender with almost all forms of inequality. Though Tocqueville warned that intellectual inequality was a fact of life, he also noted that love of equality grows constantly with equality itself. Before long the least inequality seems more inexcusable in the minds of those who dwell in democratic society than the vast disparities of the past.[12]

Democracy tends to encourage a fixation with creating total equality because it requires everyone to relate to each other through the medium of democratic equality and encourages us first to ignore and then to dislike and seek to reduce all the differences that tend to contradict this equality, particularly wealth disparities.[13] Thus Manent concludes:

> When equality ceases to be either a formal requirement for commutative justice or a synonym for all men belonging to the same species or having their equal dignity before God, when equality becomes the very horizon of social existence and the principle in whose name all is experienced and judged, when the construction of an equal society is the very task that men give themselves, the nature of man knows a new condition.[14]

The situation is further complicated by democracy's capacity to encourage what Tocqueville plainly regarded as a type of servility before the majority. This constitutes part of what he regarded as democracy's tendency to lapse into "soft despotism." In a democracy, people become servile before the majority because it is easier to obey the majority's will rather than that of a small group. Obedience to the majority, Manent stresses, allows people to preserve "the illusion that they are obeying their own will."[15] When the sovereignty of popular will is presented, many who might otherwise resist significant defraying of the foundations of commercial society take fright or simply obey.

Yet it is not simply that people tend to become servile before the democratic state. Equally problematic for commercial society is the fact that democratic peoples start looking to the state to establish equality. In democracies, people appear more prepared to tolerate incursions into freedom of contract and economic liberty as long as such incursions are approved by the only authority they recognize in a democratic society: the democratic state. Once the democratic state is declared sovereign, it is virtually impossible to place external limits upon the exercise of its sovereign power. In Tocqueville's words:

> The abstract recognition of the sovereignty of the people does not in the least increase the amount of liberty given to individuals. If we attribute to that sovereignty an amplitude which it must not have, liberty may be lost notwithstanding that principle, or even through it.
>
> When you establish that the sovereignty of the people is unlimited, you create and toss at random into human society a degree of power which is too large in itself, and which is bound to constitute an evil, in whatever hands it is placed. Entrust it to one man, to several, to all, you will still find that it is equally an evil.... There are weights too heavy for the hand of man.[16]

Observing the American commercial republic, Tocqueville recorded the presence of wealthy people in the United States and stressed that the security of possessions seemed protected by the general respect accorded to property by most Americans. Nevertheless, he added that any political authority exercised by the wealthy had little to do with their positions as holders of wealth. Even if they held political office, Tocqueville commented, they were regarded very much as the instrument of the majority and therefore of those with lesser means.[17]

Tocqueville understood that many of America's constitutional checks and balances were designed to restrict the sovereign power of its young democracy. The American Revolution, he recognized, had been followed by a struggle between two parties: those who wished to restrain popular power, and those who wanted to extend it indefinitely. The restrainers, the Federalists, found themselves on the losing side, not least in Tocqueville's view, because "they struggled against the irresistible tendency of their age and country."[18] They were nonetheless able to construct and implement a constitutional structure that limited the spread of popular power. But in the long term, Tocqueville seemed skeptical of the ability of these structures to resist the equalizing and thus anticommercial impulses of democracy. He surmised that legislatures will always end up conforming to what the majority wants.[19]

Similar themes pervade Friedrich von Hayek's commentary upon democracy's effects upon liberty and commercial society. In his view, "unlimited democracy is bound to become egalitarian."[20] Constitutionalism's emphasis upon the separation of powers, Hayek proposed, had failed to protect individual freedom in democracies because law had become understood as being anything determined by legislatures. Hayek contended that there was a distinction between lawmaking and the issuing of commands. The former involved the making of rules universally applicable "to an unknown number of future instances and renouncing the power of modifying their application to particular cases."[21] In modern democracies, Hayek theorized that the power to make these types of laws (what he called "rules of just conduct") and the powers associated with the government's ability to provide services had largely been placed in the same hands. "Such democratic government," he wrote, "necessarily ceases to be government under the law ... if the same assembly can make whatever laws it likes to suit the purposes of government."[22] Hayek critiques various early constitutional theorists ranging from Montesquieu to the drafters of the American Constitution for failing to see the necessity of separating the formulation of law from the responsibility of directing government. "From the very beginning these 'legislative' assemblies were," Hayek opined, "primarily concerned with the organization and conduct of government and they have become increasingly so."[23]

This, Hayek believes, is especially dangerous in democracies that exert power primarily according to the principle that the desires of the majority ought to receive legislative fiat. Once people recognized democratic legislatures as having the power to grant favors to particular groups, it was inevitable that democratic assemblies would eventually become constituted of coalitions of various interests able to offer particular benefits to their supporters. This was how Hayek explained the phenomenon of the vast array of lobby groups that emerge in democracies to agitate for favors from the legislature.[24] The end result would be a situation in which justice was seen as whatever gained the approval of whatever temporary majority a political party happened to assemble at any one point in time.

To this claim, we might add the observations of the English philosopher Elizabeth Anscombe that even when all issues are decided by a majority vote, the majority of voters can be in the minority on the majority of issues and the people affected by the vote can always be in the minority.[25] It is a paradox that the strength of an ostensibly all-powerful and democratically elected government is so dependent on its ability to corral together a range of different interest groups, which in turn often requires the government to do things that no one except a small minority in its coalition of interests wants the state to do. This is inescapable when a majority is built not upon ideas but upon a range of diverse, even contradictory, commitments to different, even competing, groups. A further problem is created by systems of voting that involve the amalgamation and summation of revealed policy preferences. In such systems, as William Riker illustrates, it is impossible to know whether the result of the amalgamation actually reflects the wishes of the voters or whether it has resulted from a minority's manipulation of the voting process through its decision to engage in strategic voting.[26] Hence when we think about democracy and its laws, we need to be conscious that even fair procedures cannot guarantee fair outcomes in the sense that they accurately represent majority wishes.[27] It is therefore surely somewhat naïve to venture that the rule of law will be preserved provided that all government decisions have been approved by a majority of legislators or even a majority of people. Arbitrary government in a democracy is no different than arbitrary government in an oligarchy or monarchy.

Reflecting upon the contribution of different intellectual heritages to this situation, Hayek sharply distinguished between what he regarded as the contributions of the British liberal tradition and the Continental liberal tradition.[28] The former emphasized protecting individual liberty; the second stressed the priority of ensuring that as many people as possible should be involved in determining the government and its policies. Liberalism in Continental Europe, Hayek avowed, soon became focused upon the democratization of everything. Lord Acton understood that this is not the same as protecting individual freedom:

> The true democratic principle, that none shall have power over the people, is taken to mean that none shall be able to restrain or elude its power. The true democratic principle, that the people shall not be made to do what it does not like, is taken to mean that it shall never be required to tolerate what it does not like. The true democratic principle, that every man's free will shall be as unfettered as possible, is taken to mean that the free will of the collective people shall be unfettered in nothing.[29]

In these cases, traditional safeguards of commercial society such as constitutionalism and rule of law cease to be about protecting liberty through limiting the power of the state and instead become part of a general schema for thinking about how to organize power. The problem, according to Hayek, was that "it was believed that the control of government by elected representatives of the majority made any other checks on the powers of government unnecessary, so that all the various constitutional safeguards which had been developed in the course of time could be dispensed with."[30]

Hayek's solution, which he proposed on numerous occasions, was to have two assemblies in a democracy, the composition of each being entirely different. The first would be "truly law-giving;" it would establish the rules limiting the powers of the second assembly—the government assembly—which was charged with governing. The lawmaking assembly would be charged with determining what is right, rather than the particular policy objectives of government.[31] Hayek was adamant that while the second assembly could consist of factions, the lawmaking assembly should not be composed of parties: "Where not a sum of particular concrete interests but the true public interest is concerned, 'which is no other than common right and justice, excluding all partiality or private interests' and which 'may be called the empire of laws and not of men,' ... an assembly is wanted which represents not interests but opinion about what is right."[32] As members of this assembly, Hayek had in mind people of probity and wisdom who would not be required to look after the immediate interests of different groups or lobbies. He even advanced a proposal for trying to ensure that such a lawmaking assembly could not be captured by interest groups or political parties. This involved each generation, having reached the age of forty, electing representatives to this assembly who would serve for fifteen years with no possibility of reelection. With such a legislative body being confined to articulating universally applicable rules of just conduct, Hayek hoped that it would be able to resist lobbying pressures.[33]

One can see how this arrangement might serve to protect the foundations of commercial society from democracy's equalizing tendencies. It would, for instance, help to resolve the problem of the contradiction between governments in commercial society being committed to protecting property rights, while at the same time arbitrarily interfering with the property rights of specific individuals so as to appease pressures exerted by various interest groups. Interestingly, Hayek appears to have limited his thinking about these matters to assemblies rather than courts. His law-giving assembly was designed to be independent of other groups and thus in a position to take the long term view. Surely this is what constitutional courts are supposed to do. Members of the United States Supreme Court, for instance, are appointed for life, thereby removing them from the on-going need to win the support of different external constituencies.

And yet, as previously noted, while the U.S. Supreme Court has sometimes managed to limit government interference with some of commercial society's legal and economic foundations in the United States, the court's ability to protect these foundations has been limited by pressures exerted over time by the executive and legislative branches of government, not to mention the need of the justices to forge a majority opinion among themselves. Nor have judges in a variety of jurisdictions proved immune from the impact of ideas inimical to commercial society. Hayek himself seemed confident that judges faithful to the common law tradition would be rendered immune from these and similar ideas. As Hayek's intellectual biographer Bruce Caldwell remarks, more than one scholar has described as naïve Hayek's view that judges working in common law systems are bound to arrive at conclusions drawn from the established rules as well as the facts of the particular case.[34]

The little appreciated irony is that it is questionable if a democracy can remain democratic if it progressively undermines some of the foundations of commercial society. "If government assumes tasks which are too extensive and complex to be effectively guided by majority decisions," Hayek wrote, "it seems inevitable that effective powers will devolve to a bureaucratic apparatus increasingly independent of democratic control."[35] Nowhere is this more manifest in the growth of the modern welfare state.

Democratic Despotism and the Welfare State

Part of the dynamic of democracy is that it seeks to encourage everyone to submit to the majority. The more democracy breaks down old associations and limits, the more people will look to an "external power," to use Tocqueville's phrase, to hold the social order together. This becomes especially problematic when associated with the pressures that grow day by day in democracies against any form of inequality. When full democracy is implemented, those who are not the very wealthy, or at least the "have-nots," become the legislator for those who have more.[36]

Democratic despotism, to Tocqueville's mind, is rarely violent. It would be more extensive and milder than other forms of despotism, and would degrade people without tormenting them. Nor did Tocqueville believe that the right to vote would mitigate this situation. "It does," he stated, "little good to summon those very citizens who have been made so dependent upon the central power, to choose the representatives of that power from time to time. However important, this brief and occasional exercise of free will will not prevent them little by little from gradually losing the faculty of thinking, feeling, and acting for themselves, so that they will slowly fall below the level of humanity."[37]

More than one commentator has intimated that the modern welfare state comes the closet to fulfilling Tocqueville's vision of soft despotism. In economic terms, much of the vision of the welfare state is derived from what Wilhelm Röpke poignantly described as "the conception of society as a colossal machine with its tubes, valves, and thermostats pumping incomes this way or that, or else as an enormous pot to which people contribute unequally but from which all draw equal rations."[38] From the beginning of the welfare state's emergence, its negative consequences for commercial society were noticed. In 1835, Tocqueville commented that while England's poor law helped people in need, it did not differentiate between those who were lazy and those who were genuinely indigent. It also created, he observed, a system in which the rich were expected to fund the upkeep of payments that were a source of embarrassment for many of those in need. Such a system was therefore both financially and morally destructive.[39] Similar reasoning underlies Montesquieu's comment that "if an arbitrary prince should attempt to deprive the people of nature's bounty, they would fall into a disrelish of industry; and then indolence and inaction must be their only happiness."[40]

There is nothing noble about allowing oneself to become totally dependent on others, not least because it usually means that people have to resort to morally questionable ways of attaining what they want. Adam Smith was especially conscious of this. "When an animal wants to obtain something either of a man or of another animal," he remarked, "it has no other means of persuasion but to gain the favor of those whose services it requires.... Man sometimes uses the same arts with his brethren, and when he has no other means of engaging them to act according to his inclinations, endeavors by every servile and fawning attention to gain their good will."[41] Smith may have had in mind the cunning, manipulative courtiers who populated the courts of *ancien régime* Europe. While Tocqueville's attention was upon a potential breakdown of moral sympathies, we should also bear in mind that large state welfare systems create disincentives for people to be entrepreneurial. Few would dispute that expansive welfare programs diminish the incentives for people to choose to work. What Tocqueville may not have envisaged is the size of the bureaucracy required by the modern welfare state if it is to assess and monitor the initial and continuing need of people for assistance. If laxity and fraud are to be prevented, it requires the extensive monitoring of people's choices and lives.

Further problems ensue when the welfare state becomes a regular feature of modern democratic states. Röpke postulated that the welfare state in democratic regimes was similar to progressive taxation inasmuch as there is nothing in its conception to limit it. "To expand the welfare state is not only easy," he claimed, "but it is also one of the surest means for the demagogue to win votes and political influence, and it is for all of us the most ordinary temptation to gain, at no cost to ourselves, a reputation from generosity and kindness."[42] This becomes especially dangerous for commercial society, Röpke warned, when some politicians begin to see they can utilize the largesse of the welfare state to purchase the political support they need to attain and retain power:

> There can be no doubt at all ... that there exists a broad and extremely influential group of people who are out for prestige and power, and who not only have the greatest interest in the progressive expansion of the welfare state but are determined to make the utmost of the opportunities it offers for social demagogy. I have in mind the group of people made up of so-called progressive leaders of public opinion, of officials of the public and private social security bureaucracy, of politicians adept in trimming their sails to the prevailing wind of mass sentiments and mass opinions ... Regrettably, there is every reason to believe that in modern mass democracy the joint pressure of this group is so strong that we are infinitely more likely to get too much welfare state than too little, and there is far more danger of excess than of harmful abstinence.[43]

Röpke imagined that a more critical attitude toward the welfare state might emerge when even its beneficiaries began to start to see that the cost was unsustainable and began to consider that they might be better off without large welfare payments. Unfortunately, he thought that the other future possibility might be that expectations about the welfare state would become so influential that they would paralyze "people's willingness to take care of their own needs and its financial burden considerably weakens people's ability to do so."[44] It is all too easy for people living in commercial society to adopt the line of least resistance when it comes to the welfare state. There is every possibility that the unceasing redistribution of wealth required by the welfare state will gradually undermine the attachment of property owners to a property-owning society.

Reconciling Commercial and Democratic Society

Democracy has always generated a range of positive and negative reactions. Some have opposed it on the basis that they have regarded democracy as unworkable. Others have regarded democracy as the best of a range of poor options. Then there are those who want to see democracy's equalizing tendencies spread to every segment of society. This sounds benign, even laudable to some, until we realize that it involves wanting, to cite Manent, "to realize the unrealizable, and the effort to realize the unrealizable can only be considered the destruction of all that is really human."[45]

The early nineteenth century American republic, Tocqueville believed, illustrated that the effects of democracy could be moderated by law and custom.[46] Looking at twenty-first century America, we may wonder if Tocqueville was too optimistic. Commercial society in democratic America may have not been as emasculated as in most of democratic Western Europe. Nonetheless, neither American law nor custom have proved completely successful in resisting the serious degradation of commercial society intrinsic to, for example, both Franklin Roosevelt's New Deal and Lyndon Johnson's Great Society programs. This presents particular problems for Tocqueville's thesis that one of the ways of moderating the effects of democracy is by cultivating the art of free association. While Tocqueville certainly had commercial forms of association in mind, his vision of mediating institutions also embraced a range of noncommercial organizations, all of which would curb and moderate the instincts, habits, and expectations of people living in democracies. One must ask, however, how long it will be before democracy's equalizing drive eventually wears down the links of these bonds. Building associational life, let alone preserving it, is difficult at the best of times. Intermediate associations, especially those of a commercial nature, invariably also reflect differences within society, even inequalities. As the egalitarianism of democracy becomes more pronounced, accepted, and promoted through state power, these associations' ability to resist must surely become weaker over time.

Does this mean that those who wish to promote commercial society ought to examine whether other political systems might be more respectful of commercial society's foundations? While alternatives can be contemplated, it seems extremely unlikely that people at the opening of the twenty-first century will freely opt for political systems other than democracy. We therefore need to think about how to limit its negative effects. Is it possible, we must ask, to affirm democracy's equalizing effects with regard to political participation, while resisting democracy's tendency to distort key features of commercial society?

One positive step would be to work for a dramatic limitation of the increasing number of privileges accorded the status of rights in democratic societies. It is not an exaggeration to suppose that people in democracies tend to define human beings as those who possess rights. Certainly the discourse of rights has always had a place in commercial society. Legitimate expectations attached to property, for example, are not derived solely from the mere fact of ownership or possession. They are supported by the law identifying certain protections and entitlements associated with property that we call rights. The same may be said of other features of commercial society such as economic liberty and free association.

Democracies do have an alarming tendency to what we might call rights-inflation. The United Nations' Declaration of Human Rights is neither exhaustive nor perfect in its articulation of rights. But the essential rights specified by the Declaration have surely been weakened by the multiplying number of interests, goods and desires elevated to the status of rights since 1948 by international bodies and democratically elected governments. This magnifies the expectations of people who are told that they are less than human if they do not possess a whole host of rights. Given such conditions, we should not be surprised that people start using the language of rights as a way of claiming things from others that they just happen to want and expecting the state to use its authority to legitimize such procurement. The perennial temptation for both citizens and politicians in democracies is to employ the language of rights to circumvent or subvert key elements of commercial society that, ironically enough, are more likely to realize the intended goal over the long term than a government's, interest-group's, or majority's demand for the immediate or near-to-immediate realization of a particular right.

The "right to work" is a good example. Universally recognized as something that uniquely contributes to man's material and moral well-being, we can understand the anxiousness of many that everyone who wants to work be able to do so. But to say that everyone has a right to work leaves unanswered important questions. Who, for instance, is under an obligation to provide others with work? Is it private enterprise, the state, individuals, families, or everyone? One of commercial society's benefits is the manner in which it allows tremendous growth in employment opportunities for millions of people over long periods of time, provided that its foundations—especially a free labor market—remain unfettered from undue regulation. Yet the assertion that everyone has a right to work or a right to employment often results in considerable government interference with the labor market, be it in terms of attempting to regulate the hiring and firing of employees, the implementation of government work programs, according legal privileges to trade unions, or even the adoption of specific employment goals as a part of government policy. A similar point could be made about the oft-mentioned right to a minimum wage. Defining such a right requires some determination of what constitutes a minimum in any given context. Legally mandating such a minimum as a way of actualizing this right is also, economically speaking, more than likely to price less skilled and unskilled workers out of the labor market,[47] thereby achieving the exact opposite of what promoting such a right is meant to realize.

We see, then, that while there is no shortage of rights talk, the default position of many is to assume that such rights ought to be immediately secured by the state, whatever the cost and regardless of the known consequences. Adam Smith and others took a different view. They were not concerned with limiting government for the sake of limiting government. One reason they wanted to restrain government power was to create space for a range of social, economic and legal institutions to emerge that would secure people against hunger and want over time. While governments can officially declare that everyone has the right to shelter and sufficient food, commercial institutions are more capable of actually realizing such ends, perhaps not immediately but certainly in the long run and in a sustainable manner, if they are preserved from undue state interference.

Given the centrality of rights discourse in modern democracies, it seems quixotic to imagine that we can expect such language to diminish in these societies. Under the equality of conditions intrinsic to democracy, rights must be given to all or no one. Democracy does nonetheless, at least theoretically, encourage debate and discussion of ideas and proposals across a wide spectrum of the population. It follows that those who understand the importance of commercial society ought to engage actively in the ever-burgeoning rights discussion to limit its potential negative effects upon commercial society. This is precisely the path followed by Tocqueville as a member of France's Chamber of Deputies in 1848 when he argued against inscribing a "right to work" into France's constitution. Such an act, he held, would be a warrant for the state to assume more and more control of the economy, and could theoretically result in what would effectively amount to a communist economy.[48] Thus, when people ascribe a particular entitlement with the status of a right, commercial society's advocates should politely inquire, "where does this right come from?" They should also ask people to reflect more seriously upon what set of foundational habits and arrangements is more likely to secure a right throughout a given society.

Other ways of limiting democracy's potentially negative impact upon the workings of commercial society may be found in the doctrine of federalism. This doctrine was integral to the ultimately successful efforts of the authors of the *Federalist Papers* to ensure that the form to be taken by the young United States was one of a "representative republic" which they regarded as quite different from "democracy."[49] Lord Acton took a similar view. "Liberty," he wrote, "depends on the division of power. Democracy tends to the unity of power. To keep asunder the agents, one must divide the sources; that is, one must maintain, or create, separate administrative bodies. In the view of increasing democracy, a restricted federalism is the one possible check on concentration and centralization."[50]

For commercial society, one benefit of federalism lies in the capacity of regional and national (and even pan-national) governments to check the power of the other, thereby potentially limiting their ability to undermine commercial society. Another advantage to which more attention has been paid in recent decades is the manner in which different regional governments can effectively compete against each other to offer more optimal conditions for commercial success, such as lower taxes, freer labor markets, a more marked commitment to rule of law, more secure protection of property rights, and laws preventing undue restriction of trade. The history of federalism ought nevertheless to provide us with some pause. In almost all cases of federations—ranging from the relatively commercial arrangements presided over by ancient Athens or more contemporary examples such as Australia, Canada, the United States, and even the European Union—there is a tendency for a slow, but remorseless centralization of political power. Even Switzerland, oft-cited as the exemplar of successful modern federalism, appeared to have acquired many characteristics of an increasingly centralized political entity by the end of the twentieth century.[51] In her analysis of contemporary Switzerland, the economist Victoria Curzon-Price remarks:

Switzerland has in fact introduced an extensive welfare-state and an efficient new value-added tax (VAT) at federal level. Increased taxation and growing centralization have occurred despite direct democracy and strong constitutional limits on central power. We must therefore assume that the Swiss electorate, enjoying possibly the most democratic system in the world, has consciously or not chosen this path, or allowed itself to be pushed along it by the political process ... in doing so they have probably sacrificed economic growth.[52]

There appears, then, to be no sure institutional means of guaranteeing that commercial society's foundations are protected from democracy's equalizing effects. This makes it all the more imperative to ensure that those people who have or are likely to assume positions of influence in a given democracy understand the need to engage in what may be an unending struggle to protect the foundations of commercial society against such erosion. This approach may seem counter-intuitive in light of previous observations concerning the tendency of elites in democracies to follow the lead of the democratic majority. What remains questionable is whether the ever-shifting majorities in democracies will be able to restrain themselves from using state power to provide themselves or specific groups and individuals with privileges that contribute to commercial society's degradation. More controversially, we may need to admit that the great majority of people are unable to comprehend all the reasons why a commercial society is so important for their own and their children's well-being and why the fidelity of elected representatives to their electors is only realized when such representatives are able, indeed expected, to look beyond sectional interests and not be beholden to any one group.

Any discussion of how to limit democracy's negative effects on commercial society inevitably raises the question of the role of human agency in countering such changes. This becomes even more significant when we consider that the works of some proponents of commercial society ranging from Hume to Hayek contain what may be described as strongly evolutionist strains: "evolutionist" in the sense as they reflect skepticism concerning the benefits of planned human action upon the social and economic order. This raises questions, at least at a theoretical level, about why people would want to promote commercial society if such entities are primarily the product of unplanned development. For if this is true, then there is little people can do to facilitate the emergence of commercial societies, let alone engage in activities that counter policies that undermine commercial society's foundations. Evolutionist tendencies also create difficulties in attempting to present a strong normative case for commercial society. Theories of evolution, regardless of whether they are articulated in the realm of science, philosophy or economics purport to explain events largely in terms of randomness or natural selection. If this is the case, it is difficult to provide normative reasons why such developments ought or ought not to occur. They either happen or do not happen. Integral to such deliberations is the issue of whether commercial societies are only capable of emerging in certain cultures or if, as Smith and others of his time firmly believed, commercial society actually reflects universal tendencies that, theoretically speaking, can be replicated in any culture. A related matter is whether it is possible for people with a normative commitment to commercial society—be it derived from a concern for liberty, eradicating poverty, facilitating creativity, or a combination of these and other interests—to affect changes that will realize this end. Such matters constitute the subject of this book's concluding chapter.

Notes

1. Manent, *Modern Liberty and Its Discontents*, 73.
2. Pierce Manent, *Tocqueville and the Nature of Democracy* (Rowman and Littlefield, 1996), xviii.
3. Manent, *Tocqueville*, 93.
4. Tocqueville, *Democracy*, vol. 1, 60.
5. Pierre Manent, *An Intellectual History of Liberalism* (Princeton: Princeton University Press, 1995), 63.
6. See Tocqueville, *Democracy*, vol. 2, 574–75.
7. Ibid., vol. 2, 574.
8. Ibid, vol. 2, 576.
9. See Manent, *Tocqueville*, 62.
10. Manent, *Intellectual History*, 109.
11. See J. Schumpeter, *Capitalism, Socialism and Democracy* (London: Unwin University Books, 1950).
12. See Tocqueville, *Democracy*, vol. 2, 673.
13. Manent, *Tocqueville*, 79.
14. Ibid., 64.
15. Ibid., 22.
16. Benjamin Constant, "Principles of Politics (Applicable to all Representative Governments)," in *Political Writings*, 175.
17. See Tocqueville, *Democracy*, vol. 1, 179.
18. Ibid., vol. 1, 176.
19. See ibid., vol. 1, 250–52.
20. Hayek, "Whither Democracy," in *New Studies*, 157.
21. F. A. Hayek, "The Constitution of a Liberal State," in *New Studies*, 99.
22. Ibid., 99–100.
23. Ibid., 101.
24. Ibid., 100.
25. See Elizabeth Anscombe, "On Frustration of the Majority by Fulfillment of the Majority's Will," in *Collected Philosophical Papers*, vol. 3 (Oxford: Basil Blackwell, 1981), 123–29.
26. See William Riker, *Liberalism Against Populism: A Confrontation Between the Theory of Democracy and the Theory of Social Choice* (San Francisco: W. H. Freeman Press, 1982), 26.
27. See Finnis, "The Authority of Law," 269.

28. See Hayek, "Liberalism," 120.

29. Acton, "Sir Erskine May's 'Democracy in Europe'," in *Essays in the History of Liberty*, 80.

30. Hayek, "Whither Democracy," 153.

31. See Hayek, "The Constitution of a Liberal State," 102.

32. Ibid.

33. Ibid., 100.

34. See Bruce Caldwell, *Hayek's Challenge: An Intellectual Biography of F. A. Hayek* (Chicago: University of Chicago Press, 2004), 347.

35. Hayek, "Liberalism," 144.

36. Manent, *Modern Liberty*, 128.

37. Tocqueville, *Democracy*, vol. 2, 694.

38. Wilhelm Röpke, "Robbing Peter to Pay Paul: Nature of the Welfare State," *Against the Tide* (Chicago: Henry Regnery Company, 1969), 209–10.

39. See Alexis de Tocqueville, "Mémoire sur le paupérisme," *Bulletin des Sciences économiques et sociales du Comité des travaux historiques et scientifiques* (Paris: Gaillot, 1911), 17–37.

40. Montesquieu, *Spirit*, bk. 11, chap. 1.

41. Adam Smith, *Wealth of Nations*, I.ii.2.

42. Röpke, "Robbing Peter to Pay Paul," 204.

43. Ibid., 206.

44. Ibid., 210.

45. Manent, Tocqueville, 131.

46. Tocqueville, *Democracy*, vol. 1, 262–315.

47. See, for example, Richard V. Burkhauser and T. Aldrich Finengan, "The Economics of Minimum Wage Legislation Revisited," *Cato Journal*, 13, no. 1 (1993): 123–29.

48. See Alexis de Tocqueville, "Contre l'intervention systématique de l'État,", in *Textes économique: Anthologie Critique*, ed. J. L. Benoît and É. Keslassey (Paris: Pocket, 2005), 155–75.

49. See James Madison, Alexander Hamilton, and John Jay, *The Federalist*, ed. Jacob E. Cooke (Middletown, Conn.: Wesleyan University Press, 1961), no. 10, 56–65.

50. Acton, "Letter to Mary Gladstone, February 20, 1882" in *The Letters of Lord Acton to Mary, Daughter of the Right Hon. W. E. Gladstone*, ed. Herbert Paul (London: Macmillan, 1913), 98.

51. See Victoria Curzon-Price, "Switzerland: Growth of Government, Growth of Centralization," *Economic Affairs*, 24, no. 2 (2004): 30–36.

52. Ibid., 31.

7

Culture and the Possibility of "Non-Spontaneous" Commercial Society

There is nothing absolute in the theoretical value of political institutions ... their efficiency depends almost always on original circumstances and the social condition of the people to whom they are applied.

—Alexis de Tocqueville

In 2001, Samuel Huntington's well-known book *The Clash of Civilizations* again became the subject of considerable attention when al-Qa'eda terrorists brought their war against the West, and more particularly the United States, to the symbolic heart of Western capitalism.[1] The debate fueled by Huntington's central thesis—that international affairs will have less to do with sovereign powers pursuing their national interests and be more characterized by conflicts between different civilizational groups—inevitably directs our attention to another, equally vexing matter. This is whether particular nations, even entire cultures, can alter established, centuries-old patterns of behavior in order to embrace commercial society's key moral, economic, and legal foundations. Some engaged in the notoriously hazardous exercise of advancing grand geopolitical theories continue to insist that all countries will eventually evolve, despite occasional temporary reversals, toward some type of liberal-democratic arrangement. The purpose of this concluding chapter is not to reflect upon such theories or even analyze any one particular situation or culture. It is to address an issue that puzzles those who believe that those legal, political, social, and economic arrangements that underpin commercial society *ought* to be promoted around the world. The question is whether commercial society can first be facilitated and then persist in those countries whose history and culture appear not to lend themselves to what might be called a "spontaneous" development of commercial society.

The Challenge of Culture

Much modern study of the nature of political order tends to downplay the significance of culture. Tracing the rise and fall of civilizations is often perceived primarily in terms of the workings of the economy or the pursuit of power. No doubt they have their place. Focusing upon these dimensions of life is perhaps easier because the influence of culture is more gradual and imperceptible. As the historian Christopher Dawson recognized, the journey of a wandering rabbi from Tarsus—better know today as Saint Paul—from Troy in Asia to Philippi on the European continent did far more to shape the history of Europe than anything else noticed by the historians of the time.[2] Likewise, it is difficult to dispute that Poland's crucial role in Communism's defeat in the late twentieth century owed much to that nation's successful effort since the eighteenth-century partitions to preserve its cultural identity despite attempts to dilute or even eliminate that culture—a culture that embodied certain commitments radically incompatible with any form of totalitarianism.

If a culture embodies a view of human persons as essentially passive beings, simply driven hither and thither by their emotions or the dialectics of history, it becomes more difficult to alert them to the fact that they *are* creative, active beings, capable of free choice, let alone creatures with some responsibility for themselves, others, and the future. On this basis, commentators such as George Weigel have ventured that the inability of some contemporary Western European societies to make hard domestic decisions, ranging from labor market liberalization to welfare reform, reflects profound changes in the way that some Western Europeans understand themselves. In Weigel's view, it is a crisis that reflects many Western Europeans' fixation on their present satisfaction and a basic disinterest in the long-term future of themselves and others. If this is true, then we should not be surprised, as Weigel writes, that much of Western Europe simply "declines to create the human future in the most elemental sense, by creating a next generation."[3] Why, to put Weigel's point differently, should those who refuse responsibility for the future—or those who simply do not concern themselves with it because they will have departed this life in ten, twenty, thirty, or forty years—care about unsustainable levels of welfare dependency or a paralyzed labor market? The idea that there is something wrong with foisting the payment for one's present comfort onto future generations is, by definition, logically incomprehensible to such a mindset. For if one believes that all that matters about human beings is one's own present satisfaction, then it does not seem unjust to mortgage the future of others, even one's own children. The same deadly logic may be detected as lying just beneath the surface of John Maynard Keynes' celebrated quip that "in the long run, we are all dead."

No study of political and economic order can therefore ignore culture. Like politics, culture is something distinctly human, since man's actions are uniquely creative of it. Plants and animals live and act, but have no culture. In a general sense, culture expresses everything whereby humans develop their bodily and spiritual qualities as they strive through their creative intellect and labor to bring the world under their control. Human culture may be expressed and objectified in various products, practices, and institutions that in turn influence their human creators. These manifestations include material objects, but also the different ways of living arising from the diverse manner of using things, expressing oneself, working, forming customs, practicing religion, establishing laws and juridical institutions, and cultivating the mind. Culture thus also embraces all concepts and perceptions existent within a society, especially those to which a society's members ascribe higher value. Over time, societies develop cultural traditions in the form of habits, practices and institutions that reflect their journey through life and experience of the world. Culture, therefore, necessarily has historical and social dimensions as well as distinct sociological and often ethnological characteristics. We can therefore speak of a plurality of cultures.

As persons from different cultures encounter each other on a regular basis, differences and similarities become evident. The wisdom contained in one tradition is often assimilated into another. As cultures encountered each other, Adam Smith hoped that nations would admire "the internal happiness and prosperity of the other, the cultivation of its lands, the advancement of its manufactures, the increase of its commerce, the security and number of its ports and harbors, its proficiencies in all the liberal arts and sciences. "These," he added, "are all real improvements of the world we live in. Mankind is benefited, human nature is ennobled by them. In such improvements each nation ought, not only to endeavor itself to excel, but from the love of mankind, to promote, instead of obstructing the excellence of its neighbors. These are all proper objects of national emulation, not of national prejudice and envy."[4]

Sometimes cultural interaction means that some customs become viewed as unworthy of human beings and abandoned, sometimes voluntarily, and occasionally through coercion. Being the product of human choice and action, cultures may embody failures to recognize that particular practices are in fact unreasonable. One example might be the rites of human sacrifice that prevailed in certain pre-Columbian American societies. Thus while each person lives within a culture, humans are not exhaustively defined by that culture. Whatever their cultural background, each person possesses important elements in common with the rest of humanity. In the final analysis, it is always human beings who are the authors and custodians of cultures. Moreover, being its source, people need not become prisoners of any one culture.

We also know that cultures can change significantly, sometimes quickly, and not always for the better. Within the space of twelve years, the Nazi regime transformed Germany from a society still profoundly shaped by a Judeo-Christian ethic into something rather different. The philosopher Joseph Boyle comments that the regime built upon certain social and intellectual strains such as anti-Semitism and the eugenics movement that already existed in European culture. Through initially subtle and then gradually more blatant measures to change laws and alter perceptions of reality, the Nazi state slowly made it easier for large numbers of people to ignore, even reject many moral principles that ought to have facilitated resistance to many of the government's policies. It was not that German culture lacked the moral resources to resist the tendencies fostered and reinforced by the Nazis. Instead, this moral tradition gradually ceased to be a meaningful reference point for the lived *mœurs* of much of Germany's population,[5] especially its political, intellectual, military, medical, and legal elites.[6] Reflecting from afar upon Germany in 1944, Friedrich von Hayek did not underestimate the extent to which "those common moral and political traditions which we take for granted" in a dozen years had been "destroyed, with a thoroughness which few people in this country can imagine." Fortunately, he commented, in the midst of this "moral and intellectual desert," there would be "many oases, some very fine, but almost completely isolated from each other." Hayek then added, "It will be on the Germans who have carried on in this manner ... that our hopes must rest, and to them we must give any assistance we can."[7]

Evolution or Construction?

Given culture's importance, it is necessary that those who want all to enjoy the benefits of commercial order ask whether those societies lacking strong indigenous cultures of freedom and commerce can successfully develop and protect commercial society's essential foundations. Discussion of this question requires consideration of the degree to which those more or less free and commercial societies that exist today themselves evolved spontaneously. This issue is significant not least because there exists considerable skepticism concerning the extent to which commerce-enhancing habits and institutions can be grounded upon cultures that may regard some or all of these provisions as alien. Hayek broadly claimed that the constructivist mindset of imagining that we can somehow construct a social order as if people were inanimate, unthinking objects could not but inflict the errors of utopianism and collectivism upon those subject to such experimentation. Much of Hayek's thought is based on the proposition that the emergence of free societies is heavily dependent upon a type of evolutionary process. Hayek was fond of highlighting the partly unwritten British constitution as an example of the type of unplanned development that had proved a better guarantee of freedom than many written constitutional documents. At the core of Hayek's critique of the constructionist mentality was Adam Smith's warning:

The man of system ... is apt to be very wise in his own conceit, and is so often enamored with the supposed beauty of his own ideal plan of government, that he cannot suffer the smallest deviation from any part of it.... He seems to imagine that he can arrange the different members of a great society with as much ease as the hand arranges the different pieces upon a chess-board. He does not consider that the pieces upon the chess-board have no other principle of motion besides that which the hand impresses upon them; but that, in the great chessboard of human society, every single piece has a principle of motion of its own, altogether different from that which the legislature might choose to impress upon it. If those two principles coincide and act in the same direction, the game of human society will go on easily and harmoniously, and is very likely to be happy and successful. If they are opposite or different, the game will go on miserably, and the society must be at all times in the highest degree of disorder.[8]

The British political system's relative long-term stability compared to that of continental European states, not to mention those of Africa and Latin America, certainly lends considerable credence to Hayek's thesis. Nonetheless, there are limits to its explanatory power. The fifteenth-century English jurist Sir John Fortescue astutely discerned that it is almost always the case that new regimes emerge following choices to overturn the previous political order and the subsequent need to replace it.[9] There is considerable evidence that this is indeed the case.[10] The American colonies emerged as a nation following the decision of certain leaders to reject a political system that many colonists viewed as having become tyrannical. The American Revolution's aftermath was marked by the Federalist Party's success in implementing a range of measures that were able to resist populist impulses for quite some time. In 1832, the British parliament narrowly averted the possibility of major political upheaval by passing the first major Reform Act. Choice and the making of decisions thus play a greater role in the formation of different types of constitutional arrangements than some are willing to acknowledge.

Between Determinism and Activism

Despite the examples furnished by history of apparent genuine self-determination, some remain unconvinced that certain societies are capable of embracing habits and institutions that sustain commercial society. Doubts are frequently expressed, for example, about whether those nations profoundly shaped by various expressions of Islam can embrace recognizably liberal-democratic institutions. Many theorists of commercial society have stressed how much its development owes to circumstances. Smith underscored the role of geography in shaping the growth of commercial arrangements in parts of ancient Greece. Not only, he claimed, did the relatively easy access to the sea allow these city-states to trade with each other, but they also enjoyed a landscape that lent itself more easily to self-defense against more bellicose, agrarian peoples.[11] Montesquieu's description of

Marseilles' emergence as a center of trade constitutes one of the most powerful portrayals of how circumstances often contribute to the rise of commerce:

> Marseilles, a necessary retreat in the midst of a tempestuous sea; Marseilles, a harbor which all the winds, the shelves of the sea, the disposition of the coasts, point out for a landing place, became frequented by mariners; while the sterility of the adjacent country determined the citizens to an economical commerce. It was necessary that they should be laborious to supply what nature had refused; that they should be just, in order to live among barbarous nations, from whom they were to derive their prosperity; that they should be moderate, to the end that they might always taste the sweets of a tranquil government; in fine, that they should be frugal in their manners, to enable them to subsist by trade—a trade the more certain as it was less advantageous.
>
> We everywhere see violence and oppression give birth to a commerce founded on economy, while men are constrained to take refuge in marshes, in isles, in the shallows of the sea, and even on rocks themselves. Thus it was that Tyre, Venice, and the cities of Holland were founded. Fugitives found there a place of safety; they drew, therefore, their subsistence from all parts of the world.[12]

Montesquieu's argument is that many people do not choose commerce as opposed to have it thrust upon them by circumstances. Even the virtues associated with commercial society seem, in Montesquieu's view, to spring forth from circumstances rather than from choice. They are acquired in the course of survival. Nor does Montesquieu consider the circumstances to be essentially physical. They also flow from the need to escape violence and anarchy.

However valid Montesquieu's analysis, it does create a strategic difficulty for those who desire the spread of commercial order insofar as such a thesis tends to lend credence to a doctrine of historical determinism, a viewpoint which can undermine people's willingness to attempt to affect change. Tocqueville was not blind to this, noting that such a mindset "would soon paralyze the activities of modern society and bring Christians [free men] down to the level of Turks [slaves]."[13] Tocqueville himself was deeply interested in the question of whether nations with long histories of veering between anarchy and outright authoritarianism, were capable of achieving ordered liberty. Why, Tocqueville asked, had some nations apparently embraced constitutional and commercial arrangements relatively painlessly while others had not? Was there a historical law at work or were more complex causes involved? In examining such questions, Tocqueville expended considerable energy trying to develop an analytical framework that would allow him to identify the opportunities for, and limits to, human initiative in directing a given society toward conditions favoring human liberty.

While Tocqueville's approach seems highly analytical, his purpose was normative. It was as if Tocqueville wrote for those who inherit the results of past conflicts and changes, but who have real prospects of shaping decisions that could alter the paths of entire nations. Broadly speaking, Tocqueville believed that individuals could successfully intervene at particular points to promote free institutions and their sustaining habits *if* they comprehended the cultural forces in which their societies lived, moved, and had their being. In the very writing of *Democracy in America* and *The Old Regime and the Revolution*, Tocqueville almost went out of his way to annoy his predominately French readership, seeking to force them to understand the character of France's political order and the consequences of past choices made by French leaders so that his readers could better appreciate the decisions that lay before them and the context in which such choices would be made.

The notion that human beings are able to nudge nations away from patterns of the past is rigorously defended by Tocqueville. He passionately believed that humans had free will. Tocqueville was nonetheless too insightful to believe that the emergence of free commercial societies was simply a matter of will. While he regarded human beings as naturally inclined to want to be free, Tocqueville postulated that this inclination was not always attached to a favorable cultural situation or history. Looking at early nineteenth-century English-speaking America, Tocqueville claimed that its beginnings and geography were essential for grasping its continuing development. The character of the English colonial settlement had exercised a powerful influence over the nature of the American Revolution. The specific character of this settlement was what Tocqueville called its *circumstances*. Within this category of circumstances, Tocqueville distinguished *laws* (by which he meant the judicial system, constitutions, local and national institutions) from what he called *mœurs*. This latter phrase was used by Tocqueville to embrace the whole intellectual and moral condition of a given people, including their beliefs, customs, and habits. Tocqueville further specified that of the three categories, law was more important than circumstances, but that *mœurs* were more important than laws.[14]

In devising this schema, Tocqueville seems to be trying to distinguish that which is normally unchangeable (the circumstances in which we are placed) from those things that can be altered (*mœurs* and laws). Much of his focus was upon the influence of *mœurs*, for he regarded these as especially important in determining one's scope for action to facilitate change. Hence, when Tocqueville compared the development of Mexico and America, he was aware that Mexico had formally adopted a written constitution similar to that of the United States. Yet Mexico had proved unable to overcome an apparently chronic instability. "The Mexicans," Tocqueville lamented, "wishing to establish a federal system, took the federal Constitution of their Anglo-American neighbors as a model and copied it almost completely. But when they borrowed the letter of the law, they could not at the same time transfer the spirit that gave it life."[15]

Mœurs, Institutions, and Leaders

A society's *mœurs* are, in Tocqueville's view, vital in determining its capacity to embrace many of the foundations we have identified as essential to commercial society. This is especially true in light of Tocqueville's conviction that a nation's *mœurs* tended to transcend the boundaries between "political society" and what he called "civil society." For Tocqueville, political society included the government, bureaucracy, judiciary, political associations, as well as particular laws (such as constitutions) and those habits, customs, and ideas (i.e., *mœurs*) that supported those laws. Civil society embraced everything else (except the family), including relationships between citizens and the *mœurs* that shaped those associations. It encapsulated therefore much of what we have called commercial society. Certainly there were aspects of civil society, such as the press, which were not squarely in the "private" realm precisely because they exerted powerful influence in the public square.[16] It was, however, the shared *mœurs* prevailing in a society's political and civil spheres that, Tocqueville held, tended to integrate the two.

If, then, a society was to develop the habits necessary for liberty and commerce, Tocqueville insisted that it was necessary to find prudential lawmakers and leaders who not only desired liberty to be enshrined within their society, but who also grasped the circumstances in which their nation existed, the laws that prevailed, and the *mœurs* that transcended civil and political society. In doing so, Tocqueville was not encouraging people to look for a "great man" to hasten changes. He directed attention to those groups of people—civil, political, and religious—uniquely positioned to shape the habits of societies. For Tocqueville, the tragedy of the nineteenth-century French aristocracy of which he was a member was its widespread refusal to engage in such a task. While one might imagine that those engaged in commerce would be inclined to work toward helping their societies develop a more commercial orientation, Adam Smith held that the very virtues of prudent business leaders made this likely to be a rare occurrence. Smith's commercial humanist, Smith wrote, "is not always very forward to listen to the voice even of noble and great ambition. When distinctly called upon, he will not decline the service of his country, but he will not cabal in order to force himself into it, and would be much better pleased that the public business were well-managed by some other person, than that he himself should have the trouble, and incur the responsibility, of managing it. In the bottom of his heart he would prefer the undisturbed enjoyment of secure tranquility, not to all the vain splendor of successful ambition, but to the real and solid glory of performing the greatest and most magnanimous actions."[17]

Throughout his writings, Tocqueville attempted to provide concrete examples of how certain groups can act in ways that, in particular circumstances, promote institutions and habits that support free societies. Reflecting upon England's political development, Tocqueville claimed that England's ruling aristocracy had simply refused to decline. By engaging in strategic alliances with the emerging commercial classes of the seventeenth and eighteenth centuries, it had contributed to the emergence of a commercial society associated with a parliamentary system that uniquely balanced the need for executive authority with democratic legitimacy. Moving from the civil to the religious realm, Tocqueville stressed that different choices made by religious leaders could shape the capacity of religion to mold the *mœurs* required by liberty. Tocqueville was struck by the tendency of France's Catholic clergy to slip into the habit of being apologists for non-republican regimes with absolutist inclinations. This differed remarkably, in his view, from the stance adopted by the very same Church in the United States. Different circumstances, but also prudent decisions by the clergy, Tocqueville insisted, had contributed to the formation of a United States where religion and the emerging social order were not at odds.[18]

While Tocqueville ascribed major significance to the ability of civil and religious leaders to facilitate or obstruct a nation's attachment to liberty, he did not rule out a role for the political class. On several occasions, Tocqueville emphasized that the success of American constitutionalism owed much to the careful judgment of those who founded the American Republic. Through their intervention, they were able to prevent the American Revolution from destroying those institutions and habits upon which freedom relied.[19] Tocqueville did not, therefore, view America's situation purely as the result of chance or evolution. Nor did Tocqueville believe that Napoleon's dictatorship had been inevitable.[20] In his view, the sheer disarray confronting Napoleon after his assumption of power provided a unique opportunity to establish a society that integrated the passion for liberty with the legitimate requirements of order. To France's detriment, Napoleon chose a different path.

Ironically, Tocqueville's own attempts as a politician to reshape France's political culture culminated in failure. Following his election to the Chamber of Deputies in March 1839, Tocqueville sought to create a grouping of legislators that accepted absolutism's demise, the rise of a commercial middle class, and broader participation in political life while rejecting the French Revolution's centralization of power and anti-Catholicism. One might say that this project was likely to fail, given the profound fractures characterizing nineteenth-century France. But it was also undermined by the thoughtlessness of Tocqueville's political contemporaries.[21] Tocqueville was struck at how quickly they discarded their commitment to ideas for the quest for power. He was also disappointed at his colleagues' inability to see the problems facing France through the categories of circumstances, laws, and *mœurs*: an analysis which soon made it obvious that many of France's problems proceeded from the association of democratization with centralization and a set of *mœurs* that oscillated between passivity and extreme violence, thereby encouraging either tyranny or anarchy.

Ideas, Culture, and Intellectuals

Given the opportunities for civil, religious, and political leaders to promote genuine transition toward commercial society, it is worth considering the potential role of intellectuals. Tocqueville himself clearly identified a crucial role for the makers, fomenters, and exponents of ideas. For him, it was not peasants or workers who made revolutions. Though they might provide energy for such events, they were not the guiding force. The evidence that ideas, both sound and unsound, had reshaped the destiny of nations, even entire cultures, was not lost on Tocqueville. He noted that in the pre-Christian world, paganism and pantheism had limited man's capacity for freedom insofar as they encouraged people to be terrified of nature, to regard themselves as the playthings of whimsical gods, and as part of a continual and unknowable flux of events beyond their control.[22] Tocqueville thought that such notions inhibited and undermined the individual's ability to recognize that to a considerable extent he can govern his own fate. The spread of Judeo-Christian concepts—such as man being charged with dominion over the material realm and that the state was not divine—throughout the pagan world began a process of recasting attitudes toward, for example, state authority, the poor, slaves, and women. Sometimes this had more or less immediate results, such as the gradual extension throughout the Roman Empire of the private charitable work pioneered by Jews and Christians with the sick and materially poor. In the medium term, it eventually facilitated the de-deification of the state. In other instances, such as the abolition of slavery, the consequences of such ideas took millennia to be felt.

Plainly, it is one thing to possess sound ideas and another to have the opportunity and will to implement them. Concerning intellectuals, Adam Smith wrote that their "contemplation of so great a variety of objects necessarily exercises their minds in endless comparisons and combinations, and renders their understandings ... both acute and comprehensive." But, Smith added, "Unless those few ... happen to be placed in some very particular situations, their great abilities, though honorable to themselves, may contribute very little to the good government or happiness of their society. Notwithstanding the great abilities of those few, all the nobler parts of the human character may be, in a great measure, obliterated and extinguished in the great body of the people."[23]

This is not to discount the fact that opportunities sometimes suddenly emerge for intellectuals with clear ideas to recast a nation's trajectory. One example is the market liberalization of post-war West Germany. Implemented against the Allied Military authorities' advice by Ludwig Erhard and deeply influenced by the ordo liberal school associated with Walter Eucken and Wilhelm Röpke, these major legal and economic changes were realized via administrative fiat before the first post-war elections. Struck by the uniqueness of the event, Hayek wrote:

> It must be admitted ... that Erhard could never have accomplished what he did
> under bureaucratic or democratic constraints. It was a lucky moment when the
> right person in the right spot was free to do what he thought was right, although

he could never have convinced anybody else that it was the right thing. He himself has gleefully told me how the very Sunday on which the famous decree
about the freeing of all prices accompanying the introduction of the new German
mark was to be published, the top American military commander, General Clay,
called him and told him on the telephone: "Professor Erhard, my advisers tell
me you are making a great mistake," whereupon, according to his own report,
Erhard replied: "So my advisers also tell me." The freeing of prices was unbe-
lievably successful.[24]

Yet for all their risk-taking, neither Erhard nor the ordo liberals were operating
within a cultural or intellectual vacuum. Their program and ideas drew upon distinct strains within European thought, ranging from classical natural law theory
to particular insights discernable in the works of Scottish Enlightenment
thinkers.[25] Their ideas and subsequent policies were grounded upon existing elements within the culture of ideas—however weak those particular strains may
have been after Germany's experience of Nazism, two world wars, a severe economic depression, and the failure of Weimar democracy.[26]

Similar patterns may be detected in many of those instances in which reforms
have been deliberately enacted to shift the economic and political bases of entire
societies toward more explicitly commercial orientations. The economic liberalization programs implemented by Labor governments in Australia and New
Zealand in the 1980s were put into effect through the efforts of a small number
of strategically placed individuals who took advantage of a sense of crisis to
engineer significant market-orientated changes against the wishes of many politicians on the left and right, significant opinion-forming groups, and perhaps the
majority of the population.[27] They were, however, operating in a context in which
various moral, economic, and legal foundations of commercial society were relatively intact, despite the impact of Keynesianism and welfare state policies over
a number of decades. The extremely successful economic liberalization program
enacted in Estonia following Communism's collapse in the early 1990s was also
an instance of a crisis being turned into an opportunity by reform-minded individuals. It is worth recalling here that Estonia differed from a number of other
post-Communist nations insofar as its history and culture contained strong traditions of commercial activity as far back as the medieval Hanseatic League.[28]

Some intellectuals are reluctant to recognize the extent to which their ideas
have roots in a society's moral, institutional, and cultural history. Certainly, we
should resist the notion that our minds are trapped by our cultures. To affirm
such an idea is to deny man's capacity for freedom. But that is not the same as
thinking that people somehow float outside their time and culture. It is difficult
for intellectuals to abstract themselves completely from the contingencies and
particularities of their time. Few would dispute that the languages in which people think are cultural products that shape intellectual inquiry in many ways, not
least by providing the concepts available for the use and the style of expression
shaping the articulation of such concepts.

This does not mean, however, that critical reflection about a society's future direction cannot occur within a given moral, institutional, and cultural context. Those pursuing rational inquiry normally recognize themselves as belonging to one or more intellectual traditions. They also tend to regard themselves as developing a body of thought created and developed in turn by a group of original thinkers. That said, intellectuals do not normally view themselves as simply restating traditions whose construction and application is complete. They often apply concepts and principles contained in traditions to situations that did not previously exist. Intellectuals can thus play an important role in critiquing, elaborating, and developing the resources of moral and institutional traditions in the face of political, social, and economic change.[29]

One example especially pertinent for commercial society was Christianity's development of its treatment of credit and money-lending. In this case, intellectuals made a significant contribution to shifting much of European society toward freer and more productive economies. Following Europe's first great expansion of wealth in the High Middle Ages, many began asking what conditions made the loaning of money acceptable? How did one know that the price one charged was indeed just? What was the precise nature of usury?[30] When these events and questions were combined with new insights—most particularly, the realization that money could be regarded as a form of capital rather than as sterile—Christian theologians were able to recast Western views of interest-charging.[31] After reviewing this period of history, the economic historian Franz-Xaver Kaufmann wrote, "In Europe, the Church debated the distinction between usury and interest, and from the twelfth century onwards, the scholastic literature accepted and codified them. This recognition contributed to the growing sophistication of economic discourse; for instance, concepts such as risk and opportunity came to be invoked with increasing frequency."[32] Scholars were thus able to sustain Christianity's moral objection to usury (which remains defined as a sin to this day) by drawing distinctions between it and the legitimate charging of interest. In the most authoritative study of the usury question, the theologian and jurist John T. Noonan Jr. concludes:

> As far as dogma in the technical Catholic sense is concerned, there is only one dogma at stake ... that usury, *the act of taking profit on a loan without just title*, is sinful ... This dogmatic teaching remains unchanged. What is just title, what is technically to be treated as a loan, are matters of debate, positive law, and changing evaluation. The development on these points is great. But the pure and narrow dogma is the same today as in 1200.[33]

What is especially noteworthy about the history of the treatment of usury is not simply that the European culture of the time was capable of developing in ways that allowed such dilemmas to be resolved in a manner consistent with its dominant moral tradition.[34] The very process of doing so allowed European culture to give rise to a new range of conceptual possibilities about man's potential for economic creativity.

Taken together with Tocqueville's categories of circumstances, laws and *mœurs*, the preceding analysis provides us with some criteria that allow us to consider the scope accorded by a culture for the birth and spread of commercial society. First, do a culture's *mœurs* favor commercial habits and institutions, or are they such that they can be shaped toward the promotion of commercial society's foundations? Second, is a culture capable of having certain practices grafted onto it or at least based upon indigenous institutions? Third, are there key individuals and leadership groups committed to such a transition? At a minimum, negative responses to these questions must raise doubts about the possibility of commercial societies being facilitated in a given set of cultural circumstances. The same negative answers should also generate queries about the wisdom of external forces seeking to intervene to smooth the advent and progress of such a social order. By contrast, positive answers may indicate that, at least in terms of culture, there are grounds to hope that, whatever influences exist to the contrary, commercial society is not an impossibility.

Commercial Society, Commercial Humanism

Perhaps the greatest hope for commercial society is not its unparalleled ability to enable people to rise out of poverty, but its sheer resilience in the wake of numerous efforts to impede, distort, or divert its development. Montesquieu alluded to this when he wrote, "Commerce is sometimes destroyed by conquerors, sometimes cramped by monarchs; [yet] it traverses the earth, flies from the places where it is oppressed, and stays where it has liberty to breathe."[35] Certainly it has proved relatively easy to undermine or obstruct commercial society. Yet it has transcended its European origins and taken root in every inhabited continent, albeit sometimes in partial forms. Surely this owes something to the fact that many foundations of commercial society enjoy a nature that allows them to operate independently of particular boundaries. Neither human creativity, rational self-interest, money's purchasing power, nor trade itself can be totally suffocated by their surrounding circumstances. To a large extent, they can even operate independently of the state. It is also true that the penetration of one element of commercial society into one set of cultural conditions has cumulative effects. Respecting property rights, for example, tends to engender circumstances that favor rule of law. Allowing free trade requires some protection of private property. Permitting entrepreneurship often permits people to respond to a range of incentives.

Charles de Gaulle once remarked that Communism could never succeed because the Communists "lied systematically and nothing durable had ever been based upon lies."[36] Unlike Communism, commercial society does not claim to express the fullness of the truth about human beings. Nonetheless, the foundations of commercial society do embody a considerable portion of that truth. Unlike Communism, commercial society is not anti-human by nature. It is rooted in a distinctly human order that assumes human fallibility, human creativity, human freedom, and the need for human exchange. This is what merits commercial society the title of "a system of natural liberty," to employ Adam Smith's phrase. Such claims cannot be made about command economies and are often only given token recognition in mixed economies. As Daniel Mahoney points out, "Real human needs and activities, especially commercial ones, are protected and represented in a representative commercial regime."[37]

While commerce may not constitute the entire horizon of our existence and destiny as human beings, it does offer millions the hope of economic prosperity but without asking individuals or the political order to aspire to more than they can sustain. The foundations of commercial society allow people to take advantage of their natural differences and inequalities in ways that allow more and more people to rise out of poverty. Speaking generally about the nature of human association in commercial society, Smith commented that each individual "stands at all times in need of the cooperation of assistance of great multitudes, while his whole life is scarce sufficient to gain the friendship of a few persons."[38] Here is the realism of commercial society. It recognizes the limits of what can be reasonably expected from flawed, very human beings and understands that the task of meeting the economic needs and wants of billions of people cannot be left to people giving gifts to each other. This does not mean that commercial society does not value charity, kindness, or friendship; on the contrary, it provides many with the means and circumstances for people to develop and exercise such habits.

The fact of commercial society's resilience and its potential universality might tempt some to imagine that the economic prosperity produced by commercial society will demonstrate the ultimate long-term unfeasibility of the known alternatives. Unfortunately, the fact that the validity of economic theory or policy can be disproved does not mean that its implementation will never occur. Warnings about the moral and economic perils of collective ownership go back as far as Aristotle and even beyond. In more recent centuries, Ludwig von Mises' *Socialism* (1920) was one of the first texts to provide logical proofs that collectivism's disdain for the function of market prices meant that socialist experiments were doomed to failure. It took, however, another sixty-nine years before Communism collapsed in Central-East Europe. In our own time, many neo-corporatist arrangements and institutions show no immediate signs of disappearing in continents as distant as Western Europe and South America, despite their demonstrated social and economic failures.

It is here that intellectuals who recognize the benefits of commercial society bear a tremendous responsibility, not least because of the damage facilitated by other scholars in either prescribing yet another set of collectivist or corporatist solutions to economic problems or who persist in defending economic orders that are indefensible in terms of their limited effects on poverty, their undue inhibitions of human liberty, and their steady de facto encouragement of soft despotism. The development of specific policy prescriptions that advance commercial society—be it removing corporatist structures and organizations, eliminating tariffs, or reducing the programs that seek to realize unrealizable goals such as equality of result or opportunity—are important. Such proposals assume, however, at least some familiarity with the intellectual arguments that alert people to the humanizing capacities and liberating forces of commercial society, arguments that exceed the specifics of policy prescriptions and may be of greater long-term strategic significance. Hence, while it is essential to reinstitute and strengthen the moral, economic, and legal foundations of commercial society through the adoption of sound policies, such reforms may not be enough in themselves when it comes to securing their benefits.

In part, this is because commercial society is not a simple thing to understand. Many of its premises are based on counterfactual arguments, such as the notion that everyone benefits when people pursue their rational self-interest in the economic sphere. They run contrary to long-ingrained habits of thought, such as the widespread and persistent belief that one person's gain can only be at the expense of others. They also find themselves having to struggle against what unfortunately can only be described as considerable ignorance of facts, including the persistent rise in life spans, health levels, and general material prosperity that followed the spread of commercial society in the nineteenth century. Even today, people are more likely to defer to the dreadful imagery of Charles Dickens' novels and Karl Marx's scribblings when it comes to visualizing this period of history. Sound policies are not enough in themselves to overcome such impediments. It follows that if the effects of reforms that facilitate commercial society are to persist, intellectuals committed to the vision of commercial humanism must continue to argue the case for commercial society at the level of ideas in whatever forums they find themselves.

Writing toward the end of World War II, Friedrich von Hayek considered the devastation that was Germany and realized that neither Germany nor the rest of the Europe laid low by war, hunger, and disease could possibly hope to resurrect the old liberal order through their own efforts. This, he added, made it "probable that in the cultivation of certain common standards of moral judgment, collaboration across frontiers could contribute a great deal—particularly where we have to deal with a country where traditions have been so disrupted and standards so lowered as in Germany of recent years."[39] Hayek wrote at a time where the potential for sustained cooperation across national and geographical boundaries for those committed to the power of ideas was beginning to become a reality. Following the tremendous success of his *Road to Serfdom* (1944), Hayek realized that while a considerable number of people were opposed to the emerging anticommercial consensus created by war, collectivism, New Deals, and the long Keynesian night then beginning to engulf the West, they lacked focus and organization, not to mention any detailed knowledge of where they might find like-minded people. Hayek's founding of the Mont Pèlerin Society was the first practical step toward providing the international concentration and network needed by proponents of commercial society across the globe.

This is not to say that those in favor of commercial society need to agree about everything. The Cambridge philosopher Maurice Cowling famously described the movement for greater economic liberty in Britain that began to bear fruit in the 1970s as being directed and conducted

> by about fifty people (mainly graduates and mostly men) who have come from no one type of social, sexual, or intellectual background and who included among their number a smattering of atheists and agnostics, a few converted, a few practicing and a few lapsed Catholics, a handful of Jews, observing or other-wise, a fair number of observing and a number of converted Anglicans, and a contingent for whom religion is of little significance.
>
> In opinion there has been a lack of stereotype. Many of those who have supported market economics have been authoritarian about moral and social questions. Many who supported Mr Powell economically did not support him about Europe, Ireland, Immigration or the Soviet Union. Cold Warriors and anti-Cold Warriors, Europeans and anti-Europeans, Americans and anti-Americans, and both the friends and enemies of Israel, have been distributed fairly randomly.[40]

In our own time, we find that advocates of commercial society variously describe themselves as conservatives, classical liberals, libertarians, capitalists, and so forth. They disagree, often passionately, among themselves about innumerable subjects, ranging from questions such as just how limited government should be, to matters as controversial as the legalization of intentional abortion, euthanasia, and homosexual unions.

The very fact that a significant number of people holding such a diversity of opinion about so many subjects nonetheless count themselves among those who support the advance of commercial society across the globe reveals that there are things about commercial society that people from a range of backgrounds, cultures, and intellectual disciplines recognize as being true in all times and places. We should not be surprised by this. Centuries separate Juan de Mariana (the Catholic theologian), Adam Smith (the deistic philosopher), and Friedrich von Hayek (the agnostic economist). A remarkable consistency of view nevertheless exists in their thought concerning matters such as commerce's unintended benefits, the inadvisability of excessive state economic intervention, the civilizing effects of trade, the imperative of rule of law, and the indispensability of strong private property protections. This suggests that we can speak of a commercial school, a tradition of thought accurately labeled commercial humanism. Highly skeptical of the men of system, those of the commercial school regard commercial order as integral to any society that aspires to the title of civilized. It follows that they must seek to contribute where they can to establishing, promoting, and protecting commercial society's moral, economic and legal foundations, no matter how straightened the circumstances, inhospitable the culture, or fearful the odds.

There are few more challenging or nobler ends.

Notes

1. This chapter draws upon a paper delivered by the author at the 2004 Mont Pèlerin Society General Meeting in Salt Lake City, Utah.

2. See Christopher Dawson, "The Outlook for Christian Culture," in *Christianity and European Culture: Selections from the Work of Christopher Dawson*, ed. Geraldo Russello (Washington, D.C., Catholic University of America, 1998), 5.

3. George Weigel, *Europe's Problem ... and Ours*, Third Annual William E. Simon Lecture of the Ethics and Public Policy Center, November 20, 2003, Washington, D.C. For an insightful analysis of Western Europe's apparent demographic future and its economic consequences, see Gérard-François Dumont, "Le vieillissement des populations dans l'Union européenne," *Liberté Politique*, no. 24 (2003): 39–63.

4. Smith, *Theory of Moral Sentiments*, VI.ii.3.

5. See Joseph Boyle, "Natural Law and the Ethics of Traditions," in *Natural Law Theory: Contemporary Essays*, ed. Robert P. George (Oxford: Clarendon Press, 1992), 17–18.

6. For revealing studies of the changing *mœurs* of the German medical profession in the years before and during the Nazi era, see Götz Ally, Peter Chroust, and Christian Prouss, *Cleansing the Fatherland: Nazi Medicine and Racial Hygiene* (Baltimore and London: John Hopkins University Press, 1994); Robert Jay Lifton, *The Nazi Doctors: Medical Killing and the Psychology of Genocide* (New York: Basic Books, 1986).

7. F. A. Hayek, "Historians and the Future of Europe," in *The Collected Works of F. A. Hayek*, vol. 4, *Essays on Austrian Economics and the Ideal of Freedom*, ed. Peter Klein (Chicago: University of Chicago Press, 1992), 202.

8. Smith, *Theory of Moral Sentiments*, VI.ii.2.17.

9. See Sir John Fortescue, *De Laudibus Legum Angliae*, ed. and trans. Stanley B. Chrines (Cambridge: Cambridge University Press, 1949), c.12.

10. This and the following paragraph draw upon Samuel Gregg, *On Ordered Liberty: A Treatise on the Free Society* (Lanham, Md.: Lexington Books, 2003), 78–80.

11. See Adam Smith, *Glasgow Edition of the Works and Correspondence of Adam Smith*, vol. 4, *Lectures on Rhetoric and Belle Lettres*, ed. J. C. Bryce (Oxford: Oxford University Press, 1983), Lecture XXV.

12. Montesquieu, *Spirit*, bk. 20, chap. 5.

13. Tocqueville, *Democracy*, vol. 2, 496.

14. See ibid., vol. 1, 308.

15. Ibid., vol. 1, 165.

16. For this analysis of Tocqueville's position on political and civil society, see Welch, *De Tocqueville*, 66–68.

17. Smith, *Theory of Moral Sentiments*, VI.i.13.

18. See also Manent, *Modern Liberty*, 97–115.

19. See Tocqueville, *Democracy*, vol. 1, 114, 137.

20. See Welch, *De Tocqueville*, 122–25.

21. See Jardin, *Tocqueville*, 297–315, 343–69.

22. See Tocqueville, *Democracy*, vol. 2, 452.

23. Smith, *Wealth of Nations*, V.i.f.51.

24. F. A. Hayek, "The Rediscovery of Freedom: Personal Recollections," in *The Collected Works of F. A. Hayek*, vol. 4, *Essays on Austrian Economics and the Ideal of Freedom*, ed. Peter Klein (Chicago: University of Chicago Press, 1992), 193–94.

25. See A. Peacock and H. Willgerodt, eds., *Germany's Social Market Economy: Origins and Evolution* (London: Macmillan, 1989).

26. In the long term, the ability of these influences to resist corporatist tendencies in German political culture may be questionable. As early as 1983, Hayek observed: "As far as I can judge, people in Germany are no longer so convinced that they owe everything to the return to a free-market economy. Old feelings about anti-free trade, anti-competition, and anti-internationalism are again coming to the fore." Hayek, "The Rediscovery of Freedom: Personal Recollections," 194.

27. See Kelly, *The End of Certainty*, 1–50.

28. See David J. Smith, Artis Pabriks, Aldis Purs, and Thomas Lane, *The Baltic States: Estonia, Latvia and Lithuania* (London: Routledge, 2002); Mart Laar, "How Estonia Did It," *2003 Index on Economic Freedom* (Washington, D.C.: Heritage Foundation, 2003), 35–37.

29. While it may be true that an idea has been developed in a particular tradition, this fact does not necessarily imply that such claims cannot be universally validated as being true. There is, as Boyle notes, "no inconsistency in holding that the formulation of moral norms emerges within a tradition of enquiry and that these norms apply to everyone. Similarly, there is no inconsistency in thinking that some of these universal norms can be, and even are actually, known by everybody." Boyle, "Natural Law and the Ethics of Traditions," 9.

30. See Marjorie Grice-Hutchison, *Economic Thought in Spain: Selected Essays of Marjorie Grice-Hutchinson*, eds. Lawrence S. Moss and Christopher K. Ryan (Aldershot: Edward Elgar Publishing Ltd, 1993), 9–12.

31. See Finnis, *Aquinas*, 200–210; Raymond de Roover, "The Scholastics, Usury, and Foreign Exchange," *Business History Review*, 41 (1967): 257–71.

32. F-X. Kaufmann, "Religion and Modernization in Europe," *Journal of Institutional and Theoretical Economics*, 153, no. 1 (1997), 86.

33. John T. Noonan, Jr., *The Scholastic Analysis of Usury* (Cambridge, Mass.: Harvard University Press, 1957), 399–400. Emphasis added.

34. This is not to say that moral traditions should be in the business of rationalizing particular cultural developments. It is often necessary for moral traditions to be critical of, and even oppose certain developments. Such was the case with the traditions of Western freedom in confronting first Nazism and then different variants of Marxism.

35. Montesquieu, *Spirit*, bk. 21, chap. 5.

36. Claude Mauriac, *The Other de Gaulle: Diaries 1944–1954* (London: John Day Co., 1973), 235.

37. Daniel Mahoney, "Introduction," in Manent, *Modern Liberty*, 14.

38. Adam Smith, *Wealth of Nations*, I.ii.2.

39. Hayek, "Historians and the Future of Europe," 208.

40. Maurice Cowling, *Mill and Liberalism*, 2d ed. (Cambridge: Cambridge University Press, 1963/1990), xxxvi.

INDEX

Ackroyd, Peter, 22n8
activism, 150–51
Acton, Lord, 102, 125, 135, 141
de Albornóz, Bartolomé, 12
alternative economic societies, 158
altruism, 30, 45, 53
America. *See specific countries*
Anscombe, Elizabeth, 134
Aquinas, Thomas, 5, 7, 8–9, 22n17, 30
Argentina, 110–11
Arrow, Kenneth, 31
association, freedom of, 71, 79–80, 139
Atiyah, P. S., 65, 81, 82, 106
Australia, 20, 91, 113, 141, 155
Austria, 20–21, 110, 112, 114, 122n51
Austrian economic theory, 55, 69n15

Bagehot, Walter, 38
banks and banking practices, 37–38,
    62–63, 70n36, 37, 38
Barendt, Eric, 87, 88, 90
barter system, 12, 51, 59, 132
Bartolus of Sassoferrato, 7
Bastiat, Frederic, 118
Belgium, 22n8, 51, 113, 114
Bentham, Jeremy, 78
Berlin, Isaiah, 100–101
Bernardino of Sienna, 35

Bismark, Otto von, 92
Black, Antony, 6–7, 20, 110
Bowen, R. H., 121n41
Boyle, Joseph, 148, 162n29
Brandolinus, Aurelius, 10
Burke, Edmund, 97, 99, 128

Caldwell, Bruce, 136
Calvinism, 4, 5
Canada, xv, 91, 141
capital
    altruism, and accumulation of, 30
    civility and, 21
    entrepreneurship and, 56, 63
    legal systems and, 71
    money as, 61, 156
    Nazi regime, and flow of, 76
    neo-corporatism and, 113
    self-restraint, and accumulation of, 41
    surplus capital, 37, 38, 63
    trade and, 63
    trust in banks and, 37, 38
capitalism
    Catholic Church, and analysis of rise
        of, 5, 22n8
    Christianity, and foundations of, 6–10
    civility and, 6–7, 9, 10
    contracts and, 9

163

ABOUT THE AUTHOR

SAMUEL GREGG has written and spoken extensively on moral questions in law, medicine, and finance. He has a Doctor of Philosophy degree in moral philosophy from Oxford University and has authored several books, including *Morality, Law, and Public Policy* (2000), *On Ordered Liberty* (2003), *Ethics and Economics* (1999), *A Theory of Corruption* (2004), and *Banking, Justice, and the Common Good* (2005). He also publishes in journals such as *Law and Investment Management*, *Oxford Analytica*, *Journal des Economistes et des Etudes Humaines*, *Economic Affairs*, *Evidence*, *Markets and Morality*, and *Policy*, as well as newspapers including *The Wall Street Journal Europe*, the *Washington Times*, the *Australian Financial Review*, and *Business Review Weekly*. He is Director of Research at the Acton Institute, an Adjunct Professor at the Pontifical Lateran University, a consultant for Oxford Analytica Ltd, and General Editor of the Lexington Book Series *Studies in Ethics and Economics*. In 2001, he was elected a Fellow of the Royal Historical Society, and a Member of the Mont Pèlerin Society in 2004.